Science Companion for Library, School, and Home

Second Edition

PHYLLIS J. PERRY

DEBRA ELLINGER, ILLUSTRATOR

The Scarecrow Press, Inc.
Lanham, Maryland, and Oxford
2002

SCARECROW PRESS, INC.

Published in the United States of America
by Scarecrow Press, Inc.
A Member of the Rowman & Littlefield Publishing Group
4720 Boston Way, Lanham, Maryland 20706
www.scarecrowpress.com

PO Box 317
Oxford
OX2 9RU, UK

British Library Cataloguing in Publication Information Available

Library of Congress Cataloging-in-Publication Data

Perry, Phyllis Jean.
  Science companion for library, school, and home / Phyllis J. Perry.—2nd ed.
     p. cm.
  Rev. ed. of: A teacher's science companion. 1994.
  Includes bibliographical references and index.
   ISBN 0-8108-4454-0 (alk. paper)
   1. Science—Study and teaching. 2. Science—Experiments. 3. Science
projects. I. Perry, Phyllis Jean. Teacher's science companion. II. Title.
   Q181 .P355 2002
   507.1'2—dc21

                                                          2002008349

⊗™ The paper used in this publication meets the minimum requirements of
American National Standard for Information Sciences—Permanence
of Paper for Printed Library Materials, ANSI/NISO Z39.48-1992.
Manufactured in the United States of America.

For all the children who ask questions
and
For all the librarians, teachers, parents, and other adults
who try to answer them!

Contents

Contents

11   Exploring science through your senses   161

12   Exploring science through writing   172

13   Exploring science through art   185

14   Exploring science in the library   199

     Glossary   211

     Index   219

     About the Author   227

     About the Illustrator   228

About the resource books

The resources listed at the end of each chapter are the primary content of the book which is designed first of all to serve as a librarian's, teacher's, or parent's resource. Its second function is to serve as a project book to encourage simple science investigations. Special emphasis has been given to the resources to make them as clear and easy for the reader to find as possible. For this reason, the author chose to format the resources in a simplified manner, with the title of the book first in each listing. Resources highlighted with an asterisk (*) are specifically geared toward children of preschool age.

Symbols used in this book

adult
supervision

fire

electricity

scissors

sharp object

stove

animal safety/
proper handling
of animals and
insects

dangerous
chemical

Introduction

Kids are curious, and that curiosity can be a springboard to learning. Within the school setting, teachers guide the child's educational development. Many learning opportunities can also be found in interactions between a child and other adults outside of school.

Parents, grandparents, relatives, caregivers, scout and church group leaders, librarians, neighbors, and family friends, as well as teachers may play a significant part in developing the talents of all children. These adults serve as role models, listeners, and cheerleaders, provide space and materials for activities, allow opportunities for growing independence; and encourage creativity.

Our society has become very mobile, and today it is both a rare and fortunate child who is surrounded by an extended family. Often a child's relatives and adult friends are scattered throughout the country and may have contact only by letter, telephone, and occasional visits. Even where contact is infrequent or must bridge considerable distances, there are opportunities to provide support and a positive influence.

Adults want to make the most of the time they have to spend with children. They can be guides in the backyard examining a cricket or gazing at the stars, at a museum looking at dinosaur bones, in a planetarium or library studying space travel, or in the kitchen or classroom explaining chemistry while cooking. They may provide an introduction to optics, machines, or orienteering. They may help unlock treasures and answer questions through library research.

But the curiosity of a child is far ranging, and the questions he or she poses can be specific and come so fast and furiously that few adults feel they have all the answers. Although many people who interact with children have a background in math and science, as well as lengthy and rich life-experiences to help them, they may be unfamiliar with current children's books, videos, tapes, kits, or models on specific topics outside of their own areas of expertise. Even educators find it difficult to keep up with all the new materials being released. This book provides those lists of needed up-to-date resources.

Science Companion for Library, School, and Home promotes an interdisciplinary approach to learning. In life, things are not compartmentalized. For example, the child who is interested in studying deserts or mountains in geography soon learns that maps and cartography skills are also needed. Likewise, the youth making a model of the planets quickly learns that mathematics is an essential tool. Indeed, learning about and using mathematical skills are important parts of each chapter of *Science Companion for Library, School, and Home.*

The urge to impart what one learns requires that writing also be incorporated in science education. For example, recording notes on science experiments in journals, writing detailed observations of animal behaviors, or expressing some of the joy of science through poetry are a few of the ways writing skills are used by young scientists. Likewise, sketching a wildflower in the field or making a diagram of an insect's body parts are other examples of the interdisciplinary example approach to teaching through the use of art.

Many children and adults love games. The applicability of games can be a method of using math and science principles in an exciting problem-solving setting. For this reason, a variety of games are scattered throughout the chapters in this book.

Although the use of computers at home, school, and in the library is increasingly common, Internet sites are generally not listed in the resources. These sites change and come and go so quickly that an up-to-date listing is simply not within the scope of this book.

The book begins with Chapter 1 "Exploring Chemistry in the Kitchen." This leads easily to an exploration of energy, machines, and models as emphasized in Chapter 2 "Exploring Physics." Next, the focus moves to the backyard where children make general observations, learn about habitats, and become familiar with environmental concerns and what they can do to help out planet Earth (Chapter 3 "Exploring Science in the Backyard").

In Chapters 4, 5, 6, and 7, the general exploration of plants, insects, rocks, and so forth in the backyard is narrowed to more in-depth explorations. In Chapter 4, "Exploring Botany," the child is encouraged to investigate the neighborhood garden, local parks, and beyond. Differences are noted among plants of the rain forest, the desert, and the arctic. Spores, seeds, runners, pollination, and unusual plants, including fungi and carnivorous plants, are explored.

In Chapter 5, "Exploring Ethology," the child is invited to study birds and small mammal behavior as well as the more exotic animals found in zoos.

There is an exploration of geology and paleontology (Chapter 6) through the study of rocks, fossils, and dinosaurs; and then a focus on the field of astronomy (Chapter 7). Some of the explorations in these chapters move the child from home, school, and neighborhood to a botanical garden, zoo, natural history museum, or planetarium in the community.

Chapters 8, 9, 10, and 11 take the child still farther afield. Chapter 8, "Exploring Geography and Cartography," includes learning about maps, orienteering, hiking, biking, camping, and fishing. Then, in Chapter 9 "Exploring the Watery World," aquariums, ponds, lakes, and streams are investigated. And in Chapter 10, sea life is discussed in "Exploring the Ocean."

Chapter 11, "Exploring Science through Your Senses," focuses on the child and his or her senses. In making science observations, it is important to consider how we take in information. Chapters 12 and 13 show how the information that is gained through science explorations can be shared with others through writing and art.

Finally, Chapter 14, "Exploring Science in the Library," explains how learning to use library holdings and access information in other ways can further science research projects and help answer the many questions posed by curious kids. It explains about locating magazine articles, books, reference works, specialized encyclopedias, and other resources (including the Internet) and how to present the information in effective reports.

The concluding Glossary of terms will prove useful to both adults and the young scientist while working with this book and beyond.

The purpose of *Science Companion for Library, School, and Home* is to highlight some broad areas in which librarians, teachers, parents, and other adults have exceptional opportunities to encourage and enjoy teaching children science. Each area in the book provides some hands-on ideas for projects as well as an annotated list of readily available resources that might prove helpful on the topic at hand. These resources include numerous print materials and selected videos, tapes, kits, and models as well as a listing of agencies, magazines, or other references where additional information may be secured. (An immeasurable amount of computer software on science exploration topics is not touched on in this book, but is available to the public from various sources.)

Science Companion for Library, School, and Home need not be read from beginning to end. Rather, the reader should dip into chapters in any order, as dictated by a child's interests and curiosity. One activity might lead naturally to another. Hearing about a national event, watching a television program, or spotting a rainbow, however, might spark an entirely new line of interest. With this book in hand, the caring adult and the curious child will find both ideas and resources to enrich their many science explorations.

1

Exploring chemistry in the kitchen

For many children, the idea of love and caring is very much involved with food and cooking. Even the preschooler is terribly interested in what is going on in the world of pots, pans, beaters, buzzers, spoons, and spices.

The kitchen, whether at home or in the classroom, is a wonderful place in which a child can learn about foods, nutrition, and kitchen chemistry. And what a great place to apply mathematics! There are numerous opportunities to problem solve, work with fractions, measure, and make mathematical connections.

First and foremost to being involved in kitchen chemistry are the safety factors. This includes making a safe place for the young child to watch if he or she is not tall enough to see what is going on. All children need to be taught the danger of hot burners on the stove, touching things that have just come out of the oven, sharp knives, electrical outlets, and kitchen appliances, to name a few.

Many preschools and schools also encourage classroom cooking and "kitchen chemistry." Whether an oven, hot plate, or a microwave is available, the same need for teaching safety applies. The secret to success for "kitchen chemistry" in the classroom is to have sufficient adult help. One adult for every four or five children is a good ratio.

Rather than try to work with a whole class, the chemistry experiments described below can be set up as classroom interest centers. One or two adults can supervise small groups at the chemistry center, with all children having a chance during a week to rotate through the various centers.

Take the time to explain "why" and "how" certain things are or are not to be done. This extra time in the beginning may lead to more safety-conscious children.

Opportunities for discussing nutrition, food groups, common kitchen gadgets, and kitchen chemistry will probably arise naturally at home when adults spend time in the kitchen with curious kids. In the classroom, investigations will develop out of various units of study.

A child might ask a simple question. Why does vinegar smell so funny? What does it do? This is a chance to explain about acids and bases. In your kitchen (or your school science/cooking lab) you have acids, such as sour milk, lemons, and vinegar. Ammonia and baking soda are examples of common bases. Acids and bases are chemical opposites. If you have just the right amount, one will neutralize the other. The following experiment will help show how this happens.

Creating traffic-light colors
—red to green

In a pan, add 2 cups of water and 1 cup of shredded red cabbage. Bring this to a boil, then turn down the heat and simmer the cabbage for about 15 minutes.

Pour the red liquid from the pan into a measuring cup and let it cool. When it is cool, pour a little of the red liquid into a small, clear juice glass, add a teaspoonful of baking soda, and stir.

The color will change from red to deep green. The baking soda made the acidic mixture basic. Now add a drop or two of vinegar and stir. When you have added enough vinegar, the color will turn red again, showing that the mixture is now acid.

Writing with invisible ink

This writing experiment, which also involves vinegar, allows the child to send a message in "invisible" ink.

If you dip a clean pen into some vinegar and write a message on a sheet of thick writing paper, making a good heavy line, the message will soon dry and disappear, leaving no trace.

Carefully light a candle and place the candle and holder in the kitchen sink. Then hold the paper an inch or two above the candle flame, moving the paper slowly back and forth to be certain it does not catch on fire. The writing will reappear, in dark brown.

The vinegar chemically changed the paper it touched. When it was raised to its *kindling temperature*, the compound on the paper where the vinegar had been smeared had a lower kindling temperature than the rest of the paper, so heat made the writing oxidize and turn brown.

Using Oxygen

Burning is also a chemical process. When something burns, it combines with oxygen. You can see how oxygen is used up in burning by planning a simple kitchen chemistry experiment.

Gather the following materials: a piece of old newspaper about 6 inches square, a small drinking glass or clean jelly jar, some matches, and a metal pie pan filled with ½ inch of water.

Crumple up the piece of newspaper and stuff it in the bottom of the empty drinking glass or jar. Carefully light the newspaper with a match. When it is burning well, put the glass upside down in the water in the pie pan.

The flame will go out when the oxygen in the small glass is used up. Some water from the pan will be drawn up into the glass because the air pressure inside the glass where the oxygen has been used up is less than the air pressure outside the glass.

Conducting
an oxidation experiment

You can do another simple experiment with oxygen. Usually when we think of something combining with oxygen, we think of something burning, as in the experiment above. But oxidation can take place under water. Bleaching is a chemical operation of this kind. When bleach is added to laundry, it whitens clothes. To show how this happens, you can conduct the following oxidation experiment.

Fill a drinking glass ½ full of water. Add a few drops of ink. Stir until you have an even dark-blue mixture.

Add about three drops of laundry bleach. Stir. The dark-blue mixture will lose its color, becoming almost clear again, as the dye in the ink is oxidized.

Making the most of time in the home kitchen to learn science principles is tied to timing. If a busy adult is rushing to complete a series of tasks for dinner guests who are arriving in a few minutes, he or she is probably not open to holding a long conversation with a child about the interesting shapes of the sugar crystals in the sugar bowl. But on a less hurried occasion, the adult and child can talk and enjoy experimenting together.

Crystals hold a special fascination for students and are easy to study in the kitchen or the classroom. When sugar is added to water, it gradually dissolves as the sugar separates into single molecules and spreads through the water. Because these single molecules of sugar cannot be seen, it looks like plain water. However, the sugar, unchanged chemically, is still there, and you can get it back again.

Making sugar crystals

Put 2 cups of water into a pan and bring it to a boil. Turn the heat to low. Gradually add 3 cups of granulated sugar, stirring continuously.

Put the warm mixture into a tall glass. Across the top of the glass, lay a pencil that has a short length of cotton string tied to it. The string should almost reach the bottom of the glass when it dangles down from the pencil.

Set the glass in a warm place. In a few days, the string will be covered in many-sided crystals of sugar. As the solution cools, it forms sugar crystals that are the same shape, but larger, than the granulated sugar crystals with which you started.

If everything you have used in making these sugar crystals is clean, you can enjoy eating the "rock candy."

Creating needle crystals

There are many other experiments that can be done with crystals. Many minerals have special crystal shapes by which they can be recognized. A simple experiment in crystal shape can be done with magnesium sulfate.

Buy some Epsom salts (magnesium sulfate). Put ¼ cup of water in a small pan and heat it on the stove. Add 3 or 4 tablespoons of Epsom salts, stirring the salts in the water until no more will dissolve.

Remove the mixture from the stove and stir in two drops of ordinary liquid glue. When the glue has dissolved, take a cotton ball and swab a coating of the mixture onto a piece of glass. Set the glass aside.

In a few minutes, needle-like crystals will begin to appear. You will see them growing out in all directions. When the water has dried completely, you'll have a sample of magnesium sulfate crystals.

Making an emulsion

Kitchens and classrooms have soap. The chemical nature of soap enables it to keep small globules of oil suspended in water. Usually when your clothes are dirty, the dirt clings because a film of grease holds it. When you use soap, this film is broken down and the dirt can be washed away. The following simple experiment shows how this works.

Put an inch of water in a test tube. Then add an inch of cooking oil to the test tube. The oil will float at the top because it is less dense than the water. Hold your thumb over the end of the test tube and shake vigorously. The oil breaks up into drops. If you wait and hold the test tube still, however, most of the oil drops will come together again.

Now make a cup of soapy water. Pour about an inch of soapy water into a test tube. Then add an inch of cooking oil. Hold your thumb over the end of the test tube and shake it. This time you get a milky white emulsion. It will take a long time for the oil to separate out.

There are many interesting kitchen chemistry experiments involving the properties of yeast and baking soda. Kids may wonder, for example, why soda pop is so fizzy or bubbly. Soda drinks are made by forcing carbon dioxide gas into the water that contains sweetener and flavoring. The gas is dissolved in the water. When you open the bottle or can, the carbon dioxide appears as small bubbles in the liquid and gives the drink its bubbly taste.

Making mothballs move

This is a simple experiment with carbon dioxide.

Pour one tablespoon of vinegar into a 6 oz. glass of water. Add one tablespoon of baking soda. Then drop three moth balls into the glass and wait.

You will soon see tiny bubbles forming on the moth balls. These bubbles are carbon dioxide, which form on the rough sides of the moth balls. When enough bubbles form, they act like floats and will raise the moth balls to the top of the liquid. Then some of the bubbles will break off, and the moth balls will slowly sink.

More bubbles will gather, and the moth balls will rise again. This will go on for a long time until all the chemicals are used up.

Although we have discussed the kitchen and classroom as a place for chemistry experiments, the chapter would not be complete if we didn't have at least one opportunity to enjoy some food to eat.

Sculpting snack food science

Being fanciful with food can be a lot of fun. With the tremendous variety of snack foods we have available to us, a snack food science sculpture could be an exciting class or home activity that requires no cooking at all.

Gather together some pretzels, crackers of different shapes and sizes, and some soft cheese spread. Encourage children to make fantastic snack food sculptures that can be admired and then eaten for an afternoon treat.

Depending on the age of the children and the science topics being studied, they may turn snack food into an unusual machine, a spaceship, or a sea creature.

Exploring chemistry and nutrition in the home kitchen or in the classroom can be satisfying and fun for adults and for curious kids. The resources that follow contain easy recipes for children to make simple foods. Included are books featuring foods from different countries and that are connected with special holidays, adding a social studies interest to science experimentation.

Resource Books

Acids and Bases. J. M. Patten. Vero Beach, FL: Rourke Book Co., 1996. 24 pp. Explores acids and bases.

Acids, Bases, and Salts. Brian J. Knapp. Danbury, CT: Grolier Educational, 1998. 80 pp. A basic introduction.

Adventures with Atoms and Molecules, Book 3: Chemistry experiments for young people. Robert C. Mebane and Thomas R. Rybolt. Hillside, NJ: Enslow Pub., 1991. 96 pp. Simple chemistry experiments for home or school.

Adventures with Atoms and Molecules, Book 4: Chemistry experiments for young people. Robert C. Mebane and Thomas R. Rybolt. Hillside, NJ: Enslow Pub., 1992, 96 pp. Contains chemistry experiments for home or school that demonstrate properties of atoms and molecules.

Air and Water Chemistry. Brian J. Knapp. Danbury, CT: Grolier Educational, 1998. 80 pp. Step-by-step demonstrations of theories and concepts of air and water chemistry.

Antoine Lavoisier: Founder of Modern Chemistry. Lisa Yount. Springfield, NJ: Enslow Publishers, 1997. 128 pp. Discusses Lavoisier's work on combustion and respiration.

Atoms: Building blocks of matter. Timothy L. Biel, San Diego, CA: Lucent Books, 1990. 96 pp. Presents experiments that were done by famous scientists in the fields of physics and chemistry.

Bread. Dorothy Turner. Minneapolis, MN: Carolrhoda Books, 1989. 32 pp. Tells how bread is produced and prepared and gives some background along with two recipes.

Bread, Bread, Bread. Ann Morris. New York, NY: Lothrop, Lee & Shepard Books, 1989. 32 pp. Discusses many different kinds of bread.

Carbon Chemistry. Brian J. Knapp. Danbury, CT: Grolier Educational, 1998. 80 pp. Contains step-by-step demonstrations of theories and concepts of carbon compounds.

Chemical Changes. Kathryn Whyman. New York, NY: Gloucester Press (imprint of Franklin Watts), 1986. 32 pp. Explains chemical changes.

Chemical Chaos. Nick Arnold. New York, NY: Scholastic, 1997. 158 pp. Describes extraordinary experiments that went horribly wrong and has a section on kitchen chemistry.

Chemically Active!: Experiments you can do at home. Vicki Cobb. New York, NY: J. B. Lippincott, 1985. 154 pp. Contains many experiments to try at home.

Chemicals & Reactions. Jon Richards. Brookfield, CT: Copper Beach Books, 2000. 32 pp. Describes experiments that demonstrate chemical reactions.

Chemicals in Action. Ann Fullick. Des Plaines, IL: Heinemann Library, 2000. 32 pp. A brief introduction to chemistry.

Chemistry. Shirley Cox. Vero Beach, FL: Rourke Pub., 1992. 48 pp. Explains scientific method and discusses science fair chemistry projects.

Chemistry. Ann Newmark. New York, NY: Dorling Kindersley, 1993. 64 pp. Part of the Eyewitness Book Series that provides an introduction to chemistry.

Chemistry. Chris Oxlade. Austin, TX: Raintree Steck-Vaughn, 1999. 48 pp. Introduces basic chemistry concepts through simple experiments.

Chemistry. Steve Parker. New York, NY: Franklin Watts, 1990. 40 pp. Illustrates basic principles of chemistry through experiments and tricks.

Chemistry for Every Kid: One hundred and one easy experiments that really work. Janice Pratt Vancleave. New York, NY: John Wiley & Sons, 1989. 232 pp. Gives instructions for conducting experiments.

Chemistry Magic: Learning chemistry through fun-filled experiments. Edward Palder. Kensington, MD: Woodbine House, 1987. 153 pp. Teaches through chemistry experiments.

Chemistry: The birth of a science. Tom McGowen. New York: NY: Franklin Watts, 1989. 96 pp. Traces the history of chemistry from the ancient world to the late 18th century.

Consumer Chemistry Projects for Young Scientists. David E. Newton. New York, NY: Franklin Watts, 1991. 112 pp. Suggests experiments using household items that demonstrate the basic principles of chemistry.

Cooking Wizardry for Kids. Margaret Kenda and Phyllis S. Williams. New York, NY: Barron's Inc., 1990. 314 pp. Contains instructions for nearly 200 creative kitchen projects including making invisible ink, cakes, puddings, and salads.

Cool Chemistry: Great experiments with simple stuff. Steven W. Moje. New York, NY: Sterling Publishing Co., 1999. 96 pp. Contains directions for 55 experiments including food chemistry and working with acids and bases.

Copper. Richard W. Beatty. New York, NY: Benchmark Books, 2001. 32 pp. Explores the history of copper and explains its chemistry.

Elements, Compounds, and Mixtures. Brian J. Knapp. Danbury, CT: Grolier Educational, 1998. 80 pp. A basic introduction to chemistry.

Essential Chemistry. Clive Gifford. Tulsa, OK: EDC Publishing, 1992. 64 pp. A general introduction to chemistry.

Everyday Chemicals. Terry J. Jennings. Chicago, IL: Childrens Press, 1989. 34 pp. Provides an introduction to different kinds of chemistry through activities and experiments.

Experiments with Chemistry. Helen J. Challand. Chicago, IL: Childrens Press, 1988. 48 pp. Provides an introduction to chemistry through simple experiments.

Exploring the World of Chemistry. George Burns. New York, NY: Franklin Watts, 1995. 48 pp. Suggests simple activities for exploring the field of chemistry.

Exploring the World of Chemistry: From ancient metals to high-speed computers. John Hudson Tiner. Green Forest, AR: Master Books, 2001. 142 pp. Takes the reader on a tour of chemical discoveries and discoverers.

Famous Experiments You Can Do. Robert Gardner. New York, NY: Franklin Watts, 1990. 142 pp. Shows how to replicate famous experiments to demonstrate scientific principles of chemistry and physics.

Foodworks: Over 100 science activities and fascinating facts that explore the magic of food. Ontario Science Center Staff. Reading, MA: Addison-Wesley Publishing Co. 1987. 96 pp. Contains science activities for ages 8 through 12 that explain the role of food, what it does, and how it acts in the body.

Fun with Chemistry. Paul Berman. New York, NY: Marshall Cavendish, 1993. 48 pp. A guide to projects and experiments.

Getting Ready to Cook. Stoffelina Johanna Adriana De Villiers. Milwaukee, WI: Gareth Stevens, 1985. 31 pp. Provides an introduction to utensils, cooking terms, hints, and recipes.

Holiday Cooking around the World. Easy menu ethnic cookbooks, all about 46 pages, by various authors. Each book introduces the history of a country, its festivals, and food recipes. Minneapolis, MN: Lerner Publications, Co.

Cooking the African Way. Constance Nabwire, 1988.
Cooking the Australian Way. Elizabeth Germaine, 1990.
Cooking the Austrian Way. Helga Hughes, 1990.
Cooking the Caribbean Way. Cheryl Kaufman, 1988.
Cooking the Chinese Way. Ling Yu, 1982.

Cooking the English Way. Barbara W. Hill, 1982.
Cooking the French Way. Lynne Marie Waldee, 1982.
Cooking the German Way. Helga Parnell, 1988.
Cooking the Hungarian Way. Magdolna Hargittai, 1986.
Cooking the Indian Way. Vijay Madavan, 1985.
Cooking the Japanese Way. Reiko Weston, 1983.
Cooking the Israeli Way. Josephine Bacon, 1986.
Cooking the Italian Way. Alphonse Bisignano, 1982.
Cooking the Korean Way. Okwha Chung, 1988.
Cooking the Lebanese Way. Suad Amari, 1986.
Cooking the Mexican Way. Rosa Coronado, 1982.
Cooking the Norwegian Way. Sylvia Munsen, 1982.
Cooking the Polish Way. Danuta Zamojska-Hutchins, 1984.
Cooking the Russian Way. Gregory and Rita Plotkin, 1986.
Cooking the Spanish Way. Rebecca Christian, 1982.
Cooking the Thai Way. Supenn Harrison, 1986.
Cooking the Vietnamese Way. Chi Nguyen, 1985.

The Experimenters: Twelve great chemists. Margery Evernden. Greensboro, NC: Avisson Press, 2001. 200 pp. Biographies of famous chemists.

Fun with Mixing and Chemistry. Heidi Gold-Dworkin. New York, NY: McGraw Hill, 2000. 58 pp. Contains suggestions for hands-on activities.

Getting Started in Science Fairs, From Planning to Judging. Phyllis J. Perry. Blue Ridge Summit, PA: McGraw Hill, 1995. 183 pp. Provides an introduction to scientific method and gives advice on all aspects of science fairs. Includes suggested projects.

Gold. Sarah Angliss. New York, NY: Benchmark Books, 2000. 32 pp. Explores the history and explains the chemistry of gold and how it reacts.

A Guide to the Elements. Albert Stwerlka. New York, Oxford University Press, 1998. 238 pp. Presents basic concepts of chemistry.

How to Make a Chemical Volcano and Other Mysterious Experiments. Alan Kramer. New York, NY: Franklin Watts, 1991. 112 pp. This 13-year-old author presents 29 experiments using household chemicals and materials.

Hydrogen. John Farndon. New York, NY: Benchmark Books, 2000. 32 pp. Explores the history and chemistry of hydrogen.

Ideas for Science Projects. Richard C. Adams. New York, NY: Franklin Watts, 1997. 160 pp. Introduces the scientific method.

Ideas for Science Projects. Robert Gardner. New York, NY: Franklin Watts, 1989. 144 pp. Provides an introduction to scientific method and suggests several experiments.

In Charge: A complete handbook for kids with working parents. Kathleen Sharar Kyte. New York, NY: Alfred A. Knopf, 1983. 115 pp. Advice for kids who get themselves off to school or who are alone when they come home from school. Includes tips on cooking and recipes.

Involving Dissolving: Teacher's guide. Leigh Agler. Berkeley, CA: Laurence Hall of Science, 1986. 65 pp. Contains simple chemistry problems and exercises for students in grades 1-3.

Janice VanCleave's A+ Projects in Chemistry. Janice Pratt VanCleave. New York, NY: John Wiley & Sons, 1993. 233pp. Gives step-by-step directions for 30 advanced chemistry experiments.

Janice VanCleave's Molecules. Janice Pratt VanCleave. New York, NY: John Wiley & Sons, 1993. 88 pp. Contains a collection of science experiments and projects exploring molecules.

Janice VanCleave's Science Around the Year. Janice Pratt VanCleave. New York, NY: John Wiley& Sons, 2000. 122 pp. Seasonal science projects including chemistry.

Janice VanCleave's 200 Gooey, Slippery, Slimy, Weird, and Fun Experiments. Janice Pratt VanCleave. New York, NY: John Wiley & Sons, 1992. 116 pp. Filled with experiments in biology, chemistry, physics, earth science, and astronomy.

Janice VanCleave's 202 Oozing, Bubbling, Dripping, and Bouncing Experiments. Janice Pratt VanCleave. New York, NY: John Wiley & Sons, 1996. 120 pp. Gives instruction for over 200 experiments.

Keeping the Traditions: A multicultural resource. Phyllis J. Perry. Golden, CO: Fulcrum Publishing, 2000. 262 pp. Contains information on 20 countries of the world including folktales and simple traditional recipes.

*Kids Cooking Without a Stove: A cookbook for young children (rev. ed.). Aileen Paul. Santa Fe, NM: Sunstone Press, 1985. 63 pp. Contains easy-to-follow recipes that require no cooking. Includes recipes for drinks, salads, sandwiches, desserts, and candies.

Kidsource: Science experiments. Amy Hansen. Los Angeles, CA: Lowell House Juvenile, 2000. 32 pp. Suggests both simple and complex experiments.

*Kitchen Chemistry: Science experiments to do at home (rev. ed). Robert Gardner. Englewood Cliffs, NJ: Julian Messner, 1989. 128 pp. Filled with simple science experiments.

Kitchen Fun. Catherine Ripley (Ed.). Boston, MA: Little Brown & Co., 1988. 32 pp. Contains cooking and science experiments.

Kitchen Fun for Kids: Healthy recipes and nutrition facts for 7- to 12-year-old cooks. Michael F. Jacobson, New York, NY: Henry Holt, 1991. 136 pp. Contains recipes for breakfast, lunch, and dinner and gives nutritional facts.

Let's Visit a Spaghetti Factory. Melinda Corey. Mahwah, NJ: Troll Associates, 1990. 32 pp. Tells where spaghetti and pasta come from and includes ways to cook pasta and how to make crafts from pasta.

Magic Tricks, Science Facts. Robert Friedhoffer. New York, NY: Franklin Watts, 1990. 126 pp. Presents several magic tricks that are based on principles of physics, mathematics, or chemistry.

Magnesium. Colin Uttley. New York, NY: Benchmark Books, 2000. 32 pp. Explores the history and chemistry of magnesium.

Making Bread. Ruth Thomson. New York, NY: Franklin Watts, Inc., 1987. 32 pp. Explains how to make bread.

Metals. Brian J. Knapp. Dansbury, CT: Grolier Educational, 1998. 80 pp. Step-by-step demonstrations of the chemistry of metals.

*Mummy Took Cooking Lessons, and Other Poems. John Ciardi. Boston, MA: Houghton-Mifflin, 1990. 53 pp. Contains children's poetry.

Once Upon a Recipe: Delicious, healthy foods for kids of all ages. Karen Greene, New Hope, PA: New Hope Press, 1991. 96 pp. Contains more than 50 healthy recipes with allusions to works of children's literature such as Bambi's Salad Bowl and Shakespeare's Breakfast Sandwiches.

100 Science Experiments with Paper. Steven W. Moje. New York, NY: Sterling Pub. Co., 1998. 128 pp. Describes experiments with paper that explore the fields of chemistry, electricity, and magnetism.

101 Science Surprises: Exciting experiments with everyday materials. Roy Richards. New York, NY: Sterling Pub. Co., 1993. 101 pp. Gives a variety of experiments and activities including simple chemistry experiments.

175 More Science Experiments to Amuse and Amaze Your Friends. Terry Casn, Steve Parker, and Barbara Taylor. New York, NY: Random House, 1991. 172 pp. Experiments using common household items illustrate principles of sound, electricity, magnets, weather, and chemistry.

Oxygen. John Farndon. New York, NY: Benchmark Books, 1999. 32 pp. Explores the history of oxygen and explains its chemistry.

Oxidation and Reduction. Brian J. Knapp. Danbury, CT: Grolier Educational, 1998. 80 pp. A discussion of the oxidation process.

Paper Clip Science: Simple & Fun Experiments. Steven W. Moje. New York, NY: Sterling Pub. Co, 1996, 96 pp. Contains 65 experiments that demonstrate basic physics and chemistry.

Phosphorus. Richard W. Beatty. New York, NY: Benchmark Books, 2001. 32 pp. Explores the history of phosphorus and explains its chemistry.

Preparations. Brian J. Knapp. Danbury, CT: Grolier Educational, 1998. 80 pp. Chemistry laboratory techniques and preparations are explained through step-by-step demonstrations.

Recent Revolutions in Chemistry. James A. Corrick, New York, NY: Franklin Watts, 1986, 128 pp. Discusses the different branches of chemistry and recent theories and discoveries.

Robert Gardner's Favorite Science Experiments. Robert Gardner. New York, NY: Franklin Watts, 1992. 128 pp. Contains science experiments that can be done with materials commonly found at home.

*Rookie Cookie Cookbook: Everyday recipes for kids. Betty Debnam. Kansas City, KS: Andrews & McMeel, 1989. 126 pp. Contains easy recipes and dishes that can be prepared in a microwave.

Scholastic's The Magic School Bus Gets Baked in a Cake: Book about kitchen chemistry. Linda Beech. New York, NY: Scholastic, 1995. unpaged. Discusses kitchen chemistry.

The Science Chef: 100 fun food experiments and recipes for kids. John D'Amico. New York, NY: John Wiley & Sons, 1995. 180 pp. Contains a variety of experiments involving foods.

The Science Factory. Jon Richards. Brookfield, CT: Copper Beach Books, 2000. 224 pp. Easy-to-make science experiments in various fields such as flight, sound, and chemistry.

Science Fair Projects: Chemistry. Bob Bonnet and Dan Keen. New York, NY: Sterling Pub. Co., 2000. 95 pp. Contains dozens of ideas for science fair chemistry projects.

Science Fair Success Using Supermarket Products. Salvatore Tocci. Berkeley Heights, NJ: Enslow Publishers, 2000. 128 pp. Suggests projects and experiments.

Science Fair Success Using the Internet. Marc Alan Rosner. Springfield, NJ: Enslow Publishers, 1999. 112 pp. Explains how to use Internet resources for science projects.

Science for Kids: 39 easy chemistry experiments. Robert S. Wood. Blue Ridge Summit, PA: TAB Books, 1991. 32 pp. Contains directions for 39 simple chemistry experiments.

Science Fun with a Homemade Chemistry Set. Rose Wyler. New York, NY: Julian Messner, 1987. 48 pp. Gives an introduction to the basic concepts of chemistry through simple experiments using baking powder, soap, and vinegar.

Science Projects About Chemistry. Robert Gardner. Hillside, NJ: Enslow Publishing, 1994. 128 pp. Contains directions for simple chemistry projects.

Science Projects About Kitchen Chemistry. Robert Gardner. Springfield, NJ: Enslow Publications, 1999. 128 pp. Describes science fair projects dealing with chemistry.

See for Yourself: More than 100 experiments for science fairs and projects. Vikki Cobb. New York, NY: Scholastic Reference, 2001. 192 pp. Describes experiments in various fields including chemistry.

*Sensational Science Activities with Dr. Zed. Gordon Penrose. New York, NY: Simon & Schuster Books for Young Readers, 1990. 48 pp. Explains 21 projects that can be done at home in the fields of chemistry, physics, and biology.

The Simon & Schuster Young Readers' Book of Science. Robin Kerrod. New York, NY: Simon & Schuster Books for Young Readers, 1991. 192 pp. Surveys science, including chemistry.

Simple Chemistry Experiments with Everyday Materials. Louis V., Loeschnig. New York, NY: Sterling Pub. Co., 1994. 128 pp. Suggests simple experiments.

Six-Minute Nature Experiments. Faith Hickman Brynie. New York, NY: Sterling Pub. Co., 1999. 80 pp. Experiments involving ordinary everyday materials.

The Story of Iron. Karen Fitzberald. New York, NY: Franklin Watts, 1997. 64 pp. Explores the history and chemistry of iron.

The Story of Nitrogen. Karen Fitzgerald. New York, NY: Franklin Watts, 1997. 63 pp. Explores the history and chemistry of nitrogen.

Structure of Matter, Editors of Time-Life. Alexandria, VA: Time-Life, 1992. 151 pp. Discusses the structure of matter and ways in which it can change.

Sugaring Season: Making maple syrup. Diane L. Burns. Minneapolis, MN: Carolrhoda Books, 1990. 48 pp. Describes making maple syrup from the tapping of the tree to packaging.

Sulfur. Richard W. Beatty. New York, NY: Benchmark Books, 2000. 32 pp. Explores the history of the elements and explains basic chemistry.

Tests. Brian J. Knapp. Danbury, CT: Grolier Educational, 1998. 80 pp. A discussion of simple chemical tests.

365 More Simple Science Experiments with Everyday Materials. E. Richard Churchill, Louis V. Loeschnig and Muriel Mandell. New York, NY: Black Dog & Leventhal Pub., 1998, 320 pp. Explains scientific principles through various experiments.

365 Simple Science Experiments with Everyday Materials. E. Richard Churchill, Louis V. Loeschnig, and Muriel Mandell. New York, NY: Black Dog & Leventhal Pub., 1997. 317 pp. A variety of experiments and activities to explain different scientific principles.

The Usborne Illustrated Dictionary of Chemistry. Jane Wertheim, Chris Oxlade, and Corrine Stockley. Tulsa, OK: EDC Pub., 2000. 128 pp. A dictionary of chemistry.

Vicki Lansky's Kid's Cooking. Vicki Lansky. New York, NY: Scholastic Inc., 1988. 48 pp. A helpful book on kids cooking.

The Visual Dictionary of Chemistry. Jack Challenger. New York, NY: Dorling Kindersley, 1996. 64 pp. Discusses fundamentals of chemistry.

Whizbangers and Wonderments: Science Activities for Young People. Joseph Abruscato. Boston, MA: Allyn and Bacon, 2000. 312 pp. Chapter 1 deals with kitchen chemistry.

Women in Chemistry Careers. Jetty Kahn. Mankato, MN: Capstone Books, 2000. 48 pp. Explores the careers of five women in the field of chemistry.

You Gotta Try This!: Absolutely irresistible science. Vicki Cobb and Kathy Darling. New York, NY: Morrow Junior Books, 1999. 144 pp. Contains a collection of science experiments and suggested activities.

Other Resources

In exploring foods, nutrition, and kitchen chemistry, you might want to look at some of the many periodicals devoted to different aspects of chemistry. Among these are: *Analytical Chemistry, The Journal of Biological Chemistry, Chemistry and Industry, Chemical Times and Trends, Journal of Chemical Education, Journal of the American Chemical Society,* and *Journal of Organic Chemistry.*

Acid Rain Kit. Nashua, NH: Delta Education. For grades 5 and up. Features a rain gauge, a pH test kit for acid precipitation surveys, two test tubes, activity sheets, and study guide.

Chemistry for Every Kid. Nashua, NH: Delta Education. For use in grades 2-6. Comes with everything needed for students to conduct 101 experiments described in *Chemistry for Every Kid.* Based on the Janice VanCleave book series published by John Wiley & Sons, Inc.

Chemistry Lab. Sarah Angliss. San Diego, CA: Silver Dolphin Books, 1999. 32 pp. The kit and manual provide impetus for 50 chemistry experiments.

Consumer Chemistry Lab Kit. Nashua, NH: Delta Education. This kit introduces the role of chemistry in daily living and provides a study of everyday products. Contains enough materials for a class of 40.

The Hidden Structure. Jacob Bronowski. New York, NY: Ambrose Video Pub., 1988. 1 videocassette, 52 minutes. Traces the history of chemistry.

The Magic School Bus: Ready, set, dough. Joanna Cole and Bruce Degen. New York, NY: Scholastic, 1997. 1 videocassette, 30 min. A class of students learns about kitchen chemistry by going to a bakery.

2
Exploring physics

Curious kids are always wondering how things work, so experimenting with models, gadgets, and gears will probably be of great interest to them. More abstract, but equally fascinating, are investigating optics, gravity, magnetism, electricity, radio waves, and ways of using different types of energy.

Some youngsters will be amazed by the way a clock works. Others might watch with rapt attention as someone tinkers with an automobile engine, a motorcycle, or a bicycle. Still others will be caught up in the adventure of flight.

As you explore the topics in this chapter, the child's interests will be your best guide. Many of the resource books that are listed at the end of this chapter include a large number of simple experiments or activities. Most of these require only supplies and equipment that can be commonly found around your home or classroom.

Math skills will be used through these activities as children estimate, compute, develop a spatial sense, measure, reason and problem solve, make mathematical connections, and communicate their ideas.

Explaining how a lever works

A simple experiment shows how a long lever works and demonstrates the fact that by using a lever, the child can lift a person heavier than he or she.

To set up this experiment, use a heavy 8-foot board, and put a sturdy wooden block or box under the board but close to one end.

Have a teenager or adult stand on the board at the end near the wooden support. Then have the child step onto the board at the other end. By using the lever, the child will be able to lift a person who is much heavier than he or she. To avoid accidents, have the child take special care in getting on and off the board.

Making a current detector

Many experiments with electricity require an electric current detector. The following experiment describes how to make one.

Buy a roll of inexpensive insulated "bell wire" at a hardware store. Unwind 12 inches of wire from both ends of the roll of wire. Wrap adhesive tape around the roll to prevent it from unwinding further.

Scrape the insulation from both ends of the wire so that 1 inch of bare copper wire shows.

Tape the roll of wire upright onto a piece of wood that is about 5 inches square. Push two thumbtacks gently into the top of the wood, near the front edge, about 2 inches apart.

Wrap the end of one piece of wire once around the shaft of the thumbtack so that 10 inches of wire sticks out in front. Push the thumbtack in firmly to hold the wire in place. Repeat this procedure with the other wire and thumbtack.

Set a compass, flat and level, inside the coil of wire.

Then hold one end of the wire to the end of a flashlight battery. Hold the other wire to the opposite end.

The compass needle will swing as it detects the presence of an electric current.

Making a battery

Another source of energy commonly used is a battery. The following experiment shows you how to make an 11-cent battery that is much like a flashlight battery.

Stir 1 teaspoon of salt into a glass that is filled with 3 oz. of water.

Put a postage-stamp size piece of blotting paper in the glass to soak for a few seconds in the salt water solution.

Take out the piece of blotting paper and put it between a dime and a penny and squeeze the coins together.

Then touch one wire of your current detector to the penny and the other wire to the dime. You will see the compass needle move as electricity passes from your tiny battery through the coil.

Demonstrating friction

Some of the principles of energy and simple machines can be demonstrated through activities that are easy to set up. The following experiment helps to demonstrate a little about friction.

For your demonstration of friction, cut a piece of string, pass it through a rubber band, and then tie the string around a book. Ask the child to pull the book across the table by slipping his or her finger through the rubber band and pulling.

The child will see that the rubber band stretches out long and that it is not easy to pull the book because of friction.

Then put three long, round pencils beneath the book. Have the child pull the book again. The rubber band will not stretch as far this time, and the book will be easier to pull because the pencils act like rollers and cut down friction.

Making molecules move and make heat

A simple way to show how heat travels by conduction is demonstrated in the following experiment.

Make a cup of tea or soup and pour it into a cup or bowl.

Have a child put a cold spoon into the cup or bowl of liquid and wait. Then have the child touch the spoon handle. The handle is hot even though it was never heated with the liquid.

You have demonstrated that when molecules move fast, they generate heat.

Explaining wind energy

Another example of the principles of energy and simple machines can be demonstrated by building the windmill described in the following experiment.

A child who sees or reads about a windmill as an energy source might want to make his or her own windmill. You will need scissors; a piece of light-weight cardboard, such as a file folder; a steel straightpin, and a dowel.

Cut the piece of cardboard into an 8-inch square. Mark the center. Cut from all four corners on the diagonal half-way to the center. Bend one piece of cardboard at each of the four corner points to the center.

Push your pin through all four points and gently push it into the dowel. Spin the wheel a few times around the pin so that it turns easily.

By waving your windmill through the air or taking it outside to catch the wind, it will spin away. (If the two sides of the cardboard are different colors, the "whirl" will be especially colorful.)

Performing the obedient straw trick

An understanding of the principles of physics and chemistry can also allow a child to engage in some interesting magic tricks. One of these that may amaze others is the "obedient straw" trick.

To perform the "obedient straw" trick, you will need a plastic drinking straw, a pin, and a glass of water. Use the pin to prick a double row of tiny holes in the straw about two inches from one end. (Do this before you show your trick and be sure that holes are so tiny that they will not be noticed.)

Tell a friend that you have an "obedient straw" that will only allow someone to drink from it if you so command. With the pin-pricked part of the straw out of the water, have a friend try to take a sip. Little or no water will come up the straw.

Pick up the straw and speak to it seriously saying, "Straw, I command you to let my thirsty friend have a drink of water." Replace the straw in the glass. This time be sure to put the pin-pricked part of the straw down into the water. Your friend will now be able to drink from your "obedient straw."

Using straws to produce sound

A simple experiment involving sound can also be performed with an ordinary drinking straw.

Flatten one end of a straw and cut the flat end to a point. Wet the point and put that end in your mouth. While keeping your lips on the round part of the straw, blow and listen.

Then use the scissors to cut the straw shorter. Blow again. What happens to the sound? Cut the straw still shorter. What happens to the sound now? (As the straw gets shorter, the sound gets higher.)

Performing the pencil trick

Another simple trick, this one involving optics, can be done with a pencil. Tell a friend that you can break a pencil without touching it and also make the bottom half grow larger than the top half.

Fill a glass full of water. Put a long pencil in it so that the pencil point rests at the bottom side of the glass and its eraser rests at the top opposite side of the glass.

Tell your friend that you will now break the pencil and make the bottom half grow. As seriously as possible, say, "Break and grow!"

Have your friend look into the glass. The part of the pencil where it enters the water will appear broken. The pencil below the water appears slightly larger.

Your "trick" depends on the fact that light shining on the upper part of the pencil first strikes the pencil and then travels to your eyes. This light is reflected but not bent. The light that lets you see the part of the pencil below the water travels through the water, the glass, and the air to reach your eyes. The light rays are bent. This light is slightly slower reaching your eyes and the time difference causes a distortion called refraction.

The pencil below the water looks larger because the water and the curve of the glass magnify its image.

Making a rainbow

It seems that anyone who sees a rainbow must stop to admire it Rainbows are formed when raindrops refract sunlight—when sunlight is broken into the colors of red, orange, yellow, green, blue, indigo, and violet. It isn't hard to make your own rainbow in the classroom or at home on a sunny day. The following experiment will show you how.

Fill a drinking glass with water and put it on a windowsill in the bright sunlight. Let the glass hang a little over the edge of the sill toward the room.

Put a large piece of white paper on the floor below the glass, positioning it so that the sun shines through the water onto the paper. You will be able to see a rainbow on the paper.

Once some of the underlying principles of physics are understood, the curious child may want to explore them in greater depth. Community resources may be very helpful here. For example, if a child shows interest in ham radio, there will be a local radio club with members who may supply useful information about setting up a rig or who may help your child with his or her studying to take a licensing test. If railroads are of interest, model railroad enthusiasts are equally willing to show and explain their setups to eager children.

Manufacturing companies often arrange tours for interested people to visit a plant and see their production process firsthand. Newspaper offices may have tours of their presses, and a local airport may have a variety of aeronautical displays.

Many kits and models are available commercially for those who do not want to start experimenting from scratch. Some sources for purchasing experimenting materials are listed among the "Other Resources" in this chapter.

Resource Books

Air and Flight. Barbara Taylor. New York, NY: Warwick Press, 1991. 40 pp. Contains simple experiments to demonstrate the properties of air and the principles of flight.

Albert Einstein and Relativity. Steve Parker. Philadelphia, PA: Chelsea House Publishers, 1995. 32 pp. A discussion of the contributions of Albert Einstein to the scientific world.

American Ingenuity: Henry Ford Museum and Greenfield Village. James S. Wamsley. New York, NY: H. N. Abrams, 1985. 223 pp. A guide book to the Henry Ford Museum.

An Auto Mechanic. Douglas Florian. New York, NY: Greenwillow Books, 1991. 24 pp. Shows the daily work of an auto mechanic.

Awesome Experiments in Light and Sound. Michael A. Dispezio. New York, NY: Sterling Pub. Co., 1999. 160 pp. Contains over 70 experiments on topics such as wavelengths, color spectrums, vibrations, and air particles.

Balancing. Terry Jennings. New York, NY: Gloucester Press, 1989. 28 pp. Filled with science experiments involving balancing.

Balloon Science. Etta Kaner. Redding, MA: Addison Wesley Publishing Co., 1990. 90 pp. Contains ideas for 50 balloon experiments.

Balloons: Building and experimenting with inflatable toys. Bernie Zubrowski. New York, NY: Morrow Junior Books, 1990. 80 pp. Contains experiments using balloons to demonstrate various scientific principles.

Bathtubs, Slides, Roller Coaster Rails: Simple machines that are really inclined planes. Christopher Lampton. Brookfield, CT: Millbrook Press, 1991. 32 pp. Explains the inclined plane.

The Ben Franklin Book of Easy and Incredible Experiments. Lisa Jo Rudy (Editor). New York, NY: John Wiley, 1996. 131 pp. Contains engineering experiments.

Blinkers and Buzzers: Building and experimenting with electricity and magnetism. Bernie Zubrowski. New York, NY: Morrow Junior Books, 1991. 112 pp. Filled with experiments and projects.

Boomerangs, Blades, and Basketballs. Jayne Creighton. Austin, TX: Raintree Steck-Vaughn, 2000. 48 pp. Describes aspects of sports and the principles of physics that are involved.

Cars, Trucks, and Trains. Donna Bailey. Austin, TX: Steck-Vaughn Library, 1990. 48 pp. Discusses the development of cars, trucks, and trains.

*Click, Rumble, Roar: Poems about machines. Lee Bennett Hopkins (Editor). New York, NY: Thomas Y. Crowell, 1987. 48 pp. Contains eight poems about machines.

Clocks: Building and experimenting with model timepieces. Bernard Zubrowski. New York, NY: Morrow Junior Books, 1988. 112 pp. Gives instructions for making working models of different clocks from readily available materials.

The Cool Hot Rod and Other Electrifying Experiments on Energy and Matter. Paul Doherty. New York, NY: John Wiley & Sons, 1996. 100 pp. Contains over 20 experiments exploring energy transformations.

A Day in the Life of a Racing Car Mechanic. Carol Gaskin. Mahwah, NJ: Troll Associates, 1985. 32 pp. Follows a mechanic through a day.

Electricity and Magnetism. Terry Jennings. Chicago, IL: Childrens Press, 1989. 32 pp. Provides an introduction to magnetism, magnets, compasses, batteries, and electricity.

Electricity and Magnets. Barbara Taylor. New York, NY: Franklin Watts, 1990. 32 pp. Explains the properties of electricity and magnetism.

*Energy. Terry Jennings. Chicago, IL: Childrens Press, 1989. 32 pp. Answers questions about uses of energy through activities and experiments.

Energy and Power. Barbara Taylor. New York, NY: Franklin Watts, 1990. 32 pp. Shows how oil, steam, electricity, and nuclear power are manipulated to provide energy.

Energy: Making it work. Tom Johnston. Milwaukee, WI: Gareth Stevens Pub., 1987, 32 pp. Examines energy and how one form of energy is converted into another.

Energy Projects for Young Scientists. Robert Gardner. New York, NY: Franklin Watts, 1989. 127 pp. Contains experiments related to solar, thermal, electrical, kinetic, and potential energy.

Energy Technology. Mark Lambert. New York, NY: Bookwright Press, 1991. 48 pp. Discusses both traditional and alternative energy resources.

Engineering Projects for Young Scientists. Peter H. Goodwin. New York, NY: Franklin Watts, 1989. 126 pp. Contains projects involving force, friction, motion, sound waves, light waves, and mechanics.

The Ever-Changing Atom. Roy A. Gallant. New York, NY: Benchmark Books, 2000. 80 pp. Discusses atoms and how they can be used as a source of energy.

Experimenting with Air and Flight. Ormiston H. Walker. New York, NY: Franklin Watts. 1989. 96 pp. Through experiments, explains the properties of air and the mechanics of flight.

Experimenting with Energy. Alan Ward. New York, NY: Chelsea House Publishers, 1991. 48 pp. Explains fundamental concepts of energy with simple experiments using household materials.

Experiments with Electricity. Helen J. Challand. Chicago, IL: Childrens Press, 1986. 45
pp. Provides an introduction to batteries and discusses the properties of electricity with related experiments.

Exploring Uses of Energy. Ed Catherall. Austin, TX: Steck-Vaughn Library, 1990. 48 pp.
Through simple projects and experiments, explains how energy is used, stored,
transferred, and conserved.

Fatal Forces. Nick Arnold. New York, NY: Scholastic, 1997. 159 pp. Discusses speed,
gravity, friction, pressure, and simple machines.

50 Nifty Super Science Experiments. Lisa Melton and Eric Ladizinsky. Los Angeles,
CA: Lowell House Juvenile, 1997. 80 pp. Discusses color and light dispersion experiments.

*Force and Movement. Barbara Taylor. New York, NY: Franklin Watts, 1990. 32 pp.
Contains simple experiments and activities explaining about force and the ways
things move.

Forces. Graham Peacock. New York, NY: Thomson Learning, 1994. 32 pp. Contains
interesting energy experiments.

Forces with You! Tom Johnston. Milwaukee, WI: Gareth Stevens Pub., 1987. 32 pp.
Explains various forces and their effect on our lives.

Fuel and Energy. Herta S. Breitter. Milwaukee, WI: Raintree Childrens Books, 1988.
46 pp. Explains how various types of fuel are used as sources of energy.

*Get It in Gear! The science of movement. Barbara Taylor. New York, NY: Random
House, 1991. 40 pp. Through simple experiments, explains everyday machines.

Getting Started with Model Trains. John Townsley. New York, NY: Sterling Pub. Co.,
1992. 96 pp. Tells about starting out working with model trains.

Gizmos & Gadgets. Jill Frankel Hauser. Charlotte, VT: Williamson Publishing, 1999.
144 pp. Gives instructions for making 75 contraptions that demonstrate principles of physics.

Gravity: The universal force. Don Nardo. San Diego, CA: Lucent Books, 1990. 96 pp.
Explains the force of gravity and its effects on humans.

Great Aircraft Collections of the World. Bob Ogden. New York, NY: Gallery Books,
1986. 200 pp. Discusses aeronautical museums.

The Hidden World of Forces. Jack R. White. New York, NY: Dodd Mead, 1987. 143
pp. Gives many experiments to illustrate electromagnetism, gravitation, surface
tension, and friction.

How?: More experiments for the young scientist. Dave Procknow and Kathy Procknow. Philadelphia, PA: Chelsea House Publishers, 1999. 152 pp. Filled with engineering experiments.

Inclined Planes and Wedges. Sally M. Walker and Roseann Feldmann. Minneapolis,
MN: Lerner Publications Co., 2002. 47 pp. An early bird physics book.

In the Gym. Nikki Bundey. Minneapolis, MN: Carolrhoda Books, 1999. 32 pp. Presents basic concepts of physics such as force and resistance through describing
gymnastics, games, and exercises.

In the Park. Nikki Bundey. Minneapolis, MN: Carolrhoda Books, 1998. 32 pp. Introduces basic physics through games and activities often played in parks.

In the Snow. Nikki Bundey. Minneapolis, MN: Carolrhoda Books, 1998. 32 pp. Discusses concepts of physics such as friction and gravity through examining the
mechanics of winter sports.

In the Water. Nikki Bundey. Minneapolis, MN: Carolrhoda Books, 1997. 32 pp. Presents basic concepts of physics through the mechanics of various water sports.

Invention. Lionel Bender. New York, NY: Alfred A. Knopf, 1991. 64 pp. By use of photos and text, the reader can explore inventions such as the wheel, gears, and levers.

Isaac Newton: Discovering laws that govern the universe. Michael White. Woodbridge, CT: Blackbirch Press, 1999. 64 pp. Presents the life and contributions of the famed English mathematician.

Letting Off Steam: The story of geothermal energy. Linda Jacobs. Minneapolis, MN: Carolrhoda Books, 1989. 48 pp. Explores geothermal energy and how it can be used as an alternative energy source.

Levers. Sally M. Walker. Minneapolis, MN: Lerner Publications Co., 2002. 47 pp. An early bird physics book.

Machines and How They Work. David Burnie. New York, NY: Dorling Kindersley. 1991. 64 pp. Contains information on how different machines work.

Make It Change. David Evans and Claudette Williams. New York, NY: Dorling Kindersley, 1992. 29 pp. Explores how changes occur through heating, wetting, and stirring.

Making and Using Scientific Equipment. David E. Newton. New York, NY: Franklin Watts, 1993. 157 pp. Describes equipment used in physics and other sciences and gives instructions for constructing it.

*Marbles, Roller Skates, Doorknobs: Simple machines that are really wheels. Christopher Lampton. Brookfield, CT: Millbrook Press, 1991. 32 pp. Contains many experiments involving wheels.

The Marshall Cavendish Library of Science Projects. Steve Parker. New York, NY: Marshall Cavendish, 1986. 43 pp. Contains science experiments involving mechanics, light, water, plants, earth, and the human body.

Measurement Motivators. Thomas J. Palumbo. Carthage, IL: Good Apple, 1989. 96 pp. Provides a variety of measurement activities for children in grades three through seven.

Measuring Weight and Time. Andrew King. Brookfield, CT: Copper Beech Books, 1998. 32 pp. Uses simple games and activities to introduce concepts of measurement, weight, mass, and time.

Modern Sports Science. Larry Kettelkamp. New York, NY: Morrow Junior Books, 1986. 160 pp. Helps children understand muscle mechanics.

Monster Wheels. Bill Holder and Harry Dunn. New York, NY: Sterling Pub. Co., 1990. 32 pp. Discusses modern monster trucks doing various tricks and stunts.

More Science Secrets. Judith Conaway. Mahwah, NJ: Troll Associates, 1987. 48 pp. Gives simple experiments to explore basic scientific principles.

More Wires and Watts: Understanding & using electricity. Irwin Math. New York, NY: Scribner, 1988. 96 pp. Presents fundamentals of electricity and magnetism through experiments and projects that produce working models.

Motorcycles. Alain Chirinian. Englewood Cliffs, NJ: Julian Messner, 1989. 64 pp. Discusses the 14 top motorcycles.

Move It! Henry Arthur Pluckrose. New York, NY: Franklin Watts, 1990. 28 pp. Discusses various sources of power such as wind, gravity, motors, and electricity.

Moving Things. Robin Kerrod. Morristown, NJ: Silver Burdett Press, 1987. 54 pp. Examines energy, sound, light, color, gravity, magnetism, and electricity.

The National Air and Space Museum ABC. Florence Cassen Mayers. New York, NY: H. N. Abrams, 1987. 32 pp. An ABC depicting early aviation.

Now You're Talking! Discover the world of HAM radio. Newington, CT. American Radio Relay League, 1991. 255 pp. Contains information on how to become an amateur radio operator.

Nuclear Energy/Nuclear Waste. Anne L. Galperin. New York, NY: Chelsea House Publishers, 1992. 112 pp. Shows benefits of nuclear power and the problems of nuclear waste.

On a Bike. Nikki Bundey. Minneapolis, MN: Carolrhoda Books, 1998. 32 pp. Introduces basic physics such as force, resistance, and friction through bicycling techniques.

101 Physics Tricks: Fun experiments with everyday materials. Terry Cash. New York, NY: Sterling Pub. Co., 1992. 104 pp. Activities and experiments to inform students on gravity, friction, and magnetism.

175 More Science Experiments to Amuse & Amaze Your Friends. Terry Cash and Barbara Taylor. New York, NY: Random House, 1991. 176 pp. Contains experiments using common items to demonstrate the principles of sound, electricity, and magnetism.

On the Move. Wendy Madgwick. Austin, TX: Raintree Steck-Vaughn, 1999. 32 pp. Gives instructions for activities which introduce the basic principles of physics.

The Optics Book: Fun experiments with light, vision and color. Shar Levine and Leslie Johnstone. New York, NY: Sterling Pub. Co., 1998. 80 pp. Explores the properties of light and color by means of simple experiments.

Pedal Power: The history of bicycles. Peter Lafferty and David Jefferis. New York, NY: Franklin Watts, 1990. 32 pp. Traces the history of the bicycle.

Physics for Kids: 49 easy experiments with mechanics. Robert W. Wood. Blue Ridge Summit, PA: TAB Books, 1989. 160 pp. Suggests simple physics experiments for kids.

Physics Lab in a Hardware Store. Robert Friedhoffer. New York, NY: Franklin Watts, 1996. 112 pp. Uses common tools to explore topics in physics.

Physics Lab in a Housewares Store. Robert Friedhoffer. New York, NY: Franklin Watts, 1996. 95 pp. Uses common household utensils to explore topics in physics.

Physics Projects for Young Scientists. Richard C. Adams. New York, NY: Franklin Watts, 2000. 128 pp. Explains the principles behind and gives instructions for simple physics experiments.

Power Failure. Mary LeDuc O'Neill. Mahwah, NJ: Troll Associates, 1991. 32 pp. Discusses energy today and its future.

Power Magic. Alison Alexander. New York, NY: Simon & Schuster, 1991. 30 pp. Contains experiments on exploring ways to use energy.

Power Up: Experiments, puzzles and games exploring electricity. Sandra Markle. New York, NY: Atheneum, 1989. 48 pp. Ideas for exploring electricity.

Puff and Blow. Sally Hewitt. Chicago, IL: Childrens Press, 1994. 24 pp. Contains experiments involving acoustics and physics.

Pulleys. Sally M. Walker. Minneapolis, MN: Lerner Publications Co., 2002. 47 pp. An early bird physics book.

Radio Controlled Model Airplanes. Suzanne Lord. Mankato, MN: Crestwood House, 1988. 48 pp. Discusses organizations and tools needed for building and flying model airplanes.

Rads, Ergs, and Cheeseburgers: The kids' guide to energy & the environment. Bill Yanda. Santa Fe, NM: John Muir Publications, 1991. 108 pp. A magical being discusses the various forms of energy.

Relativity and Quantum Mechanics: Principles of modern physics. Paul Fleisher. Minneapolis, MN: Lerner Publications, 2002, 63 pp. An introduction to modern physics.

Roller Coasters. Lynn M. Stone. Vero Beach, FL: Rourke Pub., 2002. 48 pp. Gives the history of roller coasters and describes the physics involved in their construction.

Rubber-Band Banjos and a Java Jive Bass: Projects and activities on the science of music and sound. Alex Sabbeth. New York, NY: John Wiley & Sons, 1997. 102 pp. Presents projects involving the science of sound and music.

*Sailboats, Flag Poles, Cranes: Using pulleys as simple machines. Christopher Lampton. Brookfield, CT: Millbrook Press, 1991. 32 pp. Discusses simple machines that use pulleys.

Secrets of the Universe: Discovering the universal laws of science. Paul Fleisher. New York, NY: Atheneum, 1987. 224 pp. Contains various experiments and activities to help children examine the laws of physics.

*Seesaws, Nutcrackers, Brooms: Simple machines that are really levers. Christopher Lampton. Brookfield, CT: Millbrook Press, 1991. 32 pp. Explains simple machines that are levers.

Science and Technology. Brian Williams. New York, NY: Kingfisher Books, 1993. Explores matter and energy, force and motion.

Science Lab in a Supermarket. Robert Friedhoffer. New York, NY: Franklin Watts, 1998. 95 pp. Presents a variety of experiments using items from a supermarket.

The Science of a Spring. John Stringer. Austin, TX: Raintree Steck-Vaughn, 2000. 32 pp. Explains why springs act the way they do based on elementary concepts of physics.

The Science of Noise. Lynne Wright. Austin, TX: Raintree Steck-Vaughn, 2000. 32 pp. Explains how different sounds are made, how they travel, and how to change sounds by altering pitch or volume.

The Science of Sound & Music. Shar Levine and Leslie Johnstone. New York, NY: Sterling Pub. Co, 2000. 80 pp. Contains instructions for experiments involving sound.

The Science of the Sky. Jonathan Bocknek. Milwaukee, WI: Gareth Stevens Pub., 2000. 32 pp. Discusses various aspects of atmospheric physics.

Science on a Shoestring. Herb Strongin. Menlo Park, CA: Addison-Wesley, 1991. 196 pp. Provides a variety of experiments.

Science Projects about the Physics of Sports. Robert Gardner. Springfield, NJ: Enslow Publishers, 2000. 128 pp. Contains science projects and experiments related to sports.

Science Projects About the Physics of Toys and Games. Robert Gardner. Springfield, NJ: Enslow Publishers, 2000. 128 pp. Explores the physics of various toys such as an air car, top, and balloon.

Screws. Sally M. Walker. Minneapolis, MN: Lerner Publications Co., 2002. 47 pp. An early bird physics book.

Simple Physics Experiments with Everyday Materials. Judy Breckenridge. New York, NY: Sterling Pub. Co., 1993. 128 pp. Contains over 60 experiments.

*Simple Science Experiments with Marbles. Eiji Orii and Masako Orii. Milwaukee, WI: Gareth Stevens Pub., 1989. 32 pp. Shows what happens when a moving object hits something.

The Skeleton and Movement. (rev. ed.) Steve Parker. New York, NY: Franklin Watts, 1991. 48 pp. Discusses the musculoskeletal system.

Soaring. Phyllis J. Perry. New York, NY: Franklin Watts, 1997. 64 pp. Traces the history of gliders and discusses the modern sport of soaring.

Solid, Liquid, or Gas? Sally Hewett. New York, Children's Press, 1998. 32 pp. Uses observation and activities to inform about properties.

Sound and Hearing. John Farndon. New York, NY: Benchmark Books, 2001. 32 pp. A collection of experiments that explore the nature of sound.

Sound and Music. Malcolm Dixon and Karen Smith. Mankato, MN: Smart Apple Media, 1999. 30 pp. Suggests simple experiments to illustrate the principles of sound.

Sound Fundamentals: Funtastic science activities for kids. Robert W. Wood. Broomall, PA: Chelsea House Pub., 1999. 125 pp. Includes 25 activities involving sound.

Sounds All Around. Wendy Pfeffer. New York, NY: HarperCollins, 1999. 32 pp. Explains how sounds are made.

Sports Science Projects: The physics of balls in motion. Madeline Goodstein. Berkeley Heights, NJ: Enslow Pub., 1999. 128 pp. Suggests experiments and science fair projects using sports balls.

Squirts and Spurts: Science fun with water. Vicki Cobb. Brookfield, CT: Millbrook Press, 2000. 48 pp. Explains how the physics of water pressure makes items like faucets and water pistols work.

Super Sound. Wendy Madgwick. Austin, TX: Raintree Steck-Vaughn, 1999. 32 pp. Gives instructions for various projects that demonstrate the properties and uses of sound.

Tell Me How Much It Weighs. Shirley Willis. New York, NY: Franklin Watts, 1999. 30 pp. Introduces the concept of weight.

Toying Around with Science: The physics behind toys and gags. Robert Friedhoffer. New York, NY: Franklin Watts, 1995. 95 pp. Explains physics using toys as examples.

Trains. Phyllis J. Perry. Berkeley Heights, NJ: Enslow Publishers, 2001. Tells about the transcontinental railroad, the steam engine, and today's high-speed trains.

Trains: The history of railroads. David Jefferis. New York, NY: Franklin Watts, 1991. 32 pp. Traces the development of trains.

Twentieth Century Science. Harry Henderson. San Diego, CA: Lucent Books, 1997. 112 pp. Gives an overview of the developments of the century that have had major impact such as the field of atomic physics.

Unusual Airplanes. Don Berliner. Minneapolis, MN: Lerner Publications Co., 1985. 48 pp. Discusses a variety of airplanes that have unusual shapes.

The Visual Dictionary of Physics. Jack Challoner. New York, NY: Dorling Kindersley, 1995. 64 pp. An Eyewitness science book.

The Way Things Work. David Macaulay. Tucson, AZ: Zephyr Press, 1988. 400 pp. Contains simple explanations of complicated scientific principles.

Weather Watcher's Library. Dean Galiano. New York, NY: Rosen Central, 2000. 48 pp. Discusses cloud dynamics and physics.

Weight and Balance. Barbara Taylor. New York, NY: Franklin Watts, 1990. 32 pp. Discusses force, gravity, and devices used to measure weight.

Weird Wheels. Alain Chirinian. Englewood Cliffs, NJ: Julian Messner, 1989. 64 pp. Shows 14 vehicles with unusual shapes and powerful engines.

Wheels. Julie Fitzpatrick. Morristown, NJ: Silver Burdett Press, 1988. 30 pp. Experiments with wheels, pulleys, and gears.

Wheels and Axles. Sally M. Walker. Minneapolis, MN: Lerner Publications Co., 2002. 47 pp. An early bird physics book.

Why Doesn't the Earth Fall Up? And other not such dumb questions about motion. Vicki Cobb. New York, NY: Lodestar Books, 1989. 40 pp. Answers nine interesting questions about motion.

Why Doesn't the Sun Burn Out? Vicki Cobb. New York, NY: Lodestar Books, 1990. 40 pp. Presents and answers nine interesting questions about energy.

Wings of History: The air museums of Europe. Louis Divone. Oakton, VA: Oakton Hills Publications. 1989. 312 pp. Discusses various aeronautical museums.

Wings, Wheels, & Sails. Tom Stacy. New York, NY: Franklin Watts, 1991. 40 pp. Discusses various forms of transportation.

Work. Sally M. Walker. Minneapolis, MN: Lerner Publications Co., 2002. 47 pp. An early bird physics book.

Work People Do., 3 vol. Betsy Imershein. Englewood Cliffs, NJ: Julian Messner, 1990. 32 pp. ea. Explains common tasks of auto mechanics.

Other Resources

American Institute of Physics
Director of Physics Program
335 East 45th Street
New York, NY 10017

All About Flight. Produced and directed by First Light Pictures, Inc. Wynnewood, PA: Schlessinger Media, 2000. 1 videocassette, 23 min. For grades K-4. Discusses topics such as gravity, lift, and thrust.

All About Forces and Gravity. Produced and directed by First Light Pictures, Inc. Wynnewood, PA: Schlessinger Media, 2000. 1 videocassette, 23 min. For grades K-4. Explains the concepts of friction and magnetism.

All About Motion and Balance. Produced and directed by First Light Pictures, Inc. Wynnewood, PA: Schlessinger Media, 2000. 1 videocassette, 23 min. For grades K-4. Explains how motion and balance are related.

AM/FM Project Kit. Fort Worth, TX: Radio Shack, Tandy Corporation. Contains a pre-assembled tuner and the remainder solderless coil spring construction. Batteries not included.

Capsela Kits. Nashua, NH: Delta Education. These kits allow students to understand gears and locomotion by building self-propelled machines.

Crystal AM Radio Kit. Fort Worth, TX: Radio Shack, Tandy Corporation. Simple materials for a crystal radio.

Electromagnet Set. Nashua, NH: Delta Education. Complete with battery and instructions for children to construct a working electromagnet.

Gears At Work. Nashua, NH: Delta Education. A guide and parts in a sturdy, plastic tote box for use in exploring the mechanics of gears.

Hands-on Explorations: Magnets. Nashua, NH: Delta Education. A manual and a variety of magnets for students to investigate poles, magnetic force, and more.

Flight and Rocketry DSM II. Nashua, NH: Delta Education. For grades 5-6, introduces the fundamentals of flight.

Flying Machines. Patrick Prentise. Rochester, NY: Eastman Kodak, 1989. 1 videocassette, 60 minutes. The viewer goes on a visit to the National Air and Space Museum's Paul E. Garber Facilty and sees how air and space craft are restored and preserved.

Force and Friction. Yorkshire Television Productions. Evanston, IL: Journal Films, 1987. 1 videocassette, 20 min. Describes the function of force in everyday life.

Henry Ford Museum & Greenfield Village. Glastonbury, CT: Video Tours, 1989. 1 videocassette, 30 minutes. Explores the Henry Ford Museum.

Investigating Electricity Kit. Nashua, NH: Delta Education. For grades 6 to 9 provides materials for hands-on investigations to study the properties of electricity.

K'Nex Simple Machines Deluxe Set. Nashua, NH: Delta Education. For students in grades 1–9 to learn about mechanical principles and to experiment with simple machines.

The Magic School Bus Plays Ball. John May, Brian Muhl, Jocelyn Stevenson. New York, NY: Scholastic, distributed by Kid Vision, 1995. 1 videocassette, 30 minutes. The class learns through watching a frictionless baseball game.

Magnetic Field Demonstrator. Nashua, NH: Delta Education. A cylinder filled with mineral oil and iron filings allows the demonstration of magnetic fields.

Motion and Balance. Produced and directed by First Light Pictures, Inc. Wynnewood, PA: Schlessenger Media, 2000. 1 videocassette, 23 min. For grades 5-8. Explains about Newton's Laws of Motion.

Physics. Kim Mitzo Thompson. Akron, OH: Twin Sisters Productions, 2001. 24-page book and 1 sound cassette. Deals with topics such as light, colors, static, electricity, and machines.

Sound. Produced and directed by First Light Pictures, Inc. Wynnewood, PA: Schlessenger Media, 2000. 1 videocassette, 23 min. For grades 5-8. Examines topics such as sound waves and the speed of sound.

Switch-On! Nashua, NH: Delta Education. Teaches the basic principles of electronics with circuit blocks made of molded heavy plastic.

30-in-1 Electronic Lab Kit. Fort Worth, TX: Radio Shack. Tandy Corporation. Teaches the basics of electronics and includes everything needed to build a radio, alarm, and timer. Batteries not included.

The Ultimate Paper Airplane. Richard Kline. San Diego, CA: Creative Learning Systems, Inc. Contains detailed diagrams and instructions for folding and flying seven models of planes.

White Wings Assembly Kit. San Diego, CA: Creative Learning Systems, Inc. Dr. Yasuaki Ninomiya, authority on paper planes, designed this kit, which contains 15 different models and includes step-by-step assembly guides and flight instructions.

3

Exploring science in the backyard

Much of a child's time is heavily regulated. This is partly due to the hectic pace of simply living in the twenty-first century. Often both parents work and alarms start everyone off each day dashing in a variety of directions. There may be buses to catch, a car pool to arrange, and day-care schedules to coordinate.

In addition, scattered through the week, for various family members, are meetings, music lessons, aerobics classes, bowling, bridge club, scouting, swimming lessons, religious activities, little league schedules, concerts, and many more activities. Although these various activities make up our "leisure time," they might not be very leisurely!

Schools are also "time conscious." Bells ring, periods end, tests and projects need to be completed within a time frame, library books need to be returned by a certain date, and so forth.

While children need discipline, they do not need to be occupied every minute of the day! Especially during the summer or while on a school vacation, a child may really appreciate the opportunity to simply play in a backyard—and the backyard is a wonderful place to begin explorations in science.

Before abandoning a young child to the joys of playing and exploring science in a backyard, it is important that safety factors be considered. If the backyard is fenced and relatively free from dangerous materials, it might be sufficient for you to explain which areas, if any, are "off limits" to the child.

Children can usually accept and respect such limits, but it is helpful to give some rationale. For instance, if a portion of the flower bed has just been seeded, the child must understand that he or she cannot dig or run there because young seedlings are starting to grow and would be damaged if trampled.

31

With a little thought, most guidelines can be positively phrased, such as "You may dig in the dirt and play with your trucks in this area," or "You may play ball in this area," rather than listing a lot of "no's" and "don'ts."

Young children may be either quite happy exploring and playing on their own or may appreciate adult company. Sometimes they may want to bring toys or equipment outside with them. Make the most of the active imagination and curiosity of a child. For example, a very young child may be content for some time to sit on a back patio with a dish of soap bubble solution and a bubble wand. After a time, this may lead to a series of questions about the size and shape of bubbles, what makes the colors that shine on them, and how high and fast they may float. This is your time to incorporate some science teaching.

If any child spends considerable time in the backyard, it is almost inevitable that her powers of observation will sharpen. Also quite early, children may develop specialized interests. This can lead to a host of questions, half of which will begin with "Why?" Your logical, thoughtful response to a child's "why?" question may immediately be met with another "why?" question.

Often these questions that are seemingly simple are in reality quite complex. For example, the question "Why is the grass green?" can take some time to explain! Knowing how to seize these opportunities can lead to wonderful outdoor learning situations.

These questions and outdoor explorations also provide great opportunities for the application of mathematics. The child will be using problem-solving techniques and reasoning skills, measuring and graphing, estimating and making connections, seeing patterns and relationships, and communicating mathematical findings. There will be plenty of opportunity to work with whole numbers and fractions.

When questions arise in your areas of expertise, it will be easy to answer the child simply, completely, and honestly. In a flush of enthusiasm over a loved and well understood subject, however, there is always a danger in telling too much. (We've all had the experience of being told far more about penguins than we ever wanted to know!)

And sometimes, when the questions arise in an unfamiliar field, you may be stumped. It's quite all right to tell a child that you don't know the answer to a very good question but will try to find out. This can be the beginning of an outing to the library. (Be sure to read Chapter 14, "Exploring Science in the Library.")

Sometimes questions can best be answered by observation. Sitting quietly and watching a honeybee move from blossom to blossom may answer some of a child's questions about pollination. It may also lead to checking out more library books to find additional information.

The child may observe that soils are different. Some soils may be reddish clay while others are rich in humus or are sandy. In Chapter 4, "Exploring Botany," some additional ideas for exploring how plants grow in different types of soil are provided.

And the activities in this chapter do not need to be limited to the backyard at home. Many teachers take students to the playground, to a nearby park, or on a more distant field trip to explore the outdoors. At the right time and in the right place, it can be amazing how much a child can learn from the observation of a square-foot of land!

Although sharp eyes and curiosity are the best equipment, if you have a budding biologist on your hands, some other items may prove useful. A notebook and pencil might be helpful, along with a magnifying glass, a butterfly net, and a specimen cage or "bug box."

Making a bug box

To make a bug box, cut four pieces of ¼-inch-thick plywood into rectangles that measure 6 inches high by 2½ inches wide. These will form the two sides, top, and bottom of your box. Into one of these pieces, 1 inch from the top edge, drill a hole, approximately 1½ inches in diameter. (This will be the hole through which specimens, leaves, and twigs are inserted.) Use

fine finishing nails to hold together the bottom and two upright sides of
your bug box. The side with the hole should be attached so that the hole
is toward the top.

For the front and back of the bug box, use very fine screen attached inside a ½-inch wooden frame with outside measurements of 6 inches tall by
7½ inches wide.

Attach the fourth piece of ¼-inch plywood to the top to complete the
box. Nail it into place. You may want to glue a handle on the top for easy
carrying.

Last, cut a small piece of plywood or smooth particle board approximately 2 inches square. Using a short screw, fasten this 2-inch piece of wood
directly above the 1½-inch hole in the side. This piece can now be pushed
aside to uncover the hole for inserting specimens and pushed back into
place again to secure the bug box.

Using his new bug box, the child might enjoy looking more closely at
the eggs that a butterfly has attached to the leaves of your willow tree. He
may also find great delight in a cricket or grasshopper that could be contained for a short time to allow a through study. Since caterpillars spend most
of their time eating, it might be possible to put one along with its favorite leaf
into a container and both watch and listen. (Yes, you can sometimes hear the
chomping noise made by a caterpillar's jaws!) Remember, however, the creature you capture must be let go so it can continue to live.

Measuring the big jump

Grasshoppers are great jumpers. Perhaps you and a curious child would like to find out just how far they can jump.

Set out a long sheet of paper, marking off a starting point. Place the grasshopper on the sheet (perhaps on a driveway, front porch, or back patio). Then make the grasshopper jump by gently touching the tail end of its abdomen with a feather.

Mark the spot where it lands and measure the distance. Try this experiment with several grasshoppers and some crickets, too. Compare their leaps. Perhaps make a graph to show this.

Setting up a vivarium at home or school

If the child really seems to enjoy crickets, an activity that would keep him or her interested would be to set up a vivarium.

Crickets make good pets. You can make a home for a cricket by putting a layer of dirt and some leaves into an empty aquarium and placing a wire mesh on top. This new home is called a *vivarium*.

To keep the cage clean, cover the cricket with a small strainer to prevent its escape while you are housekeeping. If you keep more than one cricket, you need to be sure that you have a male and a female. If you try to keep two males or two females togther, they will often fight.

Feed your pet crickets crumbs of bread, bits of lettuce and cucumber, potatoes, and even dog biscuits. Sprinkle some water onto a plant leaf for them to drink, or put in a small bottle cap of water.

The backyard is home to many busy little creatures. A spider may have provided a web in the corner of the garden. The patient child may see not only the clever spider that wove the web but also the sorts of food trapped in it. An industrious ant might be observed carrying a crumb over and through the blades of grass. A mantis, camouflaged in green and brown, may look over its shoulder at the explorers in the yard. And a beetle may be surprised in the middle of its lunch on a hollyhock.

By taking the time to observe and having some very simple equipment available, you can capitalize on the natural curiosity of a child. Remember that even at a young age, children also can be taught humaneness and responsibility. For example, a grasshopper should not be kept in an airtight jar, and after the child has had a chance to study a butterfly, it should be released back into its natural environment. You can model a respect for, as well as an interest in, nature.

Using photography

Another way to learn more about insects is to capture them on film by photographing them. In this way, the child will have a permanent record of the insect in its natural habitat.

You will want to use high-speed film and a fast setting since it is hard for a child to hold a camera very still. Also you will need practice in guessing the distance from the camera to the insect so that you can focus correctly. Many cameras have attachments for close-range photography.

You may also want to use a tripod to hold the camera perfectly steady and keep it in one position after it has been focused. For night photography, you'll need photo-flood bulbs.

Keeping a notebook in which you record the date, time, place, lighting conditions, film, and shutter speeds is a good habit for the young naturalist to acquire.

Some students won't be very interested in earthworms, butterflies, crickets, and grasshoppers. The creepy crawlies of the backyard or schoolyard don't appeal to them. But you needn't give up on exploration in the out-of-doors. These children may develop an interest in birds, flowers, trees, shrubs, or vegetables. Chapters 4 ("Exploring Botany") and 5 (Exploring Ethology") will deal with these topics.

For apartment and city dwellers who lack backyards, there can be trips to playgrounds and city parks to observe ducks, song birds, squirrels, plants, and insect life. Even on an apartment windowsill, it's possible to encourage seedlings in an egg carton planter or to participate in planting and maintaining a small herb or bulb garden planted in a large, decorative terrarium.

Relatives or friends who live some distance from a child might snap some photos of the yard filled with snow, a spring blossoming fruit tree, a prize rosebush in bloom, a robin's nest, a butterfly on a lily, a giant squash, or the biggest pumpkin from the patch, and mail these pictures to the child.

The richness of the backyard exploration might be enhanced by sharing some books together on special topics of interest and carrying out some simple experiments. Many of these may be related to classroom activities.

Resource Books

Adventures with Rocks and Minerals: Geology experiments for young people. Lloyd H. Barrow. Hillside, NJ: Enslow Publishers, 1991. 96 pp. Contains suggestions for a variety of earth science experiments.

Amazing Amphibians. Sara Swan Miller. New York, NY: Franklin Watts, 2001. 63 pp. Discusses the appearance and habits of several amphibians.

Amazing Beetles. John Still. New York, NY: Alfred A. Knopf, 1991. 32 pp. Through photographs, examines various members of the beetle world.

Animal Builders. Jim Flegg. Brookfield, CN: Newington Press, 1991. 32 pp. Tells how animals, fish, and insects build homes to protect themselves.

Animal Observations. Ray Broekel. Chicago, IL: Children's Press, 1990. 48 pp. Provides tips on observing the behavior and habitat of birds, insects, and other wildlife.

Animals, Birds, Bees, and Flowers. Alan Snow. Chicago, IL: Children's Press, 1989. 24 pp. Introduces animals, birds, insects, and plants.

Animal Skin & Scales. David M. Schwartz. Milwaukee, WI: Gareth Stevens Pub., 2000. 24 pp. Examines the outside coverings of creatures such as butterflies, earthworms, and snakes.

The Ant: Energetic worker. Luc Gomel. Watertown, MA: Charlesbridge, 2001. 25 pp. An introduction to the industrious ant.

Ant Colonies. Jill Kalz. North Mankato, MN: Smart Apple Media, 2001. 23 pp. Discusses insect societies.

Ant Colony, An. Heiderose and Andreas Fischer-Nagel. Minneapolis, MN: Carolrhoda Books, 1989. 48 pp. Describes the life cycle and the community life of ants.

Ants. Theresa Greenaway. Austin, TX: Raintree Steck-Vaughn, 2000. 32 pp. Describes the life cycle and habits of ants and tells how to collect and care for them.

Ants, Bees and Wasps. Sally Morgan. North Mankato, MN: Thameside Press, 2001. 31 pp. A basic introduction to ants, bees and wasps.

Backyard Hunter: The praying mantis. Bianca Lavies. New York, NY: Dutton, 1990. 32 pp. Describes the behavior of the mantis.

Beehives. Jill Kalz. North Mankato, MN: Smart Apple Media, 2001. 23 pp. An introduction to bee culture.

Bees and Wasps. Kate Petty. New York, NY: Gloucester Press, 1987. 29 pp. Includes discussion of the honeybee, bumblebee, and yellow jacket.

Beetle. David Hawcock. New York, NY: Random House, 1996. unpaged. This read-about, fold-out, pop-up book describes the characteristics and habitats of beetles.

Beetle. Rebecca Stefoff. New York, NY: Benchmark Books, 1997. 31 pp. Describes the physical characteristics, behaviors and habitats of different beetles.

*Beetles. Cheryl Coughlan. Mankato, MN: Pebble Books, 1999. 24 pp. Discusses features and behaviors of beetles.

Beetles. Theresa Greenaway. Austin, TX: Raintree Steck-Vaughn, 1999. 32 pp. Tells how to collect and keep beetles as pets.

Beetles. Elaine Pascoe. Woodbridge, CT: Blackbirch Press, 2000. 48 pp. Discusses the habits and life cycles of many species of beetles.

Beetles: The most common insect. Sara Swan Miller. New York, NY: Franklin Watts, 2001. 47 pp. Gives descriptions of 14 species and hints for finding and observing beetles.

Big Book of Bugs. Theresa Greenaway. New York, NY: Dorling Kindersley, 2000. 32 pp. Shows a variety of insects including beetles, wasps, and stick and leaf insects.

Bird Nests. Helen Frost. Mankato, MN: Pebble Books, 1999. 24 pp. Shows the nests of various types of birds and what materials are used in making them.

Bird Watching with Margaret Morse Nice. Michael Elsohn Ross. Minneapolis, MN: Carolrhoda Books, 1997. 48 pp. Discusses the life and career of Margaret Morse Nice and gives tips and activities involving bird watching.

Bugs, Beetles, & Butterflies. Harriet Zeifert. New York, NY: Viking, 1998. 32 pp. Gives an introduction to such creatures as the earwig, zebra butterfly and water strider.

Bugs: Stingers, suckers, sweeties, swingers. Liz Greenbacker. New York, NY: Franklin Watts, 1993. 64 pp. Examines various insects commonly found in homes.

Butterflies. Jen Green. New York, NY: Benchmark Books, 1999. 32 pp. Describes the behaviors and life cycles of butterflies.

Butterflies. Jonathan P. Latimer. Boston, Houghton Mifflin, 2000. 48 pp. A guide for identifying various butterflies.

Butterflies. Ned Simonson. New York, NY Children's Press, 2000. 48 pp. Gives information and describes various types of butterflies.

Butterflies and Moths. Larry Dane Brimner. New York, NY: Children's Press, 1999. 47 pp. Discusses the life cycles of butterflies and moths.

Butterflies Fly. Yvonne Winer. Watertown, MA: Charlesbirdge, 2001. unpaged. Contains short verses and detailed illustrations about butterflies.

Butterflies: Pollinators and nectar-sippers. Adele Richardson. Mankato, MN: Bridgestone Books, 2001. 24 pp. Discusses the characteristics, habitats, food, and enemies of butterflies.

*The Butterfly Alphabet. Kjell Bloch Sandved. New York, NY: Scholastic, 1996. unpaged. A butterfly alphabet book.

The Butterfly Alphabet Book. Brian Cassie and Jerry Pallotta. Watertown, MA: Charlesbridge, 1995. unpaged. A butterfly alphabet book.

Butterfly and Moth. Paul Ernest Sutton Whalley. New York, NY: Alfred A. Knopf, 1988. 64 pp. Using photos, the behavior and life cycles of moths and butterflies are illustrated.

The Butterfly Book: A kid's guide to attracting, raising and keeping butterflies. Kersten R. Hamilton. Santa Fe, NM: John Muir Pub., 1997. 40 pp. Explains how to attract butterflies to gardens.

Butterfly Eggs. Helen Frost. Mankato, MN: Pebble Books, 1999. 24 pp. A simple introduction to where and how butterflies lay their eggs.

Butterfly Watching. Dianne Bair. Mankato, MN: Capstone Books, 2000. 48 pp. Describes the physical characteristics of butterflies and gives tips on how to observe them.

Buzz! A book about insects. Melvin Berger. New York, NY: Scholastic, 2000. unpaged. Provides information about caterpillars, flies, bees, and butterflies.

Can You Find Me? A book about animal camouflage. Jennifer Dewey. New York, NY: Scholastic, Inc., 1989. 40 pp. Tells how insects, birds, reptiles, and mammals use camouflage.

Caterpillar. Karen Hartley. Des Plaines, IL: Heinemann Library, 1999. 32 pp. An introduction to the habitat, diet, and life cycle of a caterpillar.

Caterpillarology. Michael Elsohn Ross. Minneapolis, MN: Carolrhoda Books, 1997. 48 pp. Tells how to find, collect, and keep caterpillars.

Caterpillars. Helen Frost. Mankato, MN: Pebble Books, 1999. 24 pp. An introduction to the various stages from egg to butterfly.

Caterpillars. Jonathan P. Latimer. Boston, MA: Houghton Mifflin, 2000. 48 pp. Discusses the characteristics of caterpillars that are arranged in categories such as 'bumpy,' 'hairy,' and 'horned.'

Caterpillars. Patrick Merrick. Chanhassen, MN: The Child's World, 1998. 32 pp. Describes life cycles.

*Caterpillar to Butterfly. Elizabeth A. Rodger. New York, NY: Scholastic, 1996. unpaged. A pop-up book for young readers.

The Clover and the Bee: A book of pollination. Anne Ophelia Dowden. New York, NY: Thomas Y. Crowell, 1990. 96 pp. Explains pollination.

Cockroaches, Stinkbugs, and Other Creepy Crawlers. Christine Becker. Los Angeles, CA: Lowell House Juvenile, 1996. 64 pp. Gives tips for drawing insects.

Creepy Crawlies. Ruth Thomson. New York, NY: Macmillan, 1991. 32 pp. Provides an introduction to ants, caterpillars, flies, snails, spiders, and worms.

Crickets and Grasshoppers. Elaine Pascoe. Woodbridge, CT: Blackbirch Press, 1999. 48 pp. Describes the physical characteristics, habitat, and life cycle of crickets and grasshoppers.

Discovering Bugs. George McGavin. New York, NY: Bookwright Press, 1989. 48 pp. Describes characteristics and behavior of bugs.

Discovering Slugs and Snails. Jennifer Coldrey. New York, NY: Bookwright Press, 1987. 47 pp. Describes the physical characteristics, habitat, and behavior of slugs and snails.

Dragonfly. Barrie Watts. Morristown, NJ: Silver Burdett Press, 1989. 25 pp. Shows the development of the dragonfly through egg and nymph to adult through the use of photos and drawings.

A Dragon in the Sky: The story of a green darner dragonfly. Laurence P. Pringle. New York, NY: Orchard Books, 2001. 24 pp. An introduction to dragonflies.

Draw 50 Creepy Crawlies. Lee J. Ames. New York, NY: Doubleday, 1991. 60 pp. Includes step-by-step instructions for drawing 50 insects and spiders.

Earthworms, Dirt, and Rotten Leaves: An exploration in ecology. Molly McLaughlin. New York, NY: Atheneum, 1986. 96 pp. Describes earthworms and their habitat, and suggests simple experiments.

*The Empty Lot (Vol. 1). Dale H. Fife. Boston, MA: Little, Brown, 1991. 30 pp. In this work of fiction, Harry inspects an empty, partially wooded lot before selling it and finds birds, insects, and other small animals.

Exploring Weather. Ed Catherall. Austin, TX: Steck-Vaughn Library, 1990. 48 pp. Discusses climate and weather and includes simple activities and experiments.

The Family Butterfly Book: Discover the joy of attracting, raising and nurturing butterflies. Rick Mikula. Pownal, VT: Storey Books, 2000. 166 pp. Explains how to attract butterflies to gardens.

The Fiddlehoppers: Crickets, katydids, and locusts. Phyllis J. Perry. Danbury, CT: Franklin Watts, 1995. 64 pp. Discusses the noisemakers of the insect world.

Fingers and Feelers. Henry Arthur Pluckrose. New York, NY: Franklin Watts, 1990. 32 pp. Explores the sense of touch in the animal kingdom.

Fireflies. Caroline Arnold. New York, NY: Scholastic, 1994. 31 pp. Tells how fireflies grow and how they light up.

Frogs and Toads. Bobbie Kalman. New York, NY: Crabtree Pub. Co., 1994. 32 pp. Discusses the life cycles, behavior, and anatomy of frogs and toads.

Frogs, Toads, and Turtles. Diane L. Burns. Milwaukee, WI: Gareth Stevens Pub., 2000. 40 pp. Describes the physical characteristics, habitats, and diet of 30 kinds of frogs, toads, and turtles.

From Caterpillar to Butterfly. Deborah Heiligman. New York, NY: HarperCollins, 1996. 31 pp. Explains metamorphosis.

Garter Snakes. Mary Ann McDonald. Minneapolis, MN: Capstone Press, 1996. 48 pp. Discusses the physical characteristics, habitat, and behavior of common garter snakes.

Golden Book of Insects and Spiders. The. Lawrence P. Pringle. Racine, WI: Western Publishing Co., 1990. 45 pp. Takes a look at insects and spiders.

Grasshoppers. Graham Coleman. Milwaukee, WI: Gareth Stevens Pub., 1997. 24 pp. Examines the anatomy, behavior, habitat, and life cycles of different kinds of grasshoppers.

*Growing Like Me. Anne Rockwell. San Diego, CA: Silver Whistle, 2001. unpaged. Tells how eggs grow into birds, caterpillars into butterflies, and acorns into trees.

Hide and Seek: Creatures in camouflage. Phyllis J. Perry. Danbury, CT: Franklin Watts, 1997. 64pp. Uses color photographs to show how various animals rely on camouflage.

Hiding Toads. Suzanne Paul Dell'Oro. Minneapolis, MN: Lerner Publication, 1999. 32 pp. Discusses the life cycle of North American toads.

How Did We Find Out about Sunshine? Isaac Asimov. New York, NY: Walker & Company, 1987. 64 pp. Examines scientific discoveries for children ages 10 and more.

How Insects Build Their Amazing Homes. W. Wright Robinson. Woodbridge, CT: Blackbirch Press, 1999. 64 pp. Describes how termites, wasps, bees, and ants live in organized colonies.

How Insects Work Together. Jill Bailey. New York, NY: Benchmark Books, 1999. 32 pp. Explores the lives and survival techniques of social insects.

How Spiders and Other Silkmakers Build Their Amazing Homes. W. Wright Robinson. Woodbridge, CT: Blackbirch Press, 1999. 64 pp. Tells how these creatures produce silk and use it for webs, tents, traps, and homes.

How to Collect and Care for Beetles. Barrie Watts. New York, NY: Franklin Watts, 1989. 29pp. Tells how to collect and care for beetles.

Insect. Laurence Alfred Mound. New York, NY: Alfred A Knopf, 1990. 64 pp. Explores the world of insects.

The Insect Almanac: A year-round activity guide. Monica Russo. New York, NY: Sterling Pub. Co., 1991. 128 pp. Tells how to find, identify, and keep insects and provides seasonal activities.

Insect Metamorphosis: From egg to adult. Ron and Nancy Goor. New York, NY: Atheneum, 1990. 32 pp. Explains how insects grow and change.

Insects. Elizabeth Cooper. Austin, TX: Steck-Vaughn Library, 1990. 48 pp. Introduces and describes insects, including those that are helpful and those that are considered pests.

Insects. Terry J. Jennings. New York, NY: Gloucester Press, 1991. 24 pp. Tells how to recognize insects such as ants, butterflies, ladybugs, and bees.

Insects. Philip Steele. Mankato, MN: Crestwood House, 1991. 32 pp. Offers facts about different kinds of insects, habitats, and life cycles.

Insects. John Bonnett Wexo. Mankato, MN: Creative Education, 1991, 24 pp. Discusses the world of insects.

Insects: A guide to familiar American insects. Herbert Spencer Zim. Racine, WI: Western Publishing Co., 1991. 160 pp. Introduces the child to familiar insects.

Insects and Spiders. Linda Losit, et.al. New York, NY: Facts On File, 1989. 96 pp. Introduces insects and spiders, including centipedes, crickets, butterflies, wasps, and ants.

Inside an Ant Colony. Allan Fowler. New York, NY: Children's Press, 1998. 31 pp. Describes how social insects live.

It's a Good Thing There Are Insects. Allan Fowler. Chicago, IL: Children's Press, 1990. 32 pp. Identifies many insects and describes their useful activities.

I Wonder What It's Like to Be a Grasshopper. Erin M. Hovanec. New York, NY: PowerKids Press, 2000. 24 pp. Provides an introduction to the physical characteristics and behaviors of grasshoppers.

I Wonder What It's Like to Be an Ant. Erin M. Hovanec. New York, NY: PowerKids Press, 2000. 24 pp. Explores the life, environment, and body of an ant.

Janice VanCleave's Play and Find Out about Bugs: Easy experiments for young children. Janice Pratt VanCleave. New York, NY: John Wiley, 1999. 121 pp. Suggests simple experiments.

Jellyfish to Insects: Projects with biology. William Hemsley. New York, NY: Gloucester Press, 1991. 32 pp. Provides hands-on science projects.

Journey of a Butterfly, The. Carolyn Scrace. New York, NY: Franklin Watts, 2000. 29 pp. Presents the life cycle and annual migration of monarch butterflies.

Kid's Question and Answer Book Three, The. OWL Magazine Staff. New York, NY: Grosset & Dunlap, 1990. 80 pp. Gives answers to common questions about animals, plants, insects, and weather.

Ladybugology. Michael Elsohn Ross. Minneapolis, MN: Carolrhoda Books, 1997. 48 pp. Gives instructions for finding, collecting, and keeping ladybugs as pets.

Leaping Grasshoppers. Christine Zuchora-Walske. Minneapolis, MN: Lerner, 2000, 32 pp. Describes the physical characteristics and behavior of grasshoppers.

Let's Take a Field Trip to an Ant Colony. Kathy Furgang. New York, NY: PowerKids Press, 2000. 24 pp. Gives an introduction to an ant society including roles and duties.

The Life Cycle of a Bee. Jill Bailey. New York, NY: Bookwright Press, 1990. 32 pp. Describes the life cycle and feeding process of the bee.

Life Cycle of an Ant. Trevor Terry. New York, NY: Bookwright Press, 1988. 32 pp. Describes the common ant.

*The Listening Walk. (rev. ed.). Paul Showers. New York, NY: Harper Collins, 1991. 32 pp. Tells a story of a girl and her father who listen as they go for a walk.

Looking at Ants. Eleanor Christian. Mankato, MN: Yellow Umbrella Books, 2001. 17 pp. Tells how to set up an ant farm.

Looking at Ants. Dorothy Hinshaw Patent. New York, NY: Holiday House, 1989. 48 pp. Describes the behavior and characteristics of ants.

Magic Mud and Other Great Experiments. Gordon Penrose. New York, NY: Simon & Schuster, 1988. 48 pp. Illustrates basic scientific principles through science activities and demonstrations.

A Mealworm's Life. John Himmelman. New York, NY: Children's Press, 2001. unpaged. Discuses the life cycle of a mealworm.

Mealworms: Raise them, watch them, see them change. Adrienne Mason. Buffalo, NY: Kids Can Press, 1998. 24. Shows the metamorphosis that occurs in mealworms.

*Monarch Butterfly. Gail Gibbons. New York, NY: Holiday House, 1989. 32 pp. Describes the life cycle of the butterfly and how to raise one.

More Nature in Your Backyard: Simple activities for children. Susan S. Lang. Brookfield, CT: Millbrook Press, 1998. 48 pp. Describes simple experiments and activities for backyard science.

Mosquitoes. Dorothy Hinshaw Patent. New York, NY: Holiday House, 1986. 40 pp. Describes the development and habits of mosquitoes and discusses diseases that they carry.

Moth. Barrie Watts. Morristown, NJ: Silver Burdett Press, 1991. 25 pp. Traces the development of the moth (using photos) from the egg to caterpillar, cocoon, and finally the flying insect.

The Nature Directory: A guide to environmental organizations. Susan D. Lanier-Graham. New York, NY: Walker & Company, 1991. Contains a listing of environmental organizations.

Nature's Great Balancing Act: In our own backyard. E. Jaediker Norsgaard. New York, NY: Dutton, 1990. 64 pp. Explains interrelationships of creatures and plants and the importance of insects in the world.

Nature's Living Lights: Fireflies and other bioluminescent creatures. Alvin Silverstein. Boston, MA: Little, Brown, 1988. 42 pp. Describes bioluminescent insects, plants, and sea animals.

Naturewatch: Exploring nature with your children. Adrienne Katz. Reading, MA: Addison-Wesley Publishing Co., 1986. 128 p. Offers activities to increase one's enjoyment of nature.

Outdoor Science Adventures. Melvin Berger. New York, NY: Scholastic, 1994. 106 pp. Describes 50 science activities and experiments using common household materials.

Plants and Plant Life. Jill Bailey. Danbury, CT: Grolier Educational, 2001. 10 vols. This set of books discusses roots, stems, flowers, mosses, fruits, and other topics.

The Plant Kingdom: A guide to plant classification and biodiversity. Theresa Greenaway. Austin, TX: Raintree Steck-Vaughn, 2000. 48 pp. Discusses the life forms that make up the plant kingdom.

Rainy, Windy, Snowy, Sunny Days: Linking fiction to nonfiction. Phyllis J. Perry. Englewood, CO: Teacher Idea Press, 1996. 147 pp. Contains resources in fiction, nonfiction, and poetry to assist teachers grades K-5 teach about weather.

Salamanders. Edward J. Maruska. Plymouth, MN: Child's World, 1997. 32 pp. Introduces the salamander.

Science Fun with Mud and Dirt. Rose Wyler. Englewood Cliffs, NJ: Julian Messner, 1986. 48 pp. Provides instructions for indoor and outdoor experiments with soil and rocks.

A Shovelful of Earth. Lorus Johnson Milne. New York, NY: Henry Holt, 1987. 114 pp. Describes different soils and the plants and animals that live in them.

Small Garden Animals. Terry J. Jennings. Chicago, IL: Childrens Press, 1988. 34 pp. Describes insects, spiders, snails, and worms and suggests projects to do with them.

Snails and Slugs. Chris Henwood. New York, NY: Franklin Watts, 1988. 29 pp. Describes snails and slugs and how to keep them.

Spider's Lunch: All about garden spiders. Joanna Cole. New York, NY: Grosset & Dunlap, 1995. unpaged. Tells how a spider gets its food.

The Tiny Seed. Eric Carle. Natick, MA: Picture Book Studio, 1987. 32 pp. Describes life cycles of flowering plants.

Tongues and Tasters. Henry Arthur Pluckrose. New York, NY: Franklin Watts, 1990. 32 pp. Explores the sense of taste in the animal kingdom.

Underfoot. David M. Schwartz. Milwaukee, WI: Gareth Stevens Pub., 1999. 24 pp. Explores the world of ants, centipedes, earthworms, and moles.

Vanishing Animal Neighbors. Geraldine Marshall Gutfreund. New York, NY: Franklin Watts, 1993. 64 pp. Discusses the salamander, garter snake, and monarch butterfly.

Waiting for Wings. Lois Ehlert. San Diego, CA: Harcourt, 2001. unpaged. Discusses various aspects of butterflies.

We Watch Squirrels. Ada Graham. New York, NY: Dodd, Mead, 1985. 64 pp. Shows and explains the behavior of gray squirrels in the wild.

Wind and Weather. Barbara Taylor. New York, NY: Franklin Watts, 1991. 32 pp. Explains what makes air move, discusses weather forecasting, and air pollution.

Winter Science Projects. John Williams. Parsippany, NJ: Julian Messner, 1997. 30 pp. Contains a variety of projects including how to make a thermometer.

World's Regions and Weather. Phyllis J. Perry. Englewood, CO: Teacher Ideas Press, 1996. 157 pp. Includes fiction, nonfiction, and poetry resources to use in teaching about various kinds of weather.

Wonderful Worms. Linda Glaser. Brookfield, CT: Millbrook Press, 1992. unpaged. Discusses the physical characteristics, behavior, and life cycle of the common earthworm.

Worms. Theresa Greenaway. Austin, TX: Raintree Steck-Vaughn, 1999. 32 pp. Discusses the life cycles and habitats of worms.

Other Resources

There are a number of companies and agencies to which you can write for additional information. Ask for a catalog to learn about the free or inexpensive teaching units, posters, newsletter, and lessons that are available.

AAAS
1333 H Street, N.W.
Washington, DC 20005

Aims Education Foundation
P.O. Box 7766
Fresno, CA 93747

American Geological Institute
Director of Education
National Center for Earth Science Education
4220 King Street
Alexandria, VA 22302

American Institute of Biological Sciences
College of Natural Sciences
University of Northern Iowa
Cedar Falls, IA 50614

American Nature Study Society
Pocono Environmental Education Center
RD. 1, Box 268
Dingman's Ferry, PA 18328

Heath & Company
Science Newsletter
125 Spring Street
Lexington, MA 02173

National Association of Biology Teachers
11250 Roger Bacon Drive, #19
Reston, VA 22090

Nature Scope
National Wildlife Federation
1400 Sixteenth Street, N.W.
Washington, D.C. 20036-2266

Outdoor Biology Instructional Strategies
Lawrence Hall of Science
University of California
Berkeley, CA 94720

Butterflies and Moths. Paula Deats. Wynnewood, PA: Schlessinger Media, 1998. 1
    videocassette, 23 min. For grades 1-6. Gives facts about both butterflies and
    moths.

Butterfly Garden & Curriculum, Nashua, NH: Delta Education. A box with see-through sides so that children can watch the growth from larvae to painted lady butterfly. Coupon for larvae included. Also blackline masters and sequential lessons.

Butterfly Tower, Nashua, NH: Delta Education. Includes netting for a 6' by 14" tower and a living material card for 5 butterfly larvae.

Cricket Habitat Mini Kit, Nashua, NH: Delta Education. Plant grass seed, add live crickets, and observe a food chain.

Giant Ant Farm, Nashua, NH: Delta Education. An escape-proof plastic art farm with coupon for living ants. Farm measures 10" x 15".

Grow a Frog. Nashua, NH: Delta Education. Comes with frog house, house, and a living material card so that children can watch the development from tadpole into frog.

Plant Life for Children: All about plant structure and growth. Produced and directed by Stone House Productions. Wynnewood, PA: Schlessinger Media, 2000. 1 videocassette, 23 min. Explains the functions of roots, stems, leaves, and the manufacture by plants of sugar.

Worm Vue, Nashua, NH: Delta Education. This self-contained unit permits students to observe the subsurface activity of live worms. Includes a poster and a living material card for 200 worms.

4

Exploring Botany

Exploring botany can take many forms. It might be that a child who is not especially interested in growing things is nonetheless intrigued with how plants survive in the Arctic or is interested in the strange and unusual plant life of the rain forests. Maybe the child wonders about carnivorous plants or the ways bees carry out pollination. Such a child may approach a study of plants by reading about those special areas that are of interest.

Other curious kids will certainly want to make this exploration a hands-on activity and will want to plant seeds, till the soil, and harvest a crop. This type of activity need not require acres of land, but can be achieved even in a school room or an apartment by working in a few containers, strategically placed on a bright windowsill.

There is a special kind of wonder that is attached to putting a tiny seed into the soil and watching it slowly grow into a plant. Even though the process takes time, the curious child will be fascinated and will learn many lessons in observation and responsibility as he cares for the seedling.

Daily measuring of growth and charting changes on a piece of graph paper is a good mathematics application and will help the child see and understand the gradual unfolding process. Other students may want to keep notes on the plant's growth by writing down and dating their observations. Some may want to make detailed sketches of the growth process.

Sprouting an avocado seed

Purchase an avocado at the grocery store. Cut it in half and remove the large seed from inside. Wash the seed off and encourage the child to examine it. Carefully push three toothpicks firmly into the seed. Then put the seed, pointed end up, suspended by three toothpicks, into a glass with the base of the avocado seed submerged in water. Put it in a sunny window.

Be sure to add water now and then as it evaporates from the glass. Be patient. Soon you will see roots growing down from the seed and a green avocado plant growing up out of the seed.

Sprouting lima beans

A similar sprouting process can be observed by conducting the following experiment.

Buy some dried lima beans. Soak the beans overnight to soften the outer skins. Carefully split one of the beans open and have your curious child examine it with a hand lens. You will be able to see a baby plant curled up at the end of one-half of the bean.

Take an old jar and put a piece of blotting paper or several layers of paper toweling onto the bottom of the jar. Put a couple of inches of water into the jar and let it sit while the paper soaks up the water. Then pour off the excess water.

Next put four of your lima beans on the paper. Wait a few days to see what happens. (You may have to add a few drops of water now and then to keep the paper wet.) Gradually a root and stem will appear on each bean.

If you wish, you can then plant your tiny bean plants out in the garden or in containers. With care, they will grow into big, healthy plants.

Differing soils

Once students are interested in how seeds grow into plants and have learned to observe and note the growth, they may be ready to see what effect different soils and varying light can make on the growth of a plant.

Get three ½-gallon milk cartons. Cut off the tops, leaving a 6-inch bottom on each carton. Save the bottoms of the cartons. Label the outside of the cartons #1, #2, and #3. Put about an inch of gravel in the bottom of each carton.

Fill carton #1 with 4 inches of sand, fill carton #2 with 4 inches of rich potting soil, and fill carton #3 with a red clay soil. Chose a plant you'd like to grow and gather or purchase six seeds. Plant two seeds in each of the containers.

Make two graphs for each carton. Label each graph with the carton number and the letter A or B. (A will be for the first plant that sprouts, and B for the second plant that sprouts in each carton.) Put the number of days along the bottom of each graph. Put ¼ inch marks going up the left side of each graph.

Put the cartons in a sunny window and water them as needed. Observe the cartons each day. On the graphs, indicate on what day the seeds sprouted through the soil. Measure each plant each day and graph its height.

Did the plants sprout faster in one kind of soil or another? Did the plants grow taller and healthier in one kind of soil or another?

Varying amount of sunlight

Another factor that affects the growth of plants is the amount of sunlight they receive. The following experiment will help prove that light is a factor in plant growth.

When you have grown two seeds into plants that appear healthy and that are about the same height, you can experiment with varying light in plant growth.

Place one of your plants in a sunny window and put the other in a closet. Be sure to water each plant regularly.

After a week, what differences do you see between the two plants? What difference do you see after two weeks?

Having done some simple seed experiments, the curious child may want to purchase some seeds and plant them at home or at school. Few things are more enjoyable than growing one's own pumpkin for Halloween. Some companies offer seeds that should yield "giant" pumpkins and encourage you to get an early start by planting the seeds in containers indoors in early spring, then moving them outside when climate conditions permit.

There are a number of other hardy vegetables that will yield a very satisfactory "crop" for the young gardener. Again, if space is a problem, there are alternatives. For example, a number of tomato plants have been developed that can be grown in pots on a patio or sunny balcony. These plants will need to be staked, and will grow about 3 feet tall. With care and luck, such plants will yield about 2 dozen tomatoes.

For the child who is more interested in colorful flowers than in vegetables, there are many options, again depending on climate, amount of sun or shade, and space availability. Some examples of colorful flowers include violets and pansies, which can occupy just a small, shady place around a bird bath and beneath a shade tree in a backyard at home, or zinnias and marigolds, which will flourish in full sun in milk cartons in a sunny classroom window. Directions on seed packets or your clerk at your local nursery will give helpful advice.

Making mushroom spore prints

Not all plants grow from seeds—some grow from spores, such as mushrooms and mosses. Your curious child can learn more about mushrooms by conducting the following experiment.

If you live near the woods, you can go for a walk in August and find many different kinds of mushrooms growing. A close look at the underside of the mushroom will reveal whether it is smooth or gilled. Gather two or three of the gilled mushrooms and bring them home with you. (Remember *not* to eat wild mushrooms because some are poisonous.)

Cut the stem near the cap. Place the cap, gills down, on a sheet of paper. Put a drinking glass over the mushroom like a dome. Wait overnight.

Carefully remove the glass and lift the mushroom cap straight up from the paper. You will find a spore print left on the paper in the shape of the mushroom cap. The spores dropped out of the mushroom gills.

Growing a moss garden

If your curious child is interested in moss and its growth, the following experiment will be enlightening.

You can grow a moss garden in an empty 2-quart pickle jar. Take the lid off, and lay the jar on its side in a shallow box filled with sand.

The side of the jar resting on the sand is now the "bottom" of your terrarium. Put a layer of sand and pebbles in the bottom of the terrarium. Then cover this sandy drainage layer with woodsy soil that you collected from outside. Add a few interesting objects such as a small pinecone, an acorn, some rocks or little pieces of wood or bark.

Next, plant small pieces of moss by pressing them down into your layer of soil. Water the garden and screw the jar lid back on.

Keep your terrarium in a place where it gets only indirect light (not in a sunny windowsill!). Usually moss will grow for several months in the jar without needing more water. Depending on the temperature, you will see moisture collect on the top of the jar and fall like rain. Your mosses will grow spore cases on slender stems that you and your curious child can closely observe through a hand lens.

If the soil seems soggy, you can open the jar for a few hours to let it dry. If it seems dry in the terrarium, add some water.

The resources that follow are designed to help you and your curious child explore whatever aspects of botany are of interest. Remember that some of the resources in other chapters may also prove useful. Some students will want to learn what earthworms do for the soil. Others will be interested in how rocks break down into soils and why mountains and valleys form. Still others will be interested in plants that live in ponds and oceans. The resources listed after Chapter 3 "Exploring Science in the Backyard," Chapter 6 "Exploring Geology and Paleontology," Chapter 8 "Exploring Geography and Cartography," Chapter 9 "Exploring the Watery World," and Chapter 10 "Exploring the Ocean" might prove helpful.

There are also many interesting craft projects, such as nature mobiles and vegetable and leaf prints, that can be made with plant parts. The resources for such craft projects are listed after Chapter 13, "Exploring Science through Art." Chapter 12, "Exploring Science through Writing," includes information on keeping journals, making observations, and writing poetry. This might be of additional interest to the student of botany.

Resource Books

Adventures with Biology. Maurice Bleifeld. Springfield, NJ: Enslow Publishers, 1997. 96 pp. Presents 30 science experiments dealing with topics such as physiology, botany, heredity, and microbiology.

Agave Blooms Just Once. Gisela Jernigan. Tucson: Harbinger House, 1989. 30 pp. This A-Z illustrated book is filled with verses about plants and animals of the desert.

The Amazing Dirt Book. Paulette Bourgeois. Reading, MA: Addison-Wesley Publishing Co., 1990. 80 pp. Describes the wonders of dirt and contains several activities involving plants and soil.

Anna's Garden Songs. Mary W. Steele. New York, NY: Greenwillow Books, 1989. 31 pp. Contains 14 poems about plants in a garden.

Anticipating the Seasons. Jill Bailey. New York, NY: Facts on File, 1988. 61 pp. Explores how animals and plant life adapt to the season.

Arctic Tundra. Lynn M. Stone. Vero Beach, FL: Rourke Enterprises, 1989. 48 pp. Explains about plants and animal life of the tundra.

Atlas of Plants. Claude Delafosse. New York, NY: Scholastic, 1994. unpaged. Transparent overlays introduce over 60 different plants from around the world.

Autumn Science Projects. John Williams. Parsippany, NJ: Julian Messner, 1998. 30 pp. Includes a variety of projects including one on finding out how seeds are dispersed.

Bean and Plant. Christine Back. Morristown, NJ: Silver Burdett Press, 1985. 24 pp. Traces the development of a bean plant.

Be a Plant Detective. Linda Gamlin. New York, NY: Derrydale Books, 1989. 39 pp. Provides information on finding out about plants.

Botany: 49 more science fair projects. Robert L. Bonnet. Blue Ridge Summit, PA: TAB Books, 1991. 144 pp. Presents various experiments in botany.

Botany Projects for Young Scientists. Maurice Bleifeld. New York, NY: Franklin Watts, 1992. 144 pp. Explores photosynthesis, plant structure, and plant growth through experiments.

Cactus. Jason Cooper. Vero Beach, FL: Rourke Enterprises, 1991. 24 pp. Provides an introduction to cacti.

Cultivating a Child's Imagination Through Gardening. Nancy E. Allen Jurenka. Englewood, CO: Teacher Ideas Press, 1996. 142 pp. Contains directions for gardening experiments.

Desert Plants. Susan Reading. New York, NY: Facts on File, 1990. 62 pp. Discusses the specialized plants of the desert.

Deserts. Philip Steele. Mankato, MN: Crestwood House, 1991. 31 pp. Discusses the world's deserts and the plants and animals that grow in them.

Dig and Sow! How do plants grow? Janice Lobb. New York, NY: Kingfisher, 2000. 32 pp. Presents principles of botany and includes simple experiments.

Dumb Cane and Daffodils: Poisonous plants in the house and garden. Carol Lerner. New York, NY: Morrow Junior Books, 1990. 32 pp. Explains the characteristics, habitat, and harmful effects of several North American plants.

Earth. Kate Petty. New York, NY: Franklin Watts, 1990. 32 pp. Explains uses of soil as a home for plants and animals and as a building material.

Eating the Alphabet: Fruits and vegetables from A to Z. Lois Eklert. San Diego, CA: Harcourt Brace Jovanovich, 1989. 32 pp. Offers alphabetical examples of various fruits and vegetables.

Everglades. Christine Sotnak Rom. Mankato, MN: Crestwood House, 1988. 47 pp. Describes plants and animals of the Everglades.

Experiments With Plants. Salvatore Tocci. New York, NY: Children's Press, 2001. 47 pp. Contains ideas for botany experiments.

Experiment With Plants. Monica Byles. Minneapolis, MN: Lerner, 1994. 32 pp. Gives basic information about plants and suggests simple experiments.

Exploring the World of Plants. Penny Raife Durant. New York, NY: Franklin Watts, 1995. 48 pp. Contains ideas for plant experiments.

First Look at Growing Food. Claire Llewellyn. Milwaukee, WI: Gareth Stevens Pub., 1991. 32 pp. Presents an introduction to gardening and farming.

Floratorium. Joanne Oppenheim. New York, NY: Bantam Books, 1994. 45 pp. Takes the reader on a tour of a botanical museum.

Flowering Plants. Wendy Madgwick. Austin, TX: Steck-Vaughn Library, 1990. 47 pp. Surveys flowering plants and discusses pollination, flowers, seeds, and fruits.

Flowers. Terry J. Jennings. Chicago, IL: Children's Press, 1989. 34 pp. Contains simple experiments involving plants and flowers.

Flowers for Everyone. Dorothy Hinshaw Patent. New York, NY: Cobblehill Books, 1990. 64 pp. Discusses the growth and cultivation of flowers.

Flowers, Fruits, and Seeds. Angela Royston. Des Plaines, IL: Heinemann Library, 1999. 32 pp. Discusses buds, flowers, fruits, nuts, pods, pollination, and dispersal of seeds.

Flowers, Fruits, Seeds. Jerome Wexler. New York, NY: Prentice-Hall Books for Young Readers, 1987. 32 pp. Shows, in photographs, the different cycles from flower to fruit to seed to flower.

Flowers, Trees, and Fruits. Sally Morgan. New York, NY: Kingfisher, 1996. 32 pp. Gives basic information on the structure of plants and suggests various experiments.

Flowers, Trees and Other Plants. Angela Royston. New York, NY: Warwick Press, 1991. 40 pp. Includes projects and activities for studying growing things.

Flower Watching with Alice Eastwood. Michael Elsohn Ross. Minneapolis, MN: Carolrhoda Books, 1997. 48 pp. Explores a variety of plant life in California and Colorado.

The Forest. Isidro Sanchez and Carme Peris. New York, NY: Barron's, 1991. 32 pp. Describes a trip into the forest to learn about trees, animals, plants, and insects.

Forest Fire. Christopher Lampton. Brookfield, CT: Millbrook Press, 1991. 64 pp. Discusses forest fires and how they are in some ways beneficial.

The Four Seasons. Ruth Thomson. Milwaukee, WI: Gareth Stevens Pub., 1985. 48 pp. Describes the four seasons and their effect on plants and animals.

From Seed to Plant. Gail Gibbons. New York, NY: Holiday House, 1991. 32 pp. Explores how seeds grow into plants.

From the Water to the Land. Renato Massa. Austin, TX: Raintree Steck-Vaughn, 1997. 63 pp. Traces the evolution of plants from sea to land.

Frost: Causes and effects. Philip Steele. New York, NY: Franklin Watts, 1991. 32 pp. Explains how frost forms and its effects on humans as well as on plants and animals.

Fun with Fruits and Vegetables. Patricia Lief. Carthage, IL: Good Apple, 1991. 154 pp. An activity book involving fruits and vegetables.

Fun with Growing Things. Joan Eckstein and Joyce Gleit. New York, NY: Avon Books, 1991. 135 pp. Contains step-by-step instructions for growing plants and for projects such as leaf prints.

*A Garden Alphabet. Isabel Wilner. New York, NY: Dutton, 1991. 32 pp. Contains rhymes about gardens.

Garden Tools & Gadgets You Can Make. Percy W. Blandford. Blue Ridge Summit, PA: TAB Books, 1989. 244 pp. Provides instructions for making gardening tools.

Get Growing: Exciting indoor plant projects for kids. Lois Walker. New York, NY: John Wiley & Sons, 1991. 101 pp. Contains eleven indoor gardening projects and includes ideas for cooking and handicrafts.

Grasslands. David Lambert. Morristown, NJ: Silver Burdett Press, 1988. 48 pp. Explores plants and animal life of the grasslands.

The Great Seed Mystery for Kids. Peggy Henry. New York, NY: Avon Books, 1993. 79 pp. Contains ideas for projects and experiments.

Greening the City Streets: The story of community gardens. Barbara A. Huff. Boston, MA: Houghton Mifflin, 1990. 61 pp. Explores the urban garden movement through photos.

Growing Colors. Bruce McMillan. New York, NY: Lothrop, Lee & Shepard Books, 1988. 32 pp. Contains photos of various fruits and vegetables showing the colors in nature.

Growing Plants. Barbara Taylor. New York, NY: Warwick Press, 1991. 40 pp. Contains simple experiments to demonstrate what affects plant growth.

Growing Things. Ting Morris and Neil Morris. New York, NY: Franklin Watts, 1994. 32 pp. Discusses container gardening and plant propagation.

*Grow It for Fun. Denny Robson and Vanessa Bailey. New York, NY: Gloucester Press, 1991. 32 pp. Provides an introduction to gardening with suggestions for simple activities.

Harvesters. Irene M. Frank and David M. Brownstone. New York, NY: Facts on File, 1987. 139 pp. Discusses various occupations of collecting and cultivating food such as fishing, beekeeping, and farming.

The Hidden Life of the Meadow. David M. Schwartz. New York, NY: Crown Publishers, 1988. 36 pp. Examines plants and animals of the meadow.

Hidden Stories in Plants: Unusual and easy-to-tell stories from around the world, together with creative things to do while telling them. Anne Pellowski. New York, NY: Macmillan, 1990. 93 pp. Contains myths, folklore, and other stories with directions for making ornaments, toys, and musical instruments from plants.

How a Plant Grows. Bobbie Kalman. New York, NY: Crabtree Pub., 1997. 32 pp. Explains the functions of various parts of plants.

*How Do Apples Grow? Betsy Maestro. New York, NY: HarperCollins, 1992. 32 pp. Shows life cycle of an apple tree.

How Does Your Garden Grow? Be your own plant expert. Dominque and Philippe Joly. New York, NY: Sterling Pub. Co., 1996. 47 pp. Discusses types of gardens and describes botanical experiments.

How Plants Grow. Stephen Parker. New York, NY: Warwick Press, 1985. 32 pp. Discusses various kinds of plants and how humans and plants depend upon each other.

Ideas for Science Projects. Richard C. Adams. New York, NY: Franklin Watts, 1997. 160 pp. Gives instructions for making observations and conducting experiments.

Incredible Plants. Barbara Taylor. New York, NY: Dorling Kindersley, 1997. 44 pp. Close-up photos show the anatomy of plants.

Insects and Flowers. Hidetomo Oda. Milwaukee, WI: Raintree Childrens Books, 1986. 32 pp. Discusses plant nectar and pollination.

Introduction to Plant Science. R. O. Parker. Albany, NY: Delmar Publishers, 2000. 704 pp. Explores many aspects of the plant kingdom.

Janice VanCleave's Plants: Mind-boggling experiments you can turn into science fair projects. Janice Pratt VanCleave. New York, NY: John Wiley & Sons,1997. 90 pp. Presents facts about plants and includes ideas for experiments and projects.

A Kid's First Book of Gardening. Derek Fell. Philadelphia, PA: Running Press, 1989. 96 pp. Contains information on soils and easy-to-grow flowers and vegetables in the yard and in containers.

Kitchen Fun: Teaches children to cook successfully. Louise Price Bell. New York, NY: Derrydale Books (dist. By Crown Publishers), 1988. 26 pp. Contains a collection of easy recipes for candy, cakes, cookies, salads, and vegetables.

Leaves and Trees. Elaine Pascoe. Woodbridge, CT: Blackbirch, 2001. 48 pp. Contains suggestions for botany experiments.

*Life Cycle of a Sunflower, The. Philip Parker. New York, NY: Bookwright Pres, 1988. 32 pp. Describes sunflowers and includes simple projects.

Life in the Polar Lands. Monica Byles. New York, NY: Franklin Watts, 1990. 31 pp. Tells how humans, plants, and animals can survive at the North and South Poles.

Linnea's Windowsill Garden. Christina Bjork and Lena Anderson. New York, NY: Farrar, Straus, & Giroux, 1988. 59 pp. Tells how to create a home garden.

The Living House. Nigel S. Hester. New York, NY: Franklin Watts, 1991. 32 pp. Shows how a house can become a home for plants as well as for insects, animals, and birds.

Looking at Plants. David T. Suzuki. New York, NY: John Wiley & Sons, 1991. 96 pp. Introduces plants and suggests experiments.

Marshall Cavendish Science Project Book of Plants, The. Steve Parker. North Bellmore, NY: Marshall Cavendish, 1986. 43 pp. Contains ideas for experiments and projects.

Moonseed and Mistletoe: A book of poisonous wild plants. Carol Lerner, New York, NY: Morrow Junior Books, 1988. 32 pp. Discusses how some plants irritate the skin or cause illness when eaten.

More Than Just a Flower Garden. Dwight Kuhn. Morristown, NJ: Silver Burdett Press, 1990. 40 pp. Contains tips for starting a garden.

Morning Glories. Sylvia A. Johnson. Minneapolis, MN: Lerner Publications Co, 1985. 48 pp. Examines the stages of development of morning glories.

Mountains. Lynn M. Stone. Vero Beach, FL: Rourke Enterprises, 1989. 48 pp. Describes plants and animals of the mountains.

Mushrooms. Jason Cooper. Vero Beach, FL: Rourke Enterprises, 1991. 24 pp. Provides an introduction to mushrooms.

My First Green Book. Angela Wilkes. New York. NY: Alfred A. Knopf, 1991. 48 pp. Contains environmental activities and projects in such areas as water pollution, recycling, and wildlife gardens.

Natural Materials. Erica Burt. Vero Beach, FL: Rourke Enterprises, 1990. 32 pp. Explains how to make objects from twigs, flowers, vegetables, pebbles, shells feathers, and other things of nature.

Nature Crafts: Outdoor magic using natural materials for creative crafts. Sabine Lohf. Chicago, IL: Children's Press, 1990. 44 pp. Gives directions for crafts using flowers, leaves, vegetables, and other natural items.

Nature Projects for Young Scientists. Kenneth G. Raines, New York, NY: Franklin Watts, 1989. 142 pp. Contains nature projects and experiments involving plants and animals.

Oh, Say Can You Seed? All about flowering plants. Bonnie Worth. New York, NY: Random House, 2001. 45 pp. Part of the Cat in the Hat's learning library.

Plant. David Burnie. New York, NY: Alfred A. Knopf, 1989. 63 pp. Uses photos to describe the world of plants.

The Plant-and-Grow Project Book. Ulla Dieth. New York, NY: Sterling Pub. Co., 1993. 48 pp. Contains directions for projects rated by degree of difficulty.

Plant Biology Science Projects. David R. Hershey. New York, NY: John Wiley & Sons, 1995. 165 pp. Contains directions for science projects.

Plant Ecology. Jennifer Cochrane. New York, NY: Bookwright Press, 1987. 47 pp. Discusses conservation of natural resources.

Plant Families. Carol Lerner. New York, NY: Morrow Junior Books, 1989. 32 pp. Contains simple descriptions of 12 families of North American flowering plants.

Plant Kingdom, The: A guide to plant classification and biodiversity. Theresa Greenaway. Austin, TX: Raintree Steck-Vaughn, 2000. 48 pp. Explains the various life
forms that make up the plant kingdom.

Plant Life. Peter D. Riley. New York, NY: Franklin Watts, 1999. 32 pp. Introduces basic principles of botany and presents ideas for experiments.

Plant Partnerships. Joyce Pope. New York, NY: Facts on File, 1990. 62 pp. Contains
information on plants that depend upon animals or other plants for habitat or
survival.

Plant Projects for Young Scientists. Salvatore Tocci. New York, NY: Franklin Watts,
2000. 143 pp. Contains instructions for various botany projects.

Plants. Wendy Baker. New York, NY: Thomson Learning, 1995. 48 pp. Describes
botany experiments.

Plants. Anita Ganeri. New York, NY: Franklin Watts, 1992. 32 pp. Discusses types of
plants and how and where they grow. Includes simple projects.

Plants. Alvin Silverstein. New York, NY: Twenty-first Century Books, 1996. 64 pp.
Gives a general description and discusses specific kinds of plants.

Plants. Kathy Vanderlinden. Ontario Science Center. Buffalo, NY: Kids Can Press,
1994. 32 pp. Contains an assortment of activities to demonstrate plant growth,
reproduction and physiology.

Plants: A creative, hands-on approach to science. Claire Watts and Alexandra Parsons. New York, NY: Aladdin Books, 1993. 48 pp. Filled with directions for plant
experiments.

Plants and Flowers. Joyce Pope. Mahwah, NJ: Troll Associates, 1994. 32 pp. Describes how plants live, develop, and reproduce.

Plants and Seeds. John Stidworthy. New York, NY: Gloucester Press, 1990. 32 pp. Explains through informative text and microscopic photos the ways plants reproduce and assimilate nutrients.

Plants Around Us. Malcolm Dixon. Mankato, MN: Smart Apple Media, 1999. 30 pp.
Describes the functions of leaves and roots. Suggests activities.

Plants of the Tropics. Susan Reading. New York, NY: Facts on File, 1990. 62 pp.
Shows how plants of the tropics adapt.

Plant Stems & Roots. David M. Schwartz. Milwaukee, WI: Gareth Sevens Pub., 2000.
24 pp. Looks at the essential plant parts, stems and roots.

Plants: Origins and Evolution. Alessandro Garassino. Austin, TX: Raintree Steck-
Vaughn, 1995. 45 pp. Discusses the plant kingdom as it developed from earliest
forms to today.

Plants Without Seeds. Helen J. Challand. Chicago, IL: Children's Press, 1986. 45 pp.
Discusses algae, fungi, lichen, mosses, and ferns.

Potato. Barrie Watts. Morristown, NJ: Silver Burdett Press, 1988. 25 pp. Describes how
a potato develops.

Practical Plants. Joyce Pope. New York, NY: Facts on File, 1990. 62 pp. Examines the
many uses of plants.

Prairies. Lynn M. Stone. Vero Beach, FL: Rourke Enterprises, 1989. 47 pp. Describes
plants and animals of the prairies.

The Pumpkin Book. Gail Gibbons. New York, NY: Holiday House, 1999. 30 pp. Explains how pumpkins grow and tells how to carve them and dry their seeds.

Pumpkin, Pumpkin. Jeanne Titherington. New York, NY: Greenwillow Books, 1986. 23 pp. Tells a story of how a child named Jamie plants, grow, carves, and saves seeds from pumpkins.

Poisonous Plants. Suzanne M. Coil. New York, NY: Franklin Watts, 1991. 62 pp. Identifies poisonous plants that might be found in the home, garden, and in the wild.

Rainforests. Rodney Aldis. New York, NY: Dillon Press, 1991. 45 pp. Discusses the plants and animals of the rainforest.

Ride the Wind: Airborne journeys of animals and plants. Seymour Simon. San Diego, CA: Browndeer Press, 1997. unpaged. Information on seed dispersal.

Roses Red, Violets Blue: Why Flowers Have Colors. Sylvia A. Johnson. Minneapolis, MN: Lerner Publications Co., 1991. 64 pp. Examines the nature and function of flower colors.

Rosy's Garden: A child's keepsake of flowers. Elizabeth Laird. New York, NY: Philomel Books, 1990. 48 pp. Tells a story about how, on a visit to grandma's, a child gathers seeds, makes potpourri, and presses flowers.

Science Book of Things that Grow. Neil Ardley. San Diego, CA: Harcourt Brace Jovanovich, 1991. 29 pp. Contains many simple plant experiments.

Science Fair Projects for Elementary Schools. Patricia Hachten Wee. Lanham, MD: Scarecrow Press, 1998.

Science Fair Success with Plants. Phyllis J. Perry. Springfield, NJ: Enslow Publishers, 1999. 104 pp. Gives detailed directions for 25 interesting botany experiments.

Science for Kids: 39 easy plant biology experiments. Robert W. Wood. Blue Ridge Summit, PA: TAB Books, 1991. 123 pp. Contains information on 39 plant experiments.

Science Play!: Beginning discoveries for 2-to-6-year-olds. Jill Frankel Hauser. Charlotte, VT: Williamson Publishers, 1998. 135 pp. Contains 65 activities including some about plants.

Science Project Ideas About Trees. Robert Gardner. Springfield, NJ: Enslow Publishers, 1997. 96 pp. Contains ideas for botany experiments.

Science Projects About Plants. Robert Gardner. Springfield, NJ: Enslow Publishers, 1999. 112 pp. Over 30 experiments with plants suitable for science fairs.

Science Projects for Young People. George Barr. New York, NY: Dover Publications, 1986. 153 pp. Contains several topics for science research projects, including plants.

A Seed Grows: My first look at a plant's life cycle. Pamela Hickman. Toronto, Canada: Kids' Can Press, 1997. 15 pp. Shows life cycles of plants.

Seeds and Seedlings. Terry J. Jennings. Chicago, IL: Childrens Press, 1989. 34 pp. Includes study questions, activities, and experiments about seeds and different plants.

Seeds and Seedlings. Elaine Pascoe. Woodbridge, CT: Blackbirch Press, 1997. 48 pp. Explains how seeds form and grow and includes instructions for experiments.

Seeds to Plants: Projects with biology. Jeffrey Bates. New York, NY: Gloucester Press, 1991. 32 pp. Explores how seeds grow into plants.

Simple Earth Science Experiments with Everyday Materials. Louis V. Loeschning. New York, NY: Sterling Pub. Co., 1996. 128 pp. Contains information and suggests activities and experiments.

Six-minute Nature Experiments. Faith Hickman Brynie. New York, NY: Sterling Pub. Co., 1999. 80 pp. Contains ideas for simple science experiments using everyday materials.

Spring Science Projects. John Williams. Parsippany, NJ: Julian Messner, 1997. 30 pp. Among the variety of projects included are some on growing seeds.

Starting with Nature Plant Book. Pamela Hickman. Niagara Falls, NY: Kids Can Press, 2000. 32 pp. Presents information and ideas for projects using various plants.

Stems. Gail Saunders-Smith. Mankato, MN: Pebble Books, 1998. 24 pp. Describes the importance of roots and stems in helping flowers grow.

Strawberry. Jennifer Coldrey. Morristown, NJ: Silver Burdett Press, 1989. 25 pp. Offers, in addition to text, photos and drawings of strawberries.

Structure. Kim Taylor. New York, NY: John Wiley & Sons, 1992. 32 pp. Contains ideas for botany experiments.

Sugar: All plants make sugar, but only two do so in great quantity. Jacqueline Dineen. Hillside, NJ: Enslow Pub., 1988, 31 pp. Discusses sugar beets and cane.

Summer Science Projects. John Williams. Parsippany, NJ: Julian Messner, 1997. 30 pp. Contains a variety of projects including one on making a bottle garden.

Taking Root. Allan Fowler. New York, NY: Children's Press, 2000. 31 pp. Discusses the roots of plants and how they function.

Tiger Lilies and other Beastly Plants. Elizabeth Ring. New York, NY: Walker and Company, 1985. 32 pp. Contains full-color illustrations of many interesting plants.

Unearthing Garden Mysteries: Experiments for kids. Ellen Talmage. Golden, CO: Fulcrum Kids, 2000. 90 pp. Contains directions for botany experiments.

*Vegetable Garden. Douglas Florian. San Diego, CA: Harcourt Brace Jovanovich, 1992. 32 pp. Shows a family planting and harvesting.

Vegetables. Susan Wake. Minneapolis, MN: Carolrhoda Books, 1990. 32 pp. Discusses different vegetables and gives some easy recipes using them.

Vegetables and Oils. Jacqueline Dineen. Hillside, NJ: Enslow Pub., 1988. 31 pp. Contains information on vegetables.

*A Very Young Gardener. Jill Krementz. New York, NY: Dial Books for Young Readers, 1991. 38 pp. Tells a tale of a six-year-old who grows flowers and vegetables, looks at plants in the woods, and visits a botanical garden.

*A Walk in the Woods. Caroline Arnold. Morristown, NJ: Silver Burdett Press, 1990. 30 pp. Describes plants, animals, and seasons of the year as seen in the woods.

What Is A Plant? Bobbie Kalman. New York, NY: Crabtree Pub. Co., 2000. 32 pp. An introduction to plant life with descriptions of carnivorous and parasitic plants.

What's Inside Plants? Anita Ganeri. New York, NY: Peter Bedrick Books, 1995. 45 pp. Discusses plant physiology.

What's Inside?: Plants. Angela Royston. New York, NY: Dorling Kindersley, 1992. 17 pp. Shows the inner workings of a tulip, cactus, and thistle.

Where Food Comes From. Dorothy Hinshaw Patent. New York, NY: Holiday House, 1991. 40 pp. Shows how sun, earth, air, and water combine to help plants grow.

Why Is the Grass Green? Chris Arvetis. Chicago, IL: Children's Press, 1985. 32 pp. Explains the process of photosynthesis.

The Wonderful Woods. Rose Wyler. Englewood Cliffs, NJ: Julian Messner, 1990. 32 pp. Describes plants and animals found in the forest and suggests activities.

Wondrous Plant & Earth Experiments. Q. L. Pearce. New York, NY: T. Doherty Associates, Inc., 1989. 58 pp. Offers instructions for a large number of science experiments.

Worm's Eye View. Kipchak Johnson. Brookfield, CT: Millbrook Press, 1991. 40 pp. Describes ways to attract wildlife to your backyard and discusses the role of wild plants in ecology.

You Can Be A Woman Botanist. Kristin Rose Bozak. Culver City, CA: Cascade Press, 1999. 38 pp. Describes work opportunities available to women in botany.

Other Resources

The following magazines may be of interest as you explore plants and gardening. *Better Homes and Gardens, California, Chatelaine, Country Journal, Flower & Garden Magazine, Horticulture, The Magazine of American Gardening, Nature Canada, Organic Gardening,* and *Sunset Magazine.*

The Carrot Seed. Ruth Krauss. Ancramdale, NY: Live Oak Media, 1990. 1 book, 23 pp.; 1 sound cassette, 4 minutes. Introduces a popular story to young children about growing a carrot.

Flower Model. Nashua, NH: Delta Education. For grades 5-8, a sturdy model with removable flower parts and detailed cross-section.

Flowers, Plants and Trees. Rima Firrone. Penguin Productions: Distributed by Prism Entertainment, 1987. 1 cassette, 30 minutes. A video encyclopedia that answers questions children ask about flowers, plants, and trees.

Hydroponic Greenhouse. San Diego, CA: Creative Learning Systems, Inc. Small plastic greenhouse comes with nutrients and an illustrated manual.

Hydroponic Greenhouse. Nashua, NH: Delta Education. Greenhouse that measures 19" x 10 1/2" x 12 1/2" and nutrient mix.

Johnny Appleseed. Reeve Lindbergh. Westport, CT: Weston Woods, 2000. 1 videocassette, 18 minutes. Tells of the life and work of John Chapman, known as Johnny Appleseed.

Look What I Grew. Cambridge, MA: Intervideo, Inc. 1993. 1 videocassette, 45 minutes. A guide to raising plants in windowsill containers. Suggests easy experiments.

Plant Life For Children. Stone House Productions in cooperation with The New York Botanical Garden. Wynnewood, PA: Schlessinger Media, 2000. 1 videocassette, 23 min. For students in grades K-4, shows the transformations that a plant goes through.

Rainforest Researchers CD-Rom. Nashua, NH: Delta Education. For grades 5 - 8, allows students to explore biodiversity, plant classification, and expand their knowledge of rain forests.

Seed Mysteries. Nashua, NH: Delta Education. For grades 2-6, allows students to test a variety of seeds and to witness germination. Comes with activity guide.

Soil Test Kit. Nashua, NH: Delta Education. Allows you to test soil conditions and contains information on how to improve soil for better plant growth.

5
Exploring
ethology

Ethology is the study of animal behaviors. Interested children and adults can find numerous opportunities to observe birds and animals and to watch what they do. They can observe seasonal changes as they note a flock of migrating birds or watch animals store nuts or grow thicker coats for a winter hibernation. On a hike, they might notice a bat or owl out at night that they never see during daylight hours.

Children can sometimes observe birds and small animals in their own backyards. They may see signs of a tunneling mole or spot a wasps' nest. Other observations may require a teacher or another adult to accompany a child or group of children for a walk in the woods, to a park, or to take a visit to a zoo where more exotic creatures can be found.

Many adults and children take pleasure in observing birds. Scientists estimate there are about a 100 billion birds in the world. So whether you live in the city, the suburbs, or the country, you will encounter them.

Some children are fascinated with these wonderful creatures, and their observational skills will sharpen as they look at their colors, notice different kinds of beaks and feet, and see how they construct their nests. They may also listen to the variety of bird songs and calls and learn to identify some of them.

If you have a backyard or courtyard at home or a nature area at school, there are many projects that you can undertake to attract birds to visit.

Adding a birdbath

Putting a birdbath in your backyard or in a nature area on the school grounds can provide hours of enjoyment as you and curious children observe the birds that collect there to drink and bathe.

Many commercial birdbaths are available. You can make one by putting a shallow basin in a spot where birds come. You will need to make it secure so that it does not wobble or tip over. You might even put a clean stone in the middle of the bath where birds might stand while drinking.

With all bird feeders or baths, you need to be sure that they are placed where cats and other predators will not easily be able to hide and attack the birds.

Having a birdbath placed up on a pedestal is safer than having one on the ground. Placing the birdbath near a tree allows birds to perch and look about for danger before they visit the birdbath.

Birds eat many different kinds of foods. Ducks, gulls, terns, and herons eat fish, frogs, water plants, tiny shellfish, and insects that they find along shores, beaches, marshes, and lakes. Bobwhites, meadowlarks, and robins search in the grass and leaves for their food. Raptors, such as hawks and owls, eat rodents and other small animals. Fly catchers and swallows catch their meals as they fly. Some birds prefer beetles and caterpillars, while others prefer seeds.

Depending on where you live and what kinds of birds you are trying to attract, you can put up a bird feeder and fill it with appropriate mixes of seeds. Many feeders are available for purchase, although you might want to make one of your own.

Some feeders are simply flat trays. Another type of feeder looks like a house with a hinged roof that lifts for filling, a glass front, and a porch in front that sticks out where the birds perch while eating. Many feeders are long slender tubes with perches sticking out from the tube by small feeding holes and with a base trap where other birds can stand and eat.

While these feeders are best placed in a backyard or in a nature area of the school grounds, they can also be placed outside apartment windows or on apartment building rooftops.

Making a windowsill bird feeder

You can use a windowsill for a bird feeder. By just sprinkling seeds on the sill, you will attract small birds.

You may want to attach a small, four-sided, wooden box to your sill. A good size is 20 inches wide by 10 inches deep. Leave your box open in back and front so that you can see the birds through your window and so that the birds can easily enter. Sprinkle seeds on the floor of the box.

As a special winter treat, you may want to suspend a suet feeder inside the box. Drill holes into a short, small log or piece of wood. Fill the holes with peanut butter or suet. Screw an eye into the top of the log and tie a short piece of twine to it. Then hang the wood from another eye that is screwed into the top of your feeder box.

Feeders sometimes attract more than birds, and depending on the placement of a feeder, you may find yourself battling squirrels. Squirrels are especially fond of the sunflower seeds that are found in many birdseed mixes. They are willing to toss millet and other seeds to the ground in search of the

one special seed they like. Squirrels have no patience with the small opening through which birds are able to take seeds. So they "enlarge" these openings by gnawing through wood and plastic and destroying the feeder itself.

The best solution to prevent your bird feeder from being vandalized by
squirrels is to buy one with a baffle (or dome) suspended over the top. Then
when you place your feeder high in the air, the squirrel may jump on the dome
but probably will not be able to move from there to the bird feeder itself.

Birds' nests are wonderfully constructed, and you and your curious child
or your class of students may be lucky enough to find one that the wind has
blown to the ground or that came down with a dead tree. Do not take nests that
are still up in healthy trees because some birds use their nests more than once.

Constructing a nest box

Although you can use any kind of wood, white pine or redwood about ¾
inch or 1 inch thick is best for a nest box. Use medium screws, about 1½
inches long to join the pieces of your nest box together. It is also a good idea
to use a brown stain on your wood and let it dry thoroughly before you put
the pieces together. This stain will protect the nest box from the weather. The
directions below are for a bluebird nest box.

The back of your nest box, which you will nail to a post or tree about 8
feet above the ground, should be 5½ inches wide by 15 inches tall. The bottom should measure 4 inches by 4 inches. The front should be 5½ inches

'SIDEVIEW' AFTER ASSEMBLY

15"

6½"

5½"

TOP

SIDE
-CUT TWO-

1½"

1½"

9"

9½"

15"

BOTTOM
4" × 4"

9"

FRONT

5½"

4"

BACK
5½"

wide by 9 inches high. The front also needs to have a 1½-inch diameter hole drilled in the middle of it, 1½ inches from the top.

The two sides should be 4 inches wide and square across the bottom. But the tops should be cut on a slight slant so that the sides measure 9½ inches at the back of the side but only 9 inches at the front end of the side.

Once you have screwed together the back, two sides, and bottom of the nest box, you are ready to put on the top. The top piece of wood should measure 5 ½ inches across and be 6½ inches long. Set it in place, on the slight slant, and use a small hinge to affix it to the back, about 3 inches from the top of the back board.

Use a hook and eye as a means to close the lid tightly. Screw the eye into the top of the nest box and affix the hook to one of the sides.

This hinged top will allow you and your curious child to clean out the nest box after the young birds have flown, so that the bluebirds will have a clean place to start a new nest next year.

As you learn more about birds, questions will certainly arise. These questions may center around the migration of birds, their ability to fly, or their development from eggs. The listed resources at the end of the chapters (as well as some of the resources listed after Chapter 3 "Exploring Science in the Backyard") may be of help to you as you follow up on these interests that emerge.

You and your curious child may simply enjoy listening to birds and watching them in your backyard or in a neighborhood park. Perhaps you'll decide to study them in depth so that you can identify them.You may set up feeding stations, nest boxes, or birdbaths to attract them. Perhaps you'll even decide on a canary or other type of bird for a pet. Whatever you choose, you will derive pleasure from your exploration of birds.

You may also be fortunate enough to observe different kinds of small animals. In some neighborhoods, squirrels are frequent visitors. If you live in the suburbs or country, you may be visited by raccoons, deer, chipmunks, or coyotes. You might visit a spot where there is a beaver dam. You may discover a bee hive. Perhaps somewhere along a highway in your area is a field that has become a prairie dog community. Whatever resources you have, make the most of them. You can look for tracks as well as observe the animals.

An outing to a zoo can be another exciting way to explore science and nature! The curious child or a class of students will no doubt come away with many questions that can lead to further research and additional activities. In most zoos, there is so much to see that it is hard to take everything in, especially on a first visit. By having a few key things to look for before you go, you'll be more thorough in your visit. Don't forget to consult the explanatory signs on your walk through the zoo for a further explanation of each animal and its habitat.

Reading zoo treasure hunt signs

In most zoos there are explanatory signs and symbols. Take the time to study one of these signs carefully and point out the symbol that designates an endangered species. Explain what this means. Then, as you walk through the zoo, have the child or class of students be on the lookout for the endangered species markings. How many can you find?

It can be much like a treasure hunt because these few remaining creatures are indeed very valuable.

Examining a world map of animals

Other activities can come from a trip to the zoo, like the following activity that the child or class can conduct after the zoo visit.

As a follow-up to your zoo trip, have the child or your class list animals seen at the zoo that were of particular interest. Use reference books to learn where these animals live throughout the world.

Find a large world map. Have the child draw the zoo animals of interest or find pictures of these animals in old magazines and cut them out. Then place the animals on the world map to show them in their natural habitat. (Some animals may be found in more than one place.)

The finished map can make an interesting wall display in a library, classroom or the child's room.

There are so many wonderful animals in the zoo that it is often hard to choose a favorite. Some are so unusual that it is difficult to believe your eyes, even when you're looking at them. Another follow-up activity that might prove to be fun is explained in the following suggestion.

Drawing a combination animal

Have members of the class or a child draw a "combination animal" in its habitat. For this purpose you might make available crayons, colored pencils, magic markers, and other such mediums.

A combination animal has the characteristics of two zoo animals. For example, a hippogiraffe might have the head and neck of a giraffe on the body of a hippopotamus! Other possibilities include: the chimpanzebra, the oranguphant, and the rhinostrich. Imagination is the only limit.

While going through the zoo, the class of students or the curious child may notice any one of a number of different features of the various animals.

Sometimes it is interesting to concentrate on a single feature, such as the animals' feet. Help the child to notice the enormous size of an elephant's foot, the look of an ostrich foot, the size of the tigers' paws as they pace back and forth, the feet of a penguin as it waddles to the edge and plunges into the water, and other animals' feet on your trip through the zoo.

This should stimulate some conversation in class or at home about the way the animals interact with their environment. For example, a polar bear has hairs on his feet and often weaves back and forth from foot to foot while it is standing so that its feet do not stick to the ice.

Impressing footprints

If you, a neighbor, or a friend have a pet, you might follow up your observations of the feet of animals by making a cast of a foot print.

Mix up plaster of paris according to the directions on the box. Cut off the top of a milk carton, so that the carton stands about 3 inches high. Pour two inches of plaster of paris into the carton, and let it partially harden.

Rub a little Vaseline on the paw of a friendly dog you know. Place the dog's paw into the plaster of paris, making a good impression. (The Vaseline coating will help you to easily wipe the paw clean.) Allow the print to harden.

The next time you are on a hike in the woods, check for footprints. Can you make a guess from the prints as to what creature made it?

Some classrooms have class pets, and some do not. Some children are in a position to keep pets in their house or apartment, and others are not. Besides the pleasure and companionship that a pet provides, the care of one also teaches the child responsibility.

Setting up a miniature zoo

Even if space in the classroom, apartment restrictions, allergies, frequent traveling, and other reasons prevent you from keeping large pets at home or school, it might be possible to set up a miniature zoo.

To keep a miniature zoo, you need a corner of a room with two tables near a window that will provide air and light. In good weather, the screened window should be kept open. During cold weather, a lamp might be useful to provide warmth and light. Remember to provide shady areas in the containers for the animals during spells of hot weather.

The tables need to have tops that can be kept wiped clean. One table should have shelves above or below it where food supplies can be kept. It also needs a clear work space for mixing food, cleaning cages, and other duties.

The remainder of the work table and the surface of the other table can hold large glass jars; a dish pan, plastic bowl, or tub with gravel and water; small aquariums that have been turned into terrariums by adding a screened top, earth, and plants; and even cardboard boxes that have clear plastic across one side so that you can easily see in. These various containers can house such creatures as: crayfish, tadpoles, a small snake, horned toad, crickets, meal worms, or a lizard.

Before undertaking the setting up and maintenance of even a miniature zoo, the child or class needs to know that it takes a lot of time to feed the creatures, give them fresh water, and to clean their cages every week.

Studying the behaviors of birds and animals at school, at home, in your backyard, in a park, at the zoo, or wherever you can see them, can be a lot of fun and provides interesting topics for further research. In addition to the following resources listed to aid you in your exploration, you might also want to consult Chapter 9, "Exploring the Watery World," and Chapter 10, "Exploring the Ocean."

Resource Books

ABC Zoo. Jean Warren. Everett, WA: Warren Publishing House, 1991. 45 pp. Goes through the alphabet using zoo animals for each letter.

All About Baby Animals. Michael Chinery. New York, NY: Doubleday, 1990. 45 pp. Explores the physical characteristics and habits of more than 30 baby mammals, birds, fish, and insects.

Alligators and Crocodiles. John Bonnet Wexo, Mankato, MN: Creative Education, 1989. 24 pp. Looks at the physical characteristics and behaviors of different kinds of alligators and crocodiles.

Amazing Birds. Alexandra Parsons. New York, NY: Alfred A. Knopf, 1990. 29 pp. Introduces several unusual birds such as the vulture and hummingbird.

The Amazing Egg Book. Margaret Griffin. Reading, MA: Addison-Wesley Publishing Co., 1989. 64 pp. Explains the functions of eggs.

Amazing Tropical Birds. Gerald Legg. New York, NY: Alfred A Knopf, 1991. 29 pp. Provides text and photos of tropical birds.

America's Deserts: Guide to Plants and Animals. Marianne D. Wallace. Golden, CO: Fulcrum, 1996. 48 pp. A guide to North America's deserts.

America's Mountains: Guide to plants and animals. Marianne D. Wallace. Golden, CO: Fulcrum, 1999. 48 pp. A guide to North America's mountains from the Appalachians to the Alaska Range.

* *Animal Hideaways.* Anita Ganeri. New York, NY; Little Simon, 1995. 24 pp. See-through pages reveal secrets of animal hideaways.

Animal Migration. Nancy J. Nielsen. New York, NY: Franklin Watts, 1991. 63 pp. Shows the migratory patterns of birds, fish, and mammals.

Animals and the New Zoos. Patricia Curtis. New York, NY: Dutton, 1991. 60 pp. Explains how zoos are trying to exhibit animals in environments resembling natural habitats.

Animals Can Be Special Friends. Dorothy Chlad. Chicago, IL: Children's Press, 1985. 31 pp. Explains rules for the treatment and care of pets, wild animals, and zoo animals.

Animals in Winter. Henrietta Bancroft. New York, NY: HarperCollins, 1997. 32 pp. Explains how animals cope with winter.

Animals in Winter. Catherine de Sairigne. Ossining, NY: Young Discovery Library, 1988. 35 pp. Provides a simple introduction to birds, bats, bears, and frogs and how they live in winter.

Animals Keeping Clean. Jane Burton. New York, NY: Random House, 1989. 24 pp. Shows how animals use claws and beaks to keep themselves clean.

Animals Keeping Warm. Jane Burton. New York, NY: Random House, 1989. 24 pp. Explains how fur and feathers keep animals warm.

Animals Talking. Jane Burton. Brookfield, CT: Newington Press, 1991. 24 pp. Discusses how animals, including birds, communicate.

Animals that Hibernate. Larry Dane Brimner. New York, NY: Franklin Watts, 1991. 64 pp. Defines hibernation and explains how animals prepare to hibernate.

Animals that Hibernate. Phyllis J. Perry. Danbury, CT: Franklin Watts, 2001. 64 pp. Explains what happens to animal bodies during hibernation and how these changes help animals adapt to changing seasons.

Animals Under the Ground. Allan Fowler. New York, NY: Children's Press, 1997. 31 pp. Discusses moles, prairie dogs, and woodchucks.

Animals Under the Ground. Phyllis J. Perry. Danbury, CT: Franklin Watts, 2001. 64 pp. Introduces readers to five animals that live in underground burrows: the mole, the pocket gopher, the kangaroo rat, the prairie dog, and the badger.

Ants. Christy Steele. Austin, TX: Steadwell Books, 2001. 32 pp. Discusses ants of the rain forest.

Any Bear: A polar cub grows up at the zoo. Ginny Johnston and Judy Cutchins. New York, NY: Morrow Junior Books, 1985. 62 pp. Shows the first year in the life of a polar bear cub at the Atlanta zoo.

The Apes. John Bonnett Wexo. Mankato, MN: Creative Education, 1990. 24 pp. Provides a physical description and discusses the habitat and behaviors of gorillas, orangutans, and chimpanzees.

Apple Tree. Peter Parnall. New York, NY: MacMillan, 1987. 32 pp. Shows what happens in a tree with insects, birds, and other animals.

Archaeopteryx: The first bird. Elizabeth J. Sandell. Naples, FL: Bancroft-Sage Publishers, 1989. 31 pp. Describes the work of paleontologists who reconstruct a fossil.

Armor to Venom: Animal defenses. Phyllis J. Perry. Danbury, CT: Franklin Watts, 1997. 64 pp. Explores the variety of defense strategies that have developed in the animal world.

Autumn. Nicola Baxter. New York, NY; Children's Press, 1996. 24 pp. Discusses the time when many animals hibernate or migrate.

*Baby Animals. John Bonnett Wexo. Mankato, MN: Creative Education, 1990. 24 pp. Introduces baby zoo animals.

The Barn Owl. Bert Kitchen. New York, NY: Kingfisher, 1999. 32 pp. Discusses the hunting, feeding, nesting, mating, and moulting of barn owls.

Bats. Sue Ruff. New York, NY: Benchmark Books, 2001. 104 pp. Presents information on the physical characteristics, behavior, and habitat of bats.

Bats. Lily Wood. New York, NY: Scholastic Reference, 2001. 32 pp. Describes how bats fly, hunt, roost, and care for their young.

Bats: Mammals that Fly. Marlene Sway. New York, NY: Franklin Watts, 1999. 48 pp. Gives a general overview of 15 species of bats.

Bats: The amazing upside-downers. Phyllis J. Perry. Danbury, CT: Franklin Watts, 1998. 64 pp. Describes various kinds of bats, their flight, and hibernation.

Bat Watching: A how to guide. Diane Bair and Pamela Wright. Mankato, MN: Capstone Press, 2000. 48 pp. Tells about the behavior of bats and how to safely observe them.

Bears. John Bonnett Wexo. Mankato, MN: Creative Education, 1989. 24 pp. Discusses the physical characteristics of different species of bears, and their relationship to humans.

Beaver. Glen Rounds. New York, NY: Holiday House, 1999. unpaged. Shows the night activities of the beaver.

The Beaver. Sabrina Crewe. Austin, TX: Raintree Steck-Vaughn, 1998. 32 pp. Follows two kits from birth to adult.

Beavers. Deborah Hodge. Toronto, Canada: Kids Can Press, 1998. 32 pp. Tells about beaver habits and habitats.

Bee. Karen Hartley. Des Plaines, IL: Heinemann Library, 1998. 32 pp. Explains the life cycle, habitat, and lifespan of the bee.

Beehives. Jill Kalz. North Mankato, MN: Smart Apple Media, 2001. 23 pp. Discusses bee culture.

Bees. Larry Dane Brimner. New York, NY: Children's Press, 1999. 47 pp. Discusses the physical characteristics and behavior of bees.

Big Cats. John Bonnett Wexo. Mankato, MN: Creative Education, 1990. 24 pp. Gives the physical characteristics and describes the habitat and behaviors of lions, tigers, leopards, and cheetahs.

Big Golden Book of Backyard Birds, The. Kathleen N. Daly. Racine, WI: Western Publishing Co., 1990. 61 pp. Provides an introduction to backyard birds.

Bird. David Burnie. New York, NY: Alfred A. Knopf (dist. By Random House), 1988. 63 pp. Shows a bird's body construction, feathers, flight, beak, feet, and other noteworthy features.

The Bird Alphabet Book. Jerry Pallotta. Watertown, MA: Charlesbridge Pub., 1991, 32 pp. Presents a bird for each letter of the alphabet.

Bird-Eating Spiders. Louise Martin. Vero Beach, FL: Rourke Enterprises, 1988. 23 pp. Shows the world's largest spiders that nest in trees and feed on birds and small animals.

Bird Families. Helen Frost. Mankato, MN: Pebble Books, 1999. 24 pp. Explains where and how various species of birds make their nests.

Bird Feeder Books, The: An easy guide to attracting, identifying, and understanding your feeder birds. Donald Stokes and Lillian Stokes. Boston, MA: Little, Brown, 1987. 90 pp. Discusses birds commonly found at feeders.

Bird Migration. Liz Oram. Austin, TX: Steck-Vaughn Library, 1992. 49 pp. Discusses the migration patterns of various birds.

Bird Nests. Helen Frost. Mankato, MN: Pebble Books, 1999. 24 pp. Describes nest building and materials used to make nests.

Birds. Donna Bailey. Austin, TX: Steck-Vaughn Library, 1990. 48 pp. Gives basic information on birds, their habitats, and behaviors.

Birds. Christine Butterworth. Morristown, NJ: Silver Burdett Press, 1988. 32 pp. Discusses such birds as canaries, bowerbirds, and hummingbirds.

Birds. Ellen Doris. Danbury, CT: Grolier Educational, 1996. 72 pp. Explains how to identify birds and discusses bird behaviors.

Birds. Terry J. Jennings. Chicago, IL: Children's Press, 1989. 34 pp. Provides an introduction to birds with activities and suggested experiments.

Birds. Teri Crawford Jones. Lincolnwood, IL: Publications International, 1991. 62 pp. Introduces a variety of birds.

Birds. Wendy Meadway. New York, NY: Bookwright Press, 1990. 32 pp. Provides an introduction to birds.

Birds. Dean Morris. Milwaukee, WI: Raintree Childrens Books, 1988. 46 pp. Discusses birds, their behaviors, migrations, food gathering, and nest building.

Birds. Philip Steele. Mankato, MN: Crestwood House, 1991. 32 pp. Provides general facts about birds.

Birds: A guide to familiar American birds. Herbert S. Zim and Ira N. Gabrielson. Racine, WI: Western Publishing Co., 1991. 160 pp. Helps in the identification of birds.

Birds and Mammals. Lionel Bender. New York, NY: Gloucester Press, 1988. 36 pp. Provides an introduction to birds and mammals.

Birds Do the Strangest Things. Leonora Hornblow and Arthur Hornblow. New York, NY: Random House, 1991. 63 pp. Shows 22 birds with unusual habits or characteristics.

*Bird's Nest. Barrie Watts. Morristown, NJ: Silver Burdett Press, 1987. 24 pp. Tells the story of the blue titmouse family through photos, drawings, and text.

Birds of Antarctica: The Adelie penguin. Jennifer Owings Dewey. Boston, MA: Little, Brown, 1989. 48 pp. Discusses the Adelie penguin.

Birds of Antarctica: The wandering albatross. Jennifer Owings Dewey, Boston, MA: Little, Brown, 1989. 47 pp. Presents a year in the life of an albatross.

Birds of Prey. Jill Bailey. New York, NY: Facts on File, 1988. 61 pp. Discusses eagles, hawks, owls, and vultures.

Birds of Prey. Jonathan P. Latimer. Boston, MA: Houghton Mifflin, 1999. 48 pp. Discusses the behavior and habitat of eagles, hawks, falcons, and owls.

Birds of Prey. Kate Petty. New York, NY: Gloucester Press, 1987. 31 pp. Discusses birds of prey.

Birds—Right before Your Eyes. John R. Weissinger. Hillside, NJ: Enslow Pub., 1988. 64 pp. Gives information and contains drawings of various American birds.

Birds: The aerial hunters. Marilyn Bramwell. New York, NY: Facts on File, 1989. 96 pp. Discusses predatory and insectivorous birds.

Birds: The plant and seed eaters. Jill Bailey and Steve Parker. New York, NY: Facts on File, 1989. 96 pp. Gives a brief description of various birds that eat plants and seeds.

Birds: The waterbirds. Robin Kerrod. New York, NY: Facts on File, 1989. 96 pp. Gives a brief description of waterfowl.

Bird Watch: A book of poetry. Jane Yolen. New York, NY: Philomel Books, 1990. 36 pp. Contains poems about birds.

Birdwatch: A young person's introduction to birding. Mary MacPherson, Toronto, Canada: Summerhill Press, 1988. 136 pp. Introduces the reader to the world of bird watching.

Bird World. Struan Reid. Brookfield, CT: Millbrook Press, 1991. 64 pp. Contains an introductory survey of birds.

The Black-tailed Prairie Dog: Social life of a burrowing mammal. John L. Hoogland. Chicago, IL: University of Chicago Press, 1995, 557 pp. Full discussion of the black-tailed prairie dog.

Blue-Footed Booby: Bird of the Galapagos. Adapted by Nicholas Millhouse. New York, NY: Walker & Company, 1986. 32 pp. Describes the life cycle of a booby from its hatching on the floor of an island volcano to maturity.

The Book of North American Owls. Helen Roney Sattler. New York, NY: Clarion Books, 1995. 64 pp. Discusses 21 species of North American owls.

Building Beavers. Kathleen Martin-James. Minneapolis, MN: Lerner Publications, 2000. 32 pp. Presents the physical characteristics and habits of the North American beaver.

Busy, Buzzy Bee. Karen Wallace. New York, NY: Dorling Kindersley, 1999. 32 pp. Discusses the behavior and lives of bees.

Camels. John Bonnett Wexo. Mankato, MN: Creative Education, 1989. 24 pp. Provides an introduction to camels.

Can You Find Me? A book about animal camouflage. Jennifer Dewey. New York, NY: Scholastic Inc., 1989. 40 pp. Explains how camouflage is used by birds, fish, insects, reptiles, and mammals.

Chick. Jane Burton. New York, NY: Lodestar Books, 1992. 21 pp. Shows development of a chick from an egg.

Chicken and Egg. Christine Back and Jens Olesen. Morristown, NJ: Silver Burdett Press, 1986. 24 pp. Shows development of a chicken.

Chimpanzees and Bonobos. Ann Elwood. Mankato, MN: Creative Education, 1991. 24 pp. Gives an introduction to various chimpanzees.

City Geese. Ron Hirschi. New York, NY: Dodd, Mead, 1987. 45 pp. Examines a flock of Canadian geese.

Close to the Wild: Siberian tigers in a zoo. Thomas Cajacob and Teresa Burton. Minneapolis, MN: Carolrhoda Books, 1986, 48 pp. Shows the care and various aspects of behaviors of Siberian tigers.

Cradles in the Trees: The story of bird nests. Patricia Brennan Demuth. New York, NY: Macmillan Pub. Co., 1994, 32 pp. Explains the methods and materials used to build bird nests.

Crafty Canines: Coyotes, Foxes, and Wolves. Phyllis J. Perry. Danbury, CT: Franklin Watts, 1999. 64 pp. Describes the habitats, lifestyles, and physical features of coyotes, foxes and wolves.

The Crane. Gabriel Horn. Mankato, MN: Crestwood House, 1988. 48 pp. Contains information on various kinds of cranes.

The Crocodile and the Crane: Surviving in a crowded world. Judy Cutchins and Ginny Johnston. New York, NY: Morrow Junior Books, 1986. 54 pp. Shows how care and breeding in zoos protects endangered species.

The Crocodilians: Reminders of the age of dinosaurs. Phyllis J. Perry. Danbury, CT: Franklin Watts, 1997. Discusses crocodiles, alligators, caimans, and gavials.

A Day in the Life of a Zoo Vet. David Paige. Mahwah, NJ: Troll Associates. 1985. 32 pp. Tells the story of the day the zoo veterinarian examined an elephant and operated on an armadillo.

Dear Bronx Zoo. Joyce Altman and Sue Goldberg. New York, NY: Macmillan, 1990. 156 pp. Describes the activities at a zoo and introduces various animals.

*Dig Hole, Soft Mole. Carolyn Lesser. San Diego, CA: Harcourt Brace, 1996. unpaged. A star-nosed mole travels about underground.

Dinosaurs and Birds. G. Minelli. New York, NY: Facts on File, 1987. 57 pp. Explains evolution theories relating to dinosaurs and birds.

Discovering Songbirds. Colin S. Milkins. New York, NY: Bookwright Press, 1990. 47 pp. Introduces the characteristics and behaviors of songbirds.

Doctor Wotsit's Zoo. Felicia Law. Milwaukee, WI: Gareth Stevens Pub., 1986. 48 pp. Gives an introduction to the organization of a zoo.

The Dodo. William R. Sanford and Carl R. Geeen. Mankato, MN: Crestwood House, 1989. 48 pp. Discusses the flightless bird of Mauritius and why it became extinct.

Dolphins & Porpoises. Beth Wagner Brust, Mankato, MN: Creative Education, 1991. 24 pp. Discusses the appearance and the habits of dolphins and porpoises.

Do Tarantulas Have Teeth? Questions and answers about poisonous creatures. Melvin and Gilda Berger. New York, NY: Scholastic Reference. Discusses poisonous creatures.

Downy Woodpecker. Katherine Grier. Danbury, CT: Grolier, 1986. 47 pp. Introduces the downy woodpecker.

Ducks, Geese and Swans. John Bonnett Wexo. Mankato, MN: Creative Education, 1989. 20 pp. Looks at some waterfowl in a zoo.

Eagles. Michael Bright. New York, NY: Gloucester Press, 1991. 31 pp. Discusses various eagles.

Eagles, Hawks, and Other Birds of Prey. Lynda De Witt. New York, NY: Franklin Watts, 1989. 63 pp. A discussion of vultures, eagles, kites, hawks, falcons, and owls.

Elephants. John Bonnett Wexo. Mankato, MN: Creative Education, 1989. 24 pp. Examines the ancestors of elephants and shows their appearance and behaviors.

Endangered Animals. John Bonnett Wexo. Mankato, MN: Creative Education, 1990. 24 pp. Tells what people do to endanger animals and shows pictures of endangered species.

Exotic Birds. Marilyn Singer. New York, NY: Doubleday, 1990. 44 pp. Discusses some of the more exotic birds such as the penguin and kiwi.

Faces in the Forest. Ron Hirschi. New York, NY: Cobblehill Books, 1997. unpaged. Introduces such animals as beavers, chipmunks, spotted owls, deer, and eagles.

The Feather Book. Karen O'Conner. New York, NY: Dillon Press, 1990. 59 pp. Discusses the structure, types, and colors of feathers.

First Look at Owls, Eagles, and Other Hunters of the Sky. Millicent E. Selsam and Joyce Hunt. New York, NY: Walker & Company, 1986. 32 pp. Explains about birds of prey.

Flightless Birds. Norman S. Barrett. New York, NY: Franklin Watts, 1991. 32 pp. Discusses several flightless birds.

Flight of the Golden Plover: The amazing migration between Hawaii and Alaska. Debbie S. Miller. Anchorage, AK: Alaska Northwest Books, 1996. unpaged. Discusses transoceanic migration.

The Flight of the Snow Geese. Deborah King. New York, NY: Orchard Books, 1998. unpaged. Follows snow geese from Arctic nesting ground to the New Mexico desert.

Freshwater Giants: Hippopotamus, river dolphins, and manatees. Phyllis J. Perry. Danbury, CT: Franklin Watts, 1999. 64 pp.

The Friendly Prairie Dog. Denise Casey. New York, NY: Dodd, Mead 1987. 40 pp. Presents the habits and natural environment of prairie dogs.

Frogs. Gail Gibbons. New York, NY: Holiday House, 1993. unpaged. Explains how toads are different from frogs and tells about hibernation in frogs.

Giant Pandas. John Bonnett Wexo. Mankato, MN: Creative Education, 1989. 24 pp. Introduces the giant panda.

Giraffes. John Bonnett Wexo. Mankato, MN: Creative Education, 1991. 24 pp. Gives the physical characteristics and behaviors of the tallest of our land animals.

Good Night's Sleep, A. Allan Fowler. New York, NY: Children's Press, 1996. 31 pp. A Rookie read-about science book that discusses nocturnal animals and hibernation.

Great Northern Diver: The loon. Barbara Juster Esbensen. Boston, MA: Little, Brown, 1990. 32 pp. Provides an introduction to the loon.

The Great Zoo Hunt. Peppa Unwin. New York, NY: Doubleday, 1990. 32 pp. Provides a story where the reader helps the zookeeper locate 10 escaped animals hiding in detailed illustrations.

The Greenwich Guide to the Seasons. Graham Dolan. Chicago, IL: Heinemann Library, 2001. 22 pp. Explains some of the effects of seasons such as triggering hibernation and migration.

Have You Seen Birds? Joanne Oppenheim. New York, NY: Scholastic Inc., 1986. 32 pp. Gives simple descriptions of birds and their songs.

Hawk Highway in the Sky: Watching raptor migration. Caroline Arnold. San Diego, CA: Harcourt Brace & Co., 1997. 48. Discusses work of the HawkWatch International Raptor Migration Project.

Headhunters and Hummingbirds: An expedition into Ecuador. Robert M. Peck. New York, NY: Walker & Company, 1987. 113 pp. Explains a journalist-photographer's expedition on ornithological research in the Cutucu Mountains.

Hibernation. Paul Bennett. New York, NY: Thomson Learning, 1995. 32 pp. Discusses animals that hibernate.

Hippo. Caroline Arnold. New York, NY: Morrow Junior Books, 1989. 48 pp. Looks at hippos in the wild and those that live at the San Francisco Zoo.

Honey Farms. Lynn M. Stone. Vero Beach, FL: Rourke Corp., 1999. 24 pp. Discusses habits of honey bees and how they are raised on farms.

The Honey Makers. Gail Gibbons. New York, NY: Morrow Junior Books, 1997. 32 pp. Explains how bees produce honey.

Hooray for Beekeeping! Bobbie Kalman. New York, NY: Crabtree, Pub., 1998. 32 pp. Discusses beekeeping equipment and practices.

Hornets' Nest. Kate Scarborough. Alexandria, VA: Time-Life Books, 1997. unpaged. Discusses paper wasps and their nests.

The How and Why Wonder Book of Birds. Robert Mathewson. Los Angeles, CA: Price, Stern, Sloan, 1987. 47 pp. Provides an introduction to birds.

How Do Bats See in the Dark? Questions and answers about night creatures. New York, NY: Scholastic, 2000. 48 pp. Discusses nocturnal animals.

How Bees Make Honey. Michael Chinery. New York, NY: Benchmark Books, 1997. 32 pp. Explains how honey is made and harvested.

How to Draw Birds. Barbara Soloff-Levy. Mahwah, NJ: Watermill Press, 1987. 32 pp. gives step-by-step instructions on how to draw birds.

How to Make a Miniature Zoo (3rd ed.). Vinson Brown. New York, NY: Dodd, Mead, 1987. 244 pp. Explains how to set up small zoos in your house.

How Spiders Make Their Webs. Jill Bailey. New York, NY: Benchmark Books, 1997. 32 pp. Discusses different types of webs and their uses.

In Fields & Meadows. Paul Tessa. New York, NY: Crabtree Pub., 1997. 32 pp. A guide to finding animals by identifying their tracks and other marks.

Insect Migration. Liz Oram. Austin, TX: Raintree Steck-Vaughn, 1992. 46 pp. Discusses the reasons for insect migration.

Insect Zoo. Susan Meyers. New York, NY: Lodestar Books, 1991. 48 pp. Describes the San Francisco Insect Zoo.

*I Spy at the Zoo. Maureen Roffey. New York, NY: Aladdin Books, 1989. 29 pp. The reader finishes sentences by saying what is spied at a visit to the zoo.

It Could Still Be a Bird. Allan Fowler. Chicago, IL: Children's Press, 1990. 31 pp. Explains the essential characteristics of birds and introduces penguins, peacocks, and the ostrich.

Julius. Trygve Klingsheim (English adaptation by Dalton Exleyl). New York, NY: Delacorte Press, 1987. 62 pp. Tells a story of a young zoo chimp who is adopted by humans after being rejected by the chimps.

The Journey of a Turtle. Carolyn Scrace. New York, NY: Franklin Watts, 2000. 29 pp. Explains how green turtles migrate.

Killers—Birds. Philip Steele. Englewood Cliffs, NJ: Julian Messner, 1991. 32 pp. Explains the feeding habits of such birds as the Golden eagle, falcon, and kingfisher.

Koalas. John Bonnett Wexo. Mankato, MN: Creative Education, 1989. 24 pp. Provides an introduction to koala bears.

Ko-Hoh: The call of the trumpeter swan. Jay Featherly. Minneapolis, MN: Carolrhoda Books, 1986. 48 pp. Tells the life cycle of the trumpeter swan.

Legs: The story of a giraffe. Phyllis Barber. New York, NY: McElderry Books, 1991. 71 pp. A young giraffe is captured in Kenya and transported to a zoo.

Let's Take a Field Trip to a Beehive. Kathy Furgang. New York, NY: Power Kids Press, 2000. 24 pp. Explains how bees live and work in colonies.

Life Cycle of a Swallow. John Williams. New York, NY: Bookwright Press, 1989. 32 pp. Shows the life cycle of a swallow.

Life in a Tree. Janet Halfmann. Mankato, MN: Creative Education, 2000. 25 pp. Examines creatures such as bees and bark beetles.

The Loon. Judith Pinkerton Josephson. Mankato, MN: Crestwood House, 1988. 47 pp. Discusses the physical characteristics, behaviors, and environment of the loon.

Loon Magic for Kids. Tom Klein. Minocqua, WI: North Wood Press, 1989. 47 pp. Gives the physical characteristics, habitat, and behavior of loons.

My First Nature Book. Angela Wilkes. New York, NY: Alfred Knopf, 1990. 48 pp. Suggests simple indoor and outdoor nature-related activities.

My First Visit to an Aviary. G. Sales and J.M. Parramon. New York, NY: Barron's 1990. 31 pp. Tells how school children visit a zoo aviary.

*My First Visit to the Zoo. G. Sales and J.M. Parramon. New York, NY: Barron's, 1990. 31 pp. Tells how children visit a zoo and see the various animals.

Nature's Builders. Karen O'Callaghan. Newmarket, England: Brimax Books, 1988. 38 pp. Discusses nest building of birds.

Nature's Footprints in the Desert. Querida Lee Pearce. Englewood Cliffs, NJ: Silver Press, 1990. 22 pp. Discusses desert animals such as the tortoise, prairie dog, gila monster, and coyote.

New Zoos. Madelyn Klein Anderson. New York, NY: Franklin Watts, 1987. 71 pp. Shows how many zoos are making more natural environments for their animals.

*1,2,3 To the Zoo: A counting book. Eric Carle. New York, NY: Philomel Books, 1988. 28 pp. Each car on the train adds one more zoo animal, moving from 1 elephant to 10 birds

On the Wings: American birds in migration. Carol Lerner. New York, NY: Harper Collins, 2001. 47 pp. Discusses migration of birds.

Ostriches, Emus, Rheas, Kiwis, and Cassowaries. Ann Elwood. Mankato, MN: Creative Education, 1990. 24 pp. Provides an introduction to various zoo birds.

The Ostrich. William R. Sanford and Carl R. Green. Mankato, MN: Crestwood House, 1987. 47 pp. Discusses the physical characteristics and behaviors of the ostrich.

Ostriches and Other Flightless Birds. Caroline Arnold. Minneapolis, MN: Carolrhoda Books, 1990. 47 pp. Introduces the ostrich, rhea, emu, cassowary, kiwi, and tinamou.

Our Yard is Full of Birds. Anne F. Rockwell. New York, NY: Macmillan, 1992. unpaged. Describes birds such as the wren, phoebe, crows, and blue jays.

The Owl in the Tree. Jennifer Coldrey. Milwaukee. WI: Gareth Stevens Pub., 1988. 32 pp. shows owls in their natural habitat.

Owls. Timothy L. Biel. Mankato, MN: Creative Education, 1990. 24 pp. Discusses owls, including their attack behavior and characteristics such as their wingspan.

Owls. Kevin J. Holmes. Mankato, MN: Bridgestone Books, 1998. 24 pp. Provides a brief introduction to owls.

Owls. Deborah Kops. Woodbridge, CT: Backbirch Press, 2000. 24 pp. Discusses different kinds of owls, their eating and hunting habits.

Owls. Lynn M. Stone. Vero Beach, FL: Rourke Enterprises, 1989. 24 pp. Discusses owls and their enemies.

Owls and Other Birds of Prey. Mary E. Reid. Chicago, IL: World Book, 2000. 64 pp. Explores various birds of prey with emphasis on owls.

Owls: The silent hunters. Sara Swan Miller. New York, NY: Franklin Watts, 2000. 47 pp. Presents the physical characteristics and behaviors of 14 species of owls.

The Passenger Pigeon. Susan Dudley Morrison. Mankato, MN: Crestwood House, 1989. 48 pp. Explains how this bird became extinct.
Peeking Prairie Dogs. Christine Zuchora-Walske. Minneapolis, MN: Lerner Publications, 1999. 32 pp. Discusses the physical characteristics and behaviors of black-tailed prairie dogs.
Penguin. Caroline Arnold. New York, NY: Morrow Junior Books, 1988. 48 pp. Shows how Humberto and Domino, a pair of Magellanic penguins, live at the San Francisco Zoo.
The Penguin. Angela Royston. New York, NY: Warwick Press, 1988. 24 pp. Tells the life story of a penguin.
Penguins. John Bonnett Wexo. Mankato, MN: Creative Education, 1990. 24 pp. Gives a physical description and describes the habitat and behaviors of penguins.
The Penguins. Lynn M. Stone. Mankato, MN: Crestwood House, 1987. 47 pp. Discusses the emperor penguin.
The Peregrine Falcon. Carl R. Green and William R. Sanford. Mankato, MN: Crestwood House, 1986. 47 pp. Presents the life cycle of the peregrine falcon.
Pet Doctor. Harriet Langsam Sobol. New York, NY: G. P. Putnam's Sons, 1988. 32 pp. Follows the day of a veterinarian who is caring for cats, dogs, and birds.
*Pets and Animal Friends. Vanessa Mitchell. Milwaukee, WI: Gareth Stevens Pub., 1985. 48 pp. Shows animals at home, in the garden, on the farm, and in the zoo.
The Pets You Love. Jennifer C. Urquhart. Washington, DC: National Geographic Society, 1991. 34 pp. Discusses pleasures and responsibilities of having a pet bird, dog, rabbit, goldfish, and other family pets.
The Pileated Woodpecker. Seliesa Pembleton. New York, NY: Dillon Press, 1989. 59 pp. Shows a year in the life of a woodpecker.
Poisoners and Pretenders. Michael Chinery. New York, NY: Crabtree Pub. Co., 2000. 32 pp. Discusses defense mechanisms used to fend off predators.
*Polar Bear, Polar Bear, What Do You Hear? Bill Martin, Jr. New York, NY: Henry Holt, 1991. 28 pp. Describes how the zoo animals make sounds for each other and how children can imitate them.
Protecting Endangered Species at the San Diego Zoo. Georgeanne Irvine. New York, NY: Simon & Schuster, 1990. 45 pp. Explains projects that scientists at the zoo are working on to protect such endangered animals as the clouded leopard.
Raising Gordy Gorilla at the San Diego Zoo. Georgeanne Irvine. New York, NY: Simon & Schuster, 1990. 45 pp. Discusses the early years of a gorilla born at the San Diego Zoo.
Rhinos. John Bonnett Wexo. Mankato, MN: Creative Education, 1991. 24 pp. Provides an introduction to the habits and physical characteristics of various species of rhinos.
A Salamander's Life. John Himmelman. New York, NY: Children's Press, 1998. unpaged. Discusses winter hibernation and spring mating of salamanders.
Saving the Condor. Nancy T. Schorsch. New York, NY: Franklin Watts, 1991. 64 pp. Discusses the efforts to save the California condor.
Saving the Peregrine Falcon. Caroline Arnold. Minneapolis, MN: Carolrhoda, 1985. 48 pp. Explains efforts of scientists to prevent the extinction of this bird.
Seasons of Swans. Monica Wellington. New York, NY: Dutton, 1990. 32 pp. Tells about two swans who build a nest and raise a family.

Singing Birds and Flashing Fireflies. Dorothy Hinshaw Patent. New York, NY: Franklin Watts, 1989. 32 pp. Explains how various animals, including birds, communicate.

Snakes. John Bonnett Wexo. Mankato, MN: Creative Education, 1991. 24 pp. Discusses the bodies, locomotion, feeding, and behaviors of snakes.

The Snow Cats. Phyllis J. Perry. Danbury, CT: Franklin Watts, 1997. 64 pp. Provides an introduction to the mountain lion, snow leopard, Siberian tiger, lynx, and bobcat.

Snowy Owls. Wendy Pfeffer. Parsippany, NJ: Silver Press, 1997. unpaged. Discusses the life cycle of snowy owls.

Spider. Rebecca Stefoff. New York, NY: Benchmark Books/Marshall Cavendish, 1999. 31 pp. Discusses characteristics of spiders with emphasis on their weaving webs.

Spiderwebs to Sky-Scrapers: The science of structures. David Darling. New York, NY: Dillon Press, 1991. 57 pp. Introduces a variety of structures including birds' nests.

Spinning Spiders. Ruth Berman. Minneapolis, MN: Lerner Publishers, 1998. 32 pp. Explains how spiders use silk in weaving webs.

Spotted Owls. James E. Gerholdt. Minneapolis, MN: Abdo & Daughters, Pub., 1997. 24 pp. Gives the physical characteristics, habitats, and habits of spotted owls.

State Birds. Arthur Singer. New York, NY: Lodestar Books, 1986. 63 pp. Shows and tells about each state bird.

Swans. Althea. Chicago, IL: Longman Group, 1988. 24 pp. Discusses the appearance, habits, reproduction, and migration of swans.

A Taste of Honey. Nancy Elizabeth Wallace. Delray Beach, FL: Winslow Press, 2001. unpaged. A little bear traces the origins of honey.

10 Things I Know about Penguins. Wendy Wax and Della Rowland. Chicago, IL: Contemporary Books, 1989. 23 pp. Provides a simple introduction to penguins.

Tiger Math: Learning to graph from a baby tiger. Ann Whitehead Nagda and Cindy Bickel. New York, NY: Henry Holt, 2000. 29 pp. Shows how math is valuable in tracking growth of a baby tiger at the Denver Zoo.

Tigers. Timothy Levy Biel. Mankato, MN: Creative Education, 1990. 24 pp. Gives an introduction to tigers.

Urban Roosts: Where birds nest in the city. Barbara Bash, Boston, MA: Little, Brown, 1990. 32 pp. Discusses birds that live in the city

Vampire Bats. Patricia Merrick. Chanhassen, MN: Child's World, 2001. 32 pp. Describes the life cycle of vampire bats.

Visit of Two Giant Pandas at the San Diego Zoo, The. Georgeanne Irvine. New York, NY: Simon & Schuster, 1991. 45 pp. Relates the story of two pandas from China, Basi and Yuan Yuan, that came to visit the San Diego Zoo.

Visit to the Zoo, A. Sylvia Root Tester. Chicago, IL: Children's Press, 1987. 31 pp. Tells a story of a group that goes on a class trip to the zoo.

Wasps. Helen Frost. Mankato, MN: Pebble Books, 2001. 24 pp. An introduction to wasps.

Wasps. Jen Green. Danbury, CT: Grolier Educational, 1999. 48 pp. Discusses the behavior of wasps.

Wasps At Home. Bianca Lavies. New York, NY: Dutton Children's Books, 1991. unpaged. Discusses paper wasps and baldfaced hornets.

What Do You Do at a Petting Zoo? Hana Machotka. New York, NY: Morrow Junior Books, 1990. 32 pp. Describes the function of a petting zoo and tells about the kinds of animals found there.

What Is a Bird? Ron Hirschi. New York, NY: Walker & Company, 1987. 31 pp. Explains basic concepts of birds.

When We Went to the Zoo. Jan Ormerod. New York, NY: Lothrop, Lee & Shepard Books, 1991. 36 pp. Discusses how two children enjoy a tour of the zoo.

Where Do Birds Live? Ron Hirschi. New York, NY: Walker & Company, 1987. 32 pp. Examines the natural habitats of birds: including ponds, rivers, mountains, old trees, and yards.

Wild Goat. Caroline Arnold. New York, NY: Morrow Junior Books, 1990. 48 pp. Examines, through text and photos, Daisy and Chaim, two goats who live at the Los Angeles Zoo.

Windows on Wildlife. Ginny Johnston and Judy Cutchins. New York, NY: Morrow Junior Books, 1990. 48 pp. Shows zoos, wildlife parks, and aquariums.

Who Dug this Hole? Anita Holmes. New York, NY: Benchmark Books, 2001. 32 pp. Discusses burrowing animals.

Who Lives In—the Mountains? Ron Hirschi. New York, NY: G. P. Putnam's Sons, 1989. 32 pp. Shows the birds and animals of the high country.

Who Lives on—the Prairie? Ron Hirschi. New York, NY: G. P. Putnam's Sons, 1989. 32 pp. Discusses such birds and animals as the prairie dog, dancing birds, and weasels.

The Whooping Crane: A comeback story. Dorothy Hinshaw Patent. New York, NY: Ticknor & Fields, 1988. 88 pp. Traces attempts to save the cranes from extinction.

Wild Turkey, Tame Turkey. Dorothy Hinshaw Patent. Boston, MA: Houghton Mifflin, 1989. 57 pp. Gives the history of the North American turkey.

Wind to Flight. Peter Lafferty. New York, NY: Gloucester Press, 1989. 32 pp. Explains how the wind is used by seeds, clouds, birds, insects, and machines.

Wolves. John Bonnett Wexo. Mankato, MN; Creative Education, 1990. 24 pp. Gives a physical description and describes the habitat and behaviors of wolves.

Woodpecker Forest. Keizaburo Tejima. New York, NY: Philomel Books, 1989. 42 pp. Shows activities of woodpeckers such as nesting, hatching, and caring for young.

Woodpecker in the Backyard. Cathy Masica. New York, NY: Franklin Watts, 2000. 48 pp. Tells about the downy woodpecker.

Woodpeckers. George K. Peck. Mankato, MN: Smart Apple Media, 1998. 30 pp. Discusses the characteristics, behaviors, and habitats of woodpeckers.

Woodpeckers. Lynn M. Stone. Vero Beach, FL: Rourke Corp., 1998. 24 pp. Gives information on the flicker, gila woodpecker, and red-bellied woodpecker.

Woodpeckers. Cherie Winner. Minneapolis, MN: Carolrhoda Books, 2001. 48 pp. Presents the behaviors of many species of woodpeckers found throughout the world.

The Work of the Zoo Doctors at the San Diego Zoo. Georgeanne Irvine, New York, NY: Simon & Schuster, 1991. 45 pp. Describes the work of zoo veterinarians.

*Zachary Goes to the Zoo. Jill Krementz. New York, NY: Random House, 1986. 20 pp. Shows a child's visit to the zoo through text and photos.

Zoo. Gail Gibbons. New York, NY: Thomas Y. Crowell, 1987. 30 pp. Shows behind-the-scenes at a zoo on a typical working day.

Zoo Animals. Photos by Philip Dowell and Jerry Young. New York, NY: Macmillan, 1991. 21 pp. Through photos, shows various zoo animals including the elephant, monkey, zebra, and camel.

Zoobabies. Carolyn Fireside. New York, NY: Villard Books, 1991. 58 pp. Shows zoo animals in their infancy.

Zoo Clues: Making the most of your visit to the zoo. Sheldon L. Gerstenfeld. New York, NY: Viking Penguin, 1991. 113 pp. Gives information on favorite zoo animals.

Zoo Day. John Brennan and Leonie Keaney. Minneapolis, MN: Carolrhoda Books, 1989. 32 pp. Shows a typical zoo day through text and photos.

Zoos and Game Reserves. Miles Barton. New York, NY: Gloucester Press, 1988. 32 pp. Discusses zoos and wildlife refuges.

Zoo Workers. Judith Stamper. Mahwah, NJ: Troll Associates, 1989. 32 pp. Describes the jobs of various people who work in the zoo, such as acquiring animals, preparing food, and caring for sick animals.

Other Resources

The following magazines might be of interest as you explore the world of animals and birds: *Audubon, Conservationist, Country Journal, Field and Stream, International Wildlife, National Wildlife, Natural History, Nature Canada, Outdoor Life, Petersen's Photographic Magazine, Science, The Sporting News, Sports Afield,* and *Wilderness*.

The following magazines might be of interest as you explore zoos: *Curator, Journal of the American Veterinary Medical Association, New Scientist,* and *Zoo Biology*.

*All About Animals. Donald Thompson & Associates. Los Angeles, CA: Hi-Tops Video, 1987. 1 videocassette, 30 minutes. For ages 3-6. A classroom full of puppets visit a zoo.

Animal Guessing Games. National Geographic Society, 1988. 1 videocassette, 15 minutes. Asks and answers various questions about animals.

Animal Tracks. Nashua, NH: Delta Education. Kit includes casting plaster, 6 molds, and background information on making authentic casts.

Babies of the Pond. Jill Grunkmeyer (Producer). Sheridan, WY: Grunko Films, 1988. 1 videocassette, 45 minutes. About infant birds and pond ecology.

Captain Kangaroo—Let's go to the zoo with Captain Kangaroo. Chicago, IL: Britannica Education Corporation (distributed by MPI Home Video), 1985. 1 videocassette, 58 minutes. Contains animated and live action.

Field Guide to Bird Songs of Eastern and Central North America, A. Boston, MA: Houghton Mifflin, 1990. 2 sound cassettes. Peterson field guide series.

Lifecycle of a Frog. Nashua, NH: Delta Education. This foam model serves as a hands-on teaching tool showing a frog's lifecycle.

Loon Magic. Tom Klein. Louisville, CO: Audio Press, 1990. 2 sound cassettes. Gives a variety of information about the loon.

The National Zoo. Terence Taylor. Rochester. NY: Eastman Kodak, 1989. 1 videocassette, 50 minutes. Shows famous and unusual residents of the Smithsonian Institution's living animal collection.

Owl Pellets. Nashua, NH: Delta Education. For grades 3-8, allows for classroom study of owl pellets for learning about food webs and mammal skeletons.

Pandas in Person. Minneapolis, MN: Quality Video, 1989. 1 videocassette, 30 minutes. Examines the life styles and habits of panda bears.

Song Birds. Ithaca, NY: Library of Natural Sounds, Laboratory of Ornithology, Cornell University, 1988. 1 sound cassette. Provides the songs of several birds.

Zookeepers. Dugan Rosalini (Producer). Chicago, IL: Films Incorporated Video, 1989. 1 videocassette, 29 minutes. Shows a visit to Chicago's Lincoln Park Zoo.

Zoo-Opolis! David Lee Miller. Beverly Hills, CA: Pacific Arts Video, 1985. 1 videocassette, 88 minutes. A visit to the zoo, including a discussion with the keepers and a look at various animals.

6
Exploring geology and paleontology

It is a rare child indeed who has not gathered up rocks, pounded sandstone into dust, or asked questions about dinosaurs. These seem to be universal interests of boys and girls, and so it should be a simple task to lead them into further explorations of geology and paleontology.

To adults, rocks found in the garden, along a stream, or jutting out from the bank of a mountain roadway may look pretty much alike. However, to a curious child, each and every rock can be both beautiful and fascinating. The child may like the colors in one, the shape of another, and the smoothness of a third. Examining these rocks helps develop powers of observation and can be a springboard to a more rigorous scientific examination.

Starting a rock collection

Many children like to have a rock collection. These can be purchased, but it is fun to collect your own rocks and try to identify them. To make your own rock collection, tape or glue small pieces of rock into a shallow box. Beneath each specimen, put an identifying number.

On the cover of the box (or in a notebook) put the corresponding number and any information that you know about the rock. You might list where you found the rock, its color, hardness, and even the type of rock it is, if you know.

You can add to this collection over many months. You may even want to purchase a special rock from a shop while on vacation to put in your collection. Arrowheads, agates, turquoise, crystals, or a fern or trilobite fossil, are just a few of the inexpensive items you might want to purchase to augment your collection.

Chapter 6

Making salt crystals

Rocks are made from a mixture of minerals. For example, the salt that you eat is a mineral named halite. Making salt crystals is easy to do.

Boil 1 cup of water. Dissolve 4 tablespoons of salt in the water. Pour the cooled salty solution into a narrow jar so that it is about ⅓ full.

Tie a piece of string onto the middle of a pencil. Drop the string into the salty water and lay the pencil across the top of the jar. Put the jar in a cool place where it will not be disturbed for several days.

After about four days, little salt crystals in perfect cubes will form on the string.

If a class of students or an adult and one curious child are going to really start exploring rocks, the following few simple items should be collected and placed in your rock kit: a knife for scratching stones; a piece of glass (with smooth edges so that you won't cut yourself) to make scratches on; a magnifying glass to examine rocks; a penny; a tile; a hammer for breaking rocks open; and some ginger ale or soda pop.

Performing a hardness test on rocks

The hardness test is one that you will want to be able to apply to the rocks that you find.

Hardness 1 = You can scratch it easily with your fingernail. Talc is an example.

Hardness 2 = You can scratch it with your fingernail but it isn't easy to do so. Gypsum is an example.

Hardness 3 = You can't scratch it with your fingernail, but you can scratch it with a penny. Calcite is an example.

Hardness 4 = You can't scratch it with a fingernail or a penny, but you can scratch it with a knife. Limestone is an example.

Hardness 5 = You can just barely scratch this stone with a knife. Hornblende is an example.

Hardness 6 = You can't scratch it with a knife, but it will scratch the flat knife blade or glass. Feldspar is an example.

Hardness 7 = You can scratch glass with this rock. Quartz is an example.

Scientists carry their scale to a hardness of 10. Topaz is an example of Hardness 8. Corundum is an example of Hardness 9. (Precious corundum includes the ruby and sapphire.) Diamonds have a Hardness of 10.

Some students may be more interested in gemstones, silver, or gold than in the more ordinary garden variety rocks. Rock tumblers are available, and it might be possible to set one up and polish some rocks. If there are mines in your area (e.g., gold, silver, turquoise), you may be able to invite a gold or silver miner to visit and bring ore samples or you may be able to visit a gift shop associated with a turquoise mine or a local rock or gem shop.

Removing tarnish from a silver spoon

A child may notice that the silver at home gets a tarnish on it. This tarnish comes from a chemical reaction to sulfur dioxide, a gas that is present in the air in small quantities. The following experiment will help show the child how to remove such tarnish.

Use aluminum foil, shiny side up, to line the inside of a saucepan. Into the saucepan, put 4 cups of water, 1 tablespoon baking soda, and 1 teaspoon of salt. Stir gently.

Put a tarnished silver spoon into the saucepan. Bring the water to a boil on a hot plate or the stove.

In about 15 minutes, the tarnish will disappear. Let the water cool. Remove the spoon. Pour out the water and examine the aluminum foil.

The used foil may now look tarnished because it has a coating of aluminum sulfide. (The hot baking soda solution broke up the silver sulfide into ions of silver and ions of sulfur. The sulfur ions moved to the surface of the aluminum because aluminum is more reactive with sulfur than silver.)

Performing a limestone test

Another simple test is the test for limestone. Limestone is formed when calcite on land is dissolved in rainwater and is carried by brooks and rivers to the sea. Shellfish, corals, and a few sea plants are able to take the lime from the water. When they die, they pile up on the bottom of the ocean and over a period of time, form limestone.

Since ancient sea bottoms are now high on land, it is easy to find limestone in many places.

If you think you have found a piece of limestone for your rock collection, you can perform this test. Pour soda water onto your rock; if it is limestone, the lime will bubble and fizz.

Where there is a lot of limestone, you may also find very interesting caves. Many of these caves are open to public tours. There may be one in your area that would make a good class field trip site or you may visit one when on vacation. Do not wander into a cave on your own. Be sure you have a knowledgeable guide.

These special caves are formed when water, seeping underground, passes over limestone with calcite in it. Some of the calcite dissolves in the water. As it drips, some of the calcite sticks to the roof of a cave (forming stalactites) or dribbles into a pile on the floor of a cave (forming stalagmites). Sometimes the stalactites and the stalagmites grow together like a pillar. The Carlsbad Caverns of New Mexico, the Luray Caverns and Weyers Cave in Virginia, and Mammoth Cave in Kentucky are especially famous.

Some of our finest fossils, such as shells, corals, and other sea creatures or their prints, are found in limestone deposits. Depending on where you live, you may be able to find fossils or perhaps can visit a museum to see fossil specimens.

When children learn about fossils and prehistoric times, they often become interested in dinosaurs. Notable museums with major fossil collections can be found in New York, NY; Pittsburgh, PA; Chicago, IL; Denver, CO; Vernal, UT;

Cambridge, MA; Los Angeles, CA; New Haven, CT; Princeton, NJ; Washington, DC; Rapid City, SD; Berkeley, CA; Lawrence, KS; Lincoln, NE; Baird, TX; and Laramie, WY. Many smaller museums also have interesting collections.

You may decide to visit a natural history museum, a museum of science, a whaling museum, a local historical museum, or any one of countless other museums and collections that may be available to you. You and your curious student may wish to go on your own or you may want to be part of a guided tour.

Taking a class of students on a guided tour to a natural history museum may be a great addition to a unit of study on dinosaurs, or it may serve as a culminating activity.

Sometimes tours include behind-the-scenes glimpses of how different aspects of an exhibit are put together. Occasionally a major exhibit may come somewhere near you as part of a traveling exhibit. By being alert to these opportunities, you will maximize your viewing possibilities.

Preparing a display

After seeing a collection displayed, a child may want to prepare a simple display of his or her own. Perhaps one child or a class will want to prepare a rock collection as a display with attractive background and detailed labels providing pertinent information.

Friends, relatives, or other classes may be invited to come and view the display.

Current events may also spark interest in geology. If children hear about an earthquake, a meteor, or a volcanic eruption somewhere in the world, they may have a lot of questions. Make the most of these teachable moments by pursuing these interests when they arise.

The resources that follow should help as you explore rocks, fossils, and dinosaurs. Other resources that may also be helpful can be found in Chapter 1, Exploring Chemistry in the Kitchen; Chapter 3, Exploring Science in the Backyard; Chapter 4, Exploring Botany; and Chapter 8, Exploring Geography and Cartography.

Resource Books

Adventures with Rocks and Minerals: Geology experiments for young people. Lloyd H. Barrow. Hillside, NJ: Enslow Pub., 1991. 96 pp. Contains many earth science experiments.

*Age of Dinosaurs, The. David Lambert. New York, NY: Random House, 1987. 24 pp. Provides a brief introduction to dinosaurs.

The Age of Dinosaurs. Steve Parker. Milwaukee, WI: Gareth Stevens Pub., 1985. 48 pp. Provides an introduction to prehistoric animals.

All About Arrowheads and Spear Points. Howard E. Smith, Jr. New York, NY: Henry Holt, 1989. 56 pp. Describes different types of arrowheads and spear points.

The Amateur Geologist: Explorations and investigations. Ray Wiggers. New York, NY: Franklin Watts, 1993. 143 pp. Filled with science project ideas.

Amazing Science: Quicksand and other earthly wonders. Q. L. Pearce. Englewood Cliffs, NJ: Julian Messner, 1989. 64 pp. Explores quicksand, geysers, caves, and peat bogs.

Antarctica. April Pulley Sayre. Brookfield, CT: Twenty-First Century Books, 1998. 64 pp. Describes the landscape and geology of Antarctica.

Asteroid Impact. Doug Henderson. New York, NY: Dial Books for Young Readers, 2000. 40 pp. Explores the theory that an asteroid crashing into earth caused the extinction of dinosaurs.

Beyond the Dinosaurs! Sky Dragons, Sea Monsters, Mega-Mammals, and Other Prehistoric Beasts. Howard Zimmerman. New York, NY: Atheneum Books for Young Readers, 2001. 64 pp. Discusses prehistoric animals.

The Big Golden Book of Dinosaurs. Ian Jenkins. New York, NY: Golden Books, 2000. 48 pp. Discusses different dinosaurs and the world in which they lived.

The Big Rock. Bruce Hiscock. New York, NY: Atheneum, 1988. 30 pp. Tells about the origins of a granite rock located near the Adirondack Mountains.

Born of Heat and Pressure: Mountains and metamorphic rocks. Patricia L. Barnes-Svarney. Hillside, NJ: Enslow Pub., 1991. 64 pp. Discusses the formation of rocks and mountains.

Born Near the Earth's Surface: Sedimentary rocks. Sally M. Walker. Hillside, NJ: Enslow, Pub., 1991. 64 pp. Examines the formation and types of sedimentary rocks.

Cave. Lionel Bender. New York, NY: Franklin Watts, 1989. 32 pp. Discusses the ways in which caves are formed.

Caves. Keith Brandt. Mahwah, NJ: Troll Associates, 1985. 30 pp. Discusses the formation of caves.

*Caves. Jenny Wood. New York, NY: Puffin Books, 1990. 27 pp. Provides an introduction to caves.

The Changing Earth. Rebecca Olien. Mankato, MN: Bridgestone Books, 2002. 24 pp. Explains forces that change the earth's surface.

Clocks in the Rocks: Learning about earth's past. Patricia L. Barnes-Svarney. Hillside, NJ: Enslow Pub., 1990. 64 pp. Examines fossils, radioactive dating, and prehistoric life.

Collecting Rocks and Crystals: Hold the treasures of the earth in the palm of your hand. John Farndon. New York, NY: Sterling Pub. Co, 1999. 80 pp. Introduces different rocks and minerals and tells how they are formed and how to identify them.

Colossal Fossils: Dinosaur riddles. Charles Keller (Compiler). New York, NY: Prentice-Hall Books for Young Readers, 1987. 63 pp. Contains humorous riddles.

Copycats and Artifacts: 42 creative artisan projects to make. Marianne Ford. Boston, MA: D. R. Godine, 1986. 96 pp. Contains instructions for making projects modeled after museum artifacts.

Crystal and Gem. R. F. Symes. New York, NY: Alfred A. Knopf, 1991. 63 pp. Discusses crystals, the seven basic shapes, how they are formed, and how crystals and gems are used.

Crystals and Crystal Gardens You Can Grow. Jean Stangl. New York, NY: Franklin Watts, 1990. 64 pp. Contains ideas for experiments that explain about crystals.

Dance of the Continents. Roy A. Gallant. New York, NY: Benchmark Books, 2000. 80 pp. Describes the development of geological theory.

Dating Dinosaurs and Other Odd Things. Karen Liptak. Brookfield, CT: Millbrook Press, 1992. 72 pp. Explains the techniques used by scientists to date bones, rocks, and famous old art works.

Detecting the Past. Mike Corbishley. New York, NY: Gloucester Press, 1990. 32 pp. Explores the new developments in studying ancient rocks.

Did Comets Kill the Dinosaurs? Isaac Asimov. Milwaukee, WI: Gareth Stevens Pub., 1988. 32 pp. Offers a possible explanation for the extinction of the dinosaurs.

Digging Up Dinosaurs. Aliki. New York, NY: Thomas Y. Crowell, 1988. 32 pp. Explains how scientists study fossil remains.

Dinosaur. David Norman. New York, NY; Dorling Kindersley, 2000. 63 pp. Discusses dinosaurs in the Eyewitness series.

Dinosaur. Sarah Walker. New York, NY: Dorling Kindersley, 2001. 48 pp. An Eye Wonder book.

*Dinosaur Alphabet Book. Pat Whitehead. Mahwah, NJ: Troll Associates, 1985. 30 pp. Provides characteristics of different dinosaurs for each letter of the alphabet.

Dinosaur Bones. Bob Barner. San Francisco, CA: Chronicle Books, 2001. unpaged. A book about dinosaur finds.

Dinosaur Cousins? Bernard Most. San Diego, CA: Harcourt Brace Jovanovich, 1987. 32 pp. Provides characteristics of different dinosaurs for each letter of the alphabet.

Dinosaur Fossils. Alvin Granowsky. Austin, TX: Steck-Vaughn Library, 1992. 32 pp. Discusses fossils and the work of paleontologists.

A Dinosaur Named Sue: The find of the century. Fay Robinson. New York, NY: Scholastic, 1999. 47 pp. Describes the Tyrannosaurus rex discovered by Susan Hendrickson in South Dakota.

Dinosaur Parents, Dinosaur Young: Uncovering the mystery of dinosaur families. Kathleen Weidner Zoehfeld. New York, NY: Clarion Books, 2001. 58 pp. Investigates dinosaur behavior.

Dinosaurs. Daniel Cohen. New York, NY: Doubleday, 1986. 41 pp. Introduces dinosaurs.

Dinosaurs. Gail Gibbons. New York, NY: Holiday House, 1987. 30 pp. Discusses a variety of dinosaurs.

Dinosaurs. Will Osborne. New York, NY: Random House, 2000. 119 pp. Explains about different types of dinosaurs.

Dinosaurs. Scott Steedman. New York, NY: Franklin Watts, 1995. 30 pp. An introduction to dinosaurs.

Dinosaurs. John Bonnett Wexo. San Diego, CA: Wildlife Education, 1997. 20 pp. Describes different kinds of dinosaurs and why they became extinct.

Dinosaurs. Paul M. A. Willis. Pleasantville, NY: Reader's Digest Children's Books, 1999. 64 pp. An introduction to dinosaurs.

Dinosaurs and Birds. Giuseppe Minelli. New York, NY: Facts on File, 1987. 57 pp. Discusses evolutionary theories relating dinosaurs to birds.

Dinosaurs and Other First Animals. Dean Morris. Milwaukee, MN: Raintree Childrens Books, 1988. 47 pp. Offers an easy-to-read story about dinosaurs.

Dinosaurs at the Ends of the Earth: The story of the Central Asiatic Expeditions. Brian Floca. New York, NY: D. K. Ink, 2000. unpaged. Describes explorations to the Gobi Desert in Mongolia.

Dinosaurs Down Under: And other fossils from Australia. Caroline Arnold. Boston, MA: Houghton Mifflin, 1990. 48 pp. Explains how a museum exhibit is shipped.

Dinosaurs, Dragonflies, & Diamonds: All about natural history museums. Gail Gibbons. New York, NY: Four Winds Press, 1988. 32 pp. Discusses the behind-the-scenes work at a natural history museum and what you can expect to find there.

Dinosaurs: Opposing viewpoints. Peter and Connie Roop. St. Paul, MN: Greenhaven Press, 1987. 95 pp. Discusses possible reasons for the extinction of dinosaurs.

Dinosaurs: Poems. Lee Bennett Hopkins. San Diego, CA: Harcourt Brace Jovanovich, 1987. 46 pp. Provides a collection of 18 dinosaur poems.

Dinosaurs Walked Here, and Other Stories Fossils Tell. Patricia Lauber. New York, NY: Bradbury Press, 1987. 56 pp. Explains how fossilized remains of plants and animals reveal information about the prehistoric world.

Discover Dinosaurs: Become a dinosaur detective. Christopher McGowan. Reading, MA: Addison-Wesley, 1992. 96 pp. Describes fossils and gives suggestions for possible experiments.

Discovering Dinosaurs: All up-to-date guide, including the newest theories. Victoria Crenson. Los Angeles, CA: Price, Stern, Sloan, 1988. 79 pp. Describes the ways in which paleontologists learn from fossils.

Dorling Kindersley Guide to Dinosaurs. David Lambert. New York, NY: Dorling Kindersley, 2000. 64 pp. Tells how dinosaurs might have lived, including their hunting techniques and ways of self defense.

Dougal Dixon's Amazing Dinosaurs: The fiercest, the tallest, the toughest, the smallest. Dougal Dixon. Honesdale, PA: Boyds Mill Press, 2000. 128 pp. Describes dinosaurs, including new discoveries.

Earth. Gregory Vogt. Brookfield, CT: Millbrook Press, 1996. 31 pp. Provides information on the geology, atmosphere, seasons and orbit of planet Earth.

Earth and Beyond. Robert Snedden. Des Plaines, IL: Heinemann Library, 1999. p.cm. Describes the geology of planet earth.

Earthquake! Jules Archer. Mankato, MN: Crestwood House, 1991. 48 pp. Describes the nature, origin, and dangers associated with earthquakes.

Earthquakes. Franklyn Mansfield Branley. New York, NY: Thomas Y. Crowell, 1990. 32 pp. Explains why earthquakes occur and identifies the danger zones.

Earthquakes. Christopher Lampson. Brookfield, CT: Millbrook Press, 1991. 64 pp. Discusses the causes and results of earthquakes.

Earthquakes. Seymour Simon. New York, NY: Morrow Junior Books, 1991. 32 pp. Describes how and when earthquakes occur and how they can be predicted.

Earthquakes & Volcanoes. Ruth Deery. Carthage, IL: Good Apple, 1985. 42 pp. An activity book on earthquakes and volcanoes.

Exploring Soil and Rocks. Ed Catherall. Austin, TX: Steck-Vaughn Library, 1991. 48 pp. Contains experiments involving the composition of soil and rocks.

Exploring the World of Geology. George Burns. New York, NY; Franklin Watts, 1995. 48 pp. Suggests simple activities for exploring geology.

Family of Dinosaurs, A. Mary LeDuc O'Neill. Mahwah, NJ: Troll Associates, 1989. 29 pp. Discusses the family of dinosaurs.

Feathered Dinosaurs. Christopher Sloan. Washington, D.C.: National Geographic Society, 2000. 64 pp. Looks at evidence of dinosaurs with skeletal structure and feathers similar to birds.

Fossil. Paul D. Taylor. New York, NY: Alfred A. Knopf, 1990. 63 pp. Provides a photo essay on different types of fossils.

The Fossil Factory: A kid's guide to digging up dinosaurs, exploring evolution, and finding fossils. Niles Eldredge. Reading, MA: Addison Wesley Publishing Co., 1989. 111 pp. Describes fossils and explains how to collect them.

Fossils. Roy A. Gallant. New York, NY: Benchmark Books, 2000. 48 pp. Explains how fossils are formed and what they tell us.

Fossils. John Stidworthy. New York, NY: Marshall Cavendish, 1989. 47 pp. Provides information and suggests activities for learning about fossils

Fossils and Bones. Saviour Pirotta. Austin, TX: Raintree Steck-Vaughn, 1997. 47 pp. Tells how fossils are formed and what has been learned from studying them..

Fossils, Evidence of Vanished Worlds. Yvette Gayrard-Valy. New York, NY: H. N. Abrams, 1994. 191 pp. Provides a discussion of the development of the science of paleontology.

Fossils: Stories from bones and stones. Patricia L. Barnes-Svarney. Hillside, NJ: Enslow Publishers, 1991, 64 pp. Discusses the history and formation of fossils.

Fossils Tell of Long Ago. Aliki. New York, NY; Thomas Y. Crowell, 1990. 32 pp. Explains how fossils are formed and what they tell us.

The Geography of the Earth. Susan Brooks. New York, NY: Oxford University Press, 1996 p.cm. Gives an overview of basic geology.

Geology. Graham Peacock and Jill Jessor. New York, NY: Thomson Learning, 1995. 32 pp. Includes geology experiments.

Geology Crafts for Kids: 50 Nifty projects to explore the marvels of planet earth. Alan H. Anderson. New York, NY: Sterling Pub. Co., 1996. 144 pp. Explores topics such as plate tectonics, continental drift, erosion, and mountain and valley formations.

Geology Projects for Young Scientists. Bruce G. Smith. New York, NY: Franklin Watts, 1992. 144 pp. Suggests interesting projects and experiments for young geologists.

Geology Rocks!: 50 hands-on activities to explore the earth. Cindy Blobaum. Charlotte, VT: Williamson, 1999. 96 pp. Introduces the science of geology.

Geology: The Active Earth. National Wildlife Federation. New York, NY: Learning Triangle Press, 1997. 90 pp. Contains a geologic index to *Ranger Rick Magazine* and suggests activities in geology.

Glacier. Lionel Bender. New York, NY: Franklin Watts, 1988. 32 pp. Discusses glaciers and what they do.

Grand Canyon Journey, A: Tracing time in stone. Peter Anderson. New York, NY: Franklin Watts, 1997. 63 pp. Describes the geology and evolution of the Grand Canyon by a journey down the Bright Angel Trail.

*How and Why Wonder Book of Rocks and Minerals. Nelson W. Hyler. Los Angeles, CA: Price, Stern, Sloan, 1989. 47 pp. Provides an introduction to rocks and minerals.

How Big Is a Brachiosaurus? Fascinating Facts About Dinosaurs. Susan Carroll. New York, NY: Platt & Munk, 1986. 32 pp. Gives questions and answers about dinosaurs.

How Mountains Are Made. Kathleen Weidner Zoehfeld. New York, NY: HarperCollins, 1995. 29 pp. Tells how mountains are formed.

Hunting the Dinosaurs and Other Prehistoric Animals. Jane Burton. Milwaukee, WI: Gareth Stevens Pub., 1987. 32 pp. Discusses the work of paleontologists.

I Can Be a Geologist. Paul P. Sipiera. Chicago, IL: Children's Press, 1986. 29 pp. Discusses the education and training needed for a variety of jobs associated with geology.

*If You Find a Rock. Peggy Christian. San Diego, CA: Harcourt, 2000. unpaged. Celebrates the variety of rocks that can be found.

Incredible Journey to the Beginning of Time, The. Nicholas Harris. New York, NY: Peter Bedrick Books, 1998. p.cm. Describes the history of the earth at four locales.

Is There a Dinosaur in Your Backyard?: The world's most fascinating fossils, rocks, and minerals. New York, NY: John Wiley, 1998. 120 pp. Gives information on rocks, minerals, fossils, and rock collecting.

It Could Still Be a Rock. Allan Fowler. Chicago, IL: Children's Press, 1993. 31 pp. Discusses the size, shape, composition, and other aspects of different kinds of rocks.

Jurassic Dinosaurs, The. Dougal Dixon. Milwaukee, WI: Gareth Stevens Pub. 1987. 32 pp. Discusses 11 dinosaurs of the Jurassic Period.

Killer Asteroids. Margaret Poynter. Springfield, NJ: Enslow Publishers, 1996, 48 pp. Describes the possible consequence of a collision between our planet and an asteroid.

The Last Dinosaurs. Jane Burton and Dougal Dixon. Milwaukee, WI: Gareth Stevens Pub., 1987. 32 pp. Presents several dinosaurs and other prehistoric fossils.

Learn About Rocks and Minerals. Jack Challoner. New York, NY: Lorenz Books, 1998. 64 pp. Contains instructions for projects such as growing crystals and making concrete.

Learning about the Dinosaurs. Dougal Dixon. Milwaukee, WI: Gareth Stevens, Pub., 1989. 32 pp. Explains how paleontologists discover, reconstruct, and restore fossils.

Let's Go Dinosaur Tracking! Miriam Schlein. New York, NY: Harper-Collins, 1991. 47 pp. Shows dinosaur tracks and what they reveal.

Let's Go Rock Collecting. Roma Gans. New York, NY: HarperCollins, 1997. 30 pp. Discusses the formation and characteristics of igneous, metamorphic, and sedimentary rocks.

Let's Go to the Museum. Lisl Weil. New York, NY: Holiday House, 1989. 32 pp. Explains different jobs in a museum including director, curator, trustee, and conservator.

Living With Dinosaurs. Patricia Lauber. New York, NY: Aladdin Paperbacks, 1991. 46 pp. Discusses dinosaurs that lived in North America 75 million years ago.

A Look at Rocks: From coal to kimberlite. Jo S. Kittinger. New York, NY: Franklin Watts, 1997. 63 pp. Tells how to start a rock collection.

Making Your Own Nature Museum. Ruth B. Alford MacFarlane. New York, NY: Franklin Watts, 1989. 128 pp. Gives instructions for collecting, preserving identifying, and displaying a collection.

Martian Fossils on Earth?: The story of meteorite ALH 84001. Alfred B. Bortz. Brookfield, CT: Millbrook Press, 1997. 72 pp. Discusses the meteorite that fell in Antarctica in 1984.

Mary Anning: Fossil hunter. Sally M. Walker. Minneapolis, MN: Carolrhoda Books, 2001. 48 pp. Discusses the best and complete fossils found by Mary Anning.

Meteorite!: The last days of the dinosaurs. Richard Norris. Austin, TX: Raintree Steck-Vaughn, 2000. 64 pp. Provides one theory of the extinction of dinosaurs.

Mighty Mammals of the Past. John Stidworthy. Morristown, NJ: Silver Burdett Press, 1986. 37 pp. Discusses what we have learned about early mammals from fossilized remains.

The Moon. Michael George. Chanhassen, MN: The Child's World, 1998. 32 pp. Discusses the geology and exploration of the moon.

Mummies, Dinosaurs, Moon Rocks: How we know how old things are. James Jespersen and Jane Fitz-Randolph. New York, NY: Atheneum Books for Young Readers, 1996. 92 pp. Explains how scientists have learned to date objects.

My Best Book of Fossils, Rocks, and Minerals. Chris Pellant. New York, NY: Kingfisher, 2000. 31 pp. Provides a brief discussion of rocks, minerals, and fossils.

National Audubon Society First Field Guide: Rocks and Minerals. Edward R. Ricciuti and Margaret W. Carruthers. New York, NY: Scholastic, 1998. 159 pp. Describes over 100 types of rocks and minerals.

A Nest of Dinosaurs: The story of Oviraptor. Mark A. Norell and Lowell Dingus. New York, NY: Doubleday, 1999. 42 pp. Describes fossils found in the Gobi Desert.

The News About Dinosaurs. Patricia Lauber. New York, NY: Aladdin Books, 1994. 48 pp. Basic information about dinosaurs.

On the Tracks of Dinosaurs. James O. Farlow. New York, NY: Franklin Watts, 1991. 72 pp. Contains a discussion of fossil footprints and how these are used by paleontologists.

Origins of the Dinosaurs. Steve Parker. Danbury, CT: Grolier Educational, 2000. 57 pp. An introduction to dinosaurs.

Our Changing Planet. Nicole Valairie, Translator. New York, NY: Scholastic, 1996. 43 pp. Uses overlays to explore earth's crust, volcanoes, and earthquakes.

Our Patchwork Planet. Helen Roney Sattler. New York, NY: Lothrop, Lee & Shepard Books, 1995. 48 pp. Discusses plate tectonics.

Outside and Inside Dinosaurs. Sandra Markle. New York, NY: Atheneum Books for Young Readers, 2000. p.cm. Discusses what has been learned from studying fossils.

The Physical World. Tony Seddon. New York, NY: Doubleday, 1987. 159 pp. Examines the physical and chemical structure of our earth.

Planet Earth. Robin Kerrod. Minneapolis, MN: Lerner Pub., 2000. 32 pp. An introduction to the planet earth, including its geology.

Prehistoric Animals. Daniel Cohen, New York, NY: Doubleday, 1988. 41 pp. Discusses 20 prehistoric animals and their modern counterparts.

Prehistoric Life. Dougal Dixon. New York, NY: Oxford University Press, 1996. 46 pp. Describes animal life of prehistoric times.

Prehistoric Life. William Lindsay. New York, NY: Alfred A. Knopf, 1994. 63 pp. Discusses fossils and evolution.

Prehistoric Monsters Did the Strangest Things. Leonora and Arthur Hornblow. New York, NY: Random House, 1990. 62 pp. Introduces many strange prehistoric animals in a chronological order.

Prehistoric World. Jill Bailey. New York, NY: Oxford University Press, 1995. 160 pp. Takes an historical look at geology.

Prehistoric World. Michael Benton. New York, NY: Simon & Schuster, 1987. 128 pp. Examines prehistory from the first plants to the first animals.

*The Rock. Peter Parnall. New York, NY: Macmillan, 1991. 32 pp. Traces a rock over the years.

Rocking and Rolling. Philip Steele. Cambridge, MA: Candlewick Press, 1998. 24 pp. Discusses types of geological activity such as earthquakes, glaciers, geysers, and volcanoes.

Rocks & Fossils. Arthur B. Busbey, III. Alexandria, VA: Time-Life Books, 1996. 288 pp. Gives a description of geoscience and provides a guide to rock and mineral identification.

Rocks & Minerals. Sue Fuller. New York, NY: Dorling Kindersley, 1995. 160 pp. An introduction to rocks and minerals.

Rocks & Minerals. Neil Morris. New York, NY: Crabtree Pub. Co., 1998. 32 pp. Provides an introduction to the origins and uses of rocks and minerals.

Rocks and Minerals. Tracy Staedter. Pleasantville, NY: Reader's Digest Children's Books, 1999. 64 pp. Examines the formation of different kinds of rocks and minerals and discusses how to collect them.

*Rocks and Soil. Terry J. Jennings. Chicago, IL: Childrens Press, 1989. 34 pp. Contains ideas for activities and experiments to introduce the topics of rocks and soil.

Rocks and Soils. Robert Snedden. Austin, TX: Raintree Steck-Vaughn, 1999. 48 pp. Describes various rocks and suggests activities and experiments.

Rocks and Minerals. R. F. Symes. New York, NY: Alfred A. Knopf, 1988. 63 pp. Discusses rocks, their creation, erosion, and aspects of mining.

Rocks and Minerals. Kathryn Whyman. New York, NY: Gloucester Press, 1989. 32 pp. Provides an introduction to rocks and minerals.

Rocks, Gems, and Minerals. Lisa Sita. New York, NY: Thomson Learning, 1995. 64 pp. Explores the science of geology.

Rocks, Minerals and Fossils. Keith Lye. Morristown, NJ: Silver Burdett Press, 1991. 48 pp. Provides an introduction to rocks, minerals, and fossils.

Rocks, Rocks, Big and Small. Joanne Barkan. Morristown, NJ: Silver Burdett Press, 1990. 30 pp. Offers an introduction to rocks.

Science for Kids: 39 easy geology experiments. Robert W. Wood. Blue Ridge Summit, PA: TAB Books, 1991. 133 pp. Contains a variety of experiments for performing tests on rocks and for growing crystals.

Shaping the Earth. Dorothy Hinshaw Patent. New York, NY: Clarion Books, 2000. 88 pp. Discusses the forces that have created the geological features of the Earth's surface.

Simple Science Fun: Hands-on science made easy. Evan Forbes. Huntington Beach, CA: Teacher Created Materials, 1996. 160 pp. Suggests various experiments in both life and earth sciences.

Start Collecting Rocks and Minerals. Lee Ann Srogi. Philadelphia, PA: Running Press, 1989. 127 pp. Explains how to organize minerals, crystals, and rocks in a collection.

Super Science Book of Rocks and Soils, The. Robert Snedden. New York, NY: Thomson Learning, 1995, 32 pp. An introduction to rocks and soils.

The Tales Fossils Tell. Jonathan R. Gallant. New York, NY: Benchmark Books, 2001. 80 pp. Explains how fossils form and what they tells us.

Terrible Tyrannosaurs. Kathleen Weidner Zoehfeld. New York, NY: HarperCollins Publishers, 2001. 33 pp. Discusses Tyrannosaurus rex.

The Top and Bottom of the World. Allan Fowler. New York, NY: Children's Press, 1997. 31 pp. Discusses the geology, climate, and animal life of the Arctic and Antarctic.

Trapped in Tar: Fossils from the Ice Age. Caroline Arnold. New York, NY: Clarion Books, 1987. 57 pp. Examines the fossils of the La Brea Tar Pits in California through text and photos.

Triassic Dinosaur World. Tamara Green. Milwaukee, WI: Gareth Stevens, 1998. 32 pp. Takes the reader back 210 million years and describe the world of that time.

A Visit to the Natural History Museum. Sandra Ziegler. Chicago, IL: Children's Press, 1988. 31 pp. Using the format of a tour, the reader learns about the reconstruction of dinosaurs, plants, and an Indian lodge.

Volcano. Christopher Lampton. Brookfield, CT: Millbrook Press, 1991. 64 pp. Discusses four types of volcanoes.

Volcanoes and Earthquakes. Mary Elting with Rachel Folsom and Robert Moll. New York, NY: Simon & Schuster, 1990. 40 pp. Discusses how volcanic activity and earthquakes occur and how they are predicted.

Volcanoes and Earthquakes. Zuza Vrbova. Mahwah, NJ: Troll Associates, 1990. 32 pp. Offers an introduction to volcanoes and earthquakes.

Walking With Dinosaurs. Tim Haines. New York, NY: Dorling Kindersley, 2000. p.cm. Describes the environment in which dinosaurs flourished.

What Did Dinosaurs Eat?: And other things you want to know about dinosaurs. Elizabeth MacLeod. Tonawanda, NY: Kids Can Press, 2001. 32 pp. Answers common questions that children ask about dinosaurs.

What Is A Dinosaur? Niki Walker. New York, NY: Crabtree Pub., 1999. 32 pp. Identifies what is and what is not a dinosaur.

Where Are all of the Dinosaurs? Mary O'Neill. Mahwah, NJ: Troll Associates, 1989. 32 pp. Examines fossils to explain why dinosaurs disappeared.

Why Do Volcanoes Erupt? Questions about our unique planet answered by Dr. Philip Whitfield with the Natural History Museum. Philip Whitfield. New York, NY: Viking Penguin, 1990. 36 pp. Answers many questions about volcanoes.

The World in One Day. Russell Ash. New York, NY: Dorling Kindersley, 1997. 32 pp. Gives statistics on what happens to the world in a single day with respect to geology, biology, etc.

Zion National Park. Ruth Radlauer. Chicago, IL: Children's Press, 1988. 48 pp. Discusses the rock formations of Utah's Zion Park.

Other Resources

All About Fossils. Wynnewood, PA: Schlessinger Media, 2000. 1 videocassette, 23 minutes. Designed for primary and intermediate students, explains the ways fossils are formed.

American Museum of Natural History. Glastenbury, CT: Video Tours, 1990. 1 videocassette, 40 minutes. Explores the fascinating exhibits of the American Museum of Natural History.

Before You Visit a Museum. Stamford, CT: The Group, 1987. 1 videocassette, 14 minutes. Pt. 1 Finding your way around. Pt. 2, Getting the most from your visit.

Classroom Dinosaur. Nashua, NH: Delta Education. From corrugated cardboard students can assemble a 5-foot skeleton of a Brontosaurus or Tyranosaurus Rex.

Crystal Growing Lab Investigation. Nashua, NH: Delta Education. For grades 6–9. A way to study the world of minerals as students grow their own amazing large crystals, crystal clusters, and crystal geodes.

Desktop Seismograph. Nashua, NH: Delta Education. For grades 6–12. A scaled-down recorder with attached support and suspended weight records shock waves from earthquakes that you create.

Dinosaurs: Lessons from bones. Hightstown, NJ: American School Publishers, 1991. 1 videocassette, 24 minutes. Shows fossil research in the field and in the museum.

Dinosaur World. Geoffrey T. Williams. Los Angeles, CA: Price, Stern, Sloan, 1986. 1 book, 32 pp. 1 sound cassette, 20 minutes. A tapekit about the world of dinosaurs.

Earth Science in Action. Wynnewood, PA: Schlessinger Media, 2000. 1 videocassette, 23 min. Discusses rocks and what they can tell us about earth's history.

Hands on Exploration: Fossils. Nashua, NH: Delta Education. Over 100 samples introduce 12 fossil varieties. Includes fossils, a guidebook, and two hand lenses.

Rock Collections. Nashua, NH: Delta Education. Rock collections come in various sizes and prices.

Rock Identification Kit. Nashua, NH: Delta Education. Contains steel pans and 40 unidentified, marble-sized rocks with magnifiers, and a 128-page book to facilitate identification.

Sedimentator. Nashua, NH; Delta Education. For grades 1–6. A plastic demonstration tube for teaching the soil sedimentation process. Includes student and teacher guides.

Volcano. Anne McLeod. A CAFÉ production for BBC Worldwide America. D.K. Visions in association with Oregon Public Broadcasting. 1 videocassette, 35 min. Uses a mixture of animation and live footage to show the origin of volcanoes.

7
Exploring astronomy

An evening of backyard sky watching or a night school session to look at the heavens can be a lot of fun. If you live in a city where there are many lights, you may have to postpone your astronomy session until you are on a week-end backpack trip in the mountains or vacationing at a summer cabin by a lake. But even in the city, with a trained eye, a teacher or other adult can help children find out a lot about the mysteries of the sky.

Perhaps the curious child in your life comments early one evening that the star he or she can see from your backyard over the mountains at the edge of town is especially bright and seems to be up earlier than all the others. Perhaps late one night while driving home on an especially clear night, you point out to the child that a lot of the constellations, or star pictures, are easy to see this evening. Maybe a class discussion begins when a student reports that he or she saw a "falling star" last night. Or perhaps on a family camping trip a child comments that he or she has never seen so many stars in the sky before. Any of these may be an opening to begin some exploring of astronomy.

As in all areas with curious kids, the adult needs to be guided by the interest shown. Don't tell too much or go into such complex answers that it becomes boring. If the child is really interested, the questions will keep coming, and you'll know that this is an area for some in-depth exploration.

If a unit of study in the classroom or an individual child's interest at home persists over several weeks, the class of students or the child will come to realize that the sky looks "different" each and every night. A child may ask why it changes. Another student may also notice that the moon seems to change its shape and ask questions about that aspect of the night sky.

One of the first steps in sky watching is to orient yourself with respect to north, south, east, and west. Using shadows is a good way to do this.

Making a shadow board

The following experiment will explain how to make a shadow board which will help you orient yourself.

You can help a child make a shadow board by cutting and fastening a stick or dowel upright in the center of an 8-inch-square board.

Take the board outside and put it on a level spot of ground. In the United States at noontime, there will be a short shadow, which indicates the north–south line, since the sun is directly toward the south at this time. This will help you orient yourself for sky watching by knowing the directions in your own back yard.

At night, you can look for the Big Dipper above the northern horizon all during the year. Older youth may need to learn about azimuth (the position of an object relative to north) and altitude (where an object lies between the horizon and the zenith). Various references included in the Resource books section of this chapter will show you how to make a simple device for determining azimuth and altitude.

Once you are certain about the directions from the spot where you and the child will be observing, many simple activities are possible.

Drawing a sky map

From a convenient window in your house, you and your curious child can make a map of the eastern skyline showing trees, buildings, or other features.

Then make a similar map of the western skyline.

Note on your eastern sky map where the sun rises each day, and date your observation. Similarly, note on your western sky map where the sun sets each night and date your observations.

You may skip days or even weeks between your observations.

You will find that during winter, the sun rises south of east and sets south of west. On the first day of spring, it will rise due east and set due west.

Such mapping and graphing experiences may be very intriguing to a child who comes to have a sense of discovery about the objects in the sky.

Making a cardboard sundial

If a child or a group of students show an interest in the sun and its position, you might want to continue your study by using a sundial to tell time. You can purchase one or you may find it challenging to make one. There are many ways to go about this. You can make a simple, sundial (which won't last) from cardboard or you can make a heavy duty one from wood or metal.

You need to know your latitude to make a working sundial. The directions below are for making a sundial at a latitude of 40 degrees.

Cut a 6-inch-square piece of stiff cardboard. Use a protractor to draw a line marking a 40-degree angle for the longest side of a triangle, which will be about 7¼ inches long. Cut out this right-angled triangle.

Take a piece of cardboard that is 12 inches long by 6 inches wide. Draw a half-circle on it that has a 6-inch radius. Cut out the semicircle.

Use tape to attach your triangle to the semicircle. The sloping side of the triangle should point to the center of the semicircle.

Place the sundial outside. Use a compass to align the triangle north and south. The tallest side of the 40-degree angle should point north.

Then mark the position of the sun's shadow on the base of your sundial every hour. You can begin at 6 A.M. on the left side of the triangle. At the back of your triangle should be 12 noon. Number again to about 6 P.M. on the right side of the triangle. Your marks should be at an equal distance around the half-circle with 12 noon pointing true north.

Now by looking at the shadow cast on the base of your sundial, you can tell time on a sunny day.

A visit to a planetarium with a curious child or a classroom of students can be a very special treat. It is a judgment call as to whether you do preparation before the visit or whether you follow-up afterwards with explorations into areas that seemed of particular interest. Both kinds of activities can be useful.

If you have access to a planetarium, there is probably a brochure available that details the shows that are planned during the next several months. One of these shows may have considerably more interest for a child or a class than another.

Constructing a star box

You can replicate the feeling of being in a planetarium by making a star box out of a large empty refrigerator packing box that you can get from a shopkeeper.

Cut a door into one side of the refrigerator packing box. Devise a simple way to hold it shut, such as a strip of duct tape.

Paint the inside of the box black and let it dry thoroughly.

Choose favorite constellations and make accurate patterns of them. Then duplicate the patterns onto the inside walls and top of the box by using glow-in-the-dark pieces of tape for stars.

You can decorate the outside of the box in any fashion.

Cut a hole in the top of the box large enough to allow you to dangle a light that is attached to an extension cord that is the right length to comfortably reach a nearby electric outlet.

Put a stool or small chair inside the box. You can turn on the light just long enough to activate the glow tape, then turn out the light and sit inside the box. You will be surrounded by black space and glowing stars!

Watching the moon may also prove interesting. Many calendars will list the date of the next new moon, full moon, and crescent moons. During the new moon phase, the moon is between the sun and the earth with the lighted half of the moon away from the earth. The new moon is invisible, but a night or two after the new moon, you will be able to see the new crescent moon in the sky right after sunset. On each succeeding night, the moon appears higher and you will be able to see more of the surface until there is a full moon. The moon then begins to slowly fade again toward a new moon (waning crescent moon).

Only rarely will you and your curious child happen to be together in the right place during a lunar eclipse. If this were to occur, there would be considerable publicity about the event. Similarly you may happen to see a comet or the northern lights.

Answering the question:
Why is the sky blue?

It is much more likely that your curious child may ask, "Why is the sky blue?" or "What is that ring around the moon?" These questions lead to more questions and investigations about how the clouds in our own atmosphere affect how we see the sky and moon in the distance. Clearly you would capitalize on such special events.

To answer the question, "Why is the sky blue?" you can do a simple experiment. Put a spoon in a full glass of water. Hold the glass up and look through it from the side. The spoon handle looks broken where it enters the water. This is due to the fact that light rays bend as they go from the thin air to the thicker liquid.

In the same way, light rays from the sun bend as they enter the earth's atmosphere and are scattered by the air and dust. Light rays from the sun are made up of all the colors of the rainbow. In our atmosphere, blue light is scattered most, so the sky looks blue.

Planets are another fruitful source of investigation. Planets do not produce light, they reflect sunlight, and so they must be close to us or very large to be seen. Mars, Venus, Jupiter, and Saturn can be seen easily. Charts are available that will let you know which planets can be seen in the evening or the early morning and where to look for them in the sky.

Modeling the planets

It is hard for students to conceptualize the sizes of the various planets. The following experiment explains a way to model the approximate sizes of the planets in a small space so that children can have some understanding of the sun and its family.

Label a basketball, which has a 10-inch diameter, "The Sun" and put it on a table.

Take a strip of wood about 1 foot long and 3 inches wide. Hammer nine tall, thin nails into the strip of wood, equidistant from each other, with all but a ½ inch of the nail sticking upright from the wood. Put the strip of wood next to the basketball. Use strips of paper to write the names of the planets. Label each nail with the planet's name, beginning on the left with Mercury, Venus, Earth, Mars, Jupiter, Saturn, Uranus, Neptune, and Pluto. (Although this will correctly show the order of the planets from closest to farthest from the sun, it will not correctly show the distances.)

Make a model of each of the planets out of clay and put the model on the top of the nail with the correct label. Most of the planets will be very tiny. Mercury should be shown with a diameter of 1 mm; Venus, 2 mm; Earth, slightly more than 2 mm; Mars and Pluto about 1½ mm; Neptune, about 5 mm; Uranus, about 6 mm; Saturn, about 13 mm; and Jupiter, about 16 mm.

If you like, you might make a cardboard ring to go around Saturn, holding it in place with toothpicks stuck into the ball of clay.

Learning about the stars may be the most exciting part of sky watching. For this, however, you will need a cloudless night away from city lights. If a telescope is available, the opportunities will be increased. But even without a telescope, a child will enjoy finding constellations in the sky and will be able to see that some stars are "brighter" than others.

The Dipper Group has excellent stars for springtime viewing. A good summer group for observation is Cygnus, Draco, and Scorpio. The Pegasus group is good for fall viewing, and the Orion Group is a good cluster for winter viewing. In all seasons, you can study the Polar Group including the Big and Little Dipper and Cassiopeia.

Projecting constellations

When a youngster knows a constellation well, he or she might draw it to scale on a small paper circle the size of a bottom of an empty tin can.

Tape the finished drawing to the bottom of the can. Use a hammer and a nail to puncture holes right through the drawing and into the can for each star. Use different sized nails; large ones to show bright stars and smaller ones to show not-so-bright stars.

Then, go into a dark room. Put a flashlight inside the can and turn it on. You will be able to project the constellation onto the wall!

Clocking time exposure of star trails

Watching the stars as they appear still in the sky is fun, but you and your curious child can also track a star with a camera as it travels in the night sky.

If you have a camera with a time exposure adjustment, you may get a picture of star trails in the northern sky. Select a location away from city lights, on a dark night with little or no moon.

Mount the camera on a tripod and aim it at Polaris. Open the stop to its widest aperture, open the shutter, and leave it open for an hour.

Your photograph will show a circular star pattern.

Your class or a curious youngster might also be interested in comets and meteors. Many books are available on all these topics. Perhaps a museum in your area has a meteorite that you can view.

Sometimes sky watching leads to increased interest in space exploration and man-made satellites. This could open up a whole new area of exploration.

In addition to the resources listed below, you might want to consult the Resource books section in the following chapters for more specific details: Chapter 6 "Exploring Geology and Paleontology" for more information on meteorites, Chapter 8 "Exploring Geography and Cartography" for more books on mapping and orienteering, and Chapter 12 "Exploring Science through Writing" for star legends.

Resource Books

About Stars and Planets. James Muirden. New York, NY: Warwick Press, 1986. 32 pp. Provides an introduction to stars and planets.

Adventure in Space: The flight to fix the Hubble. Elaine Scott. New York, NY: Hyperion Books for Children, 1995. 64 pp. Discusses the repair of the Hubble space telescope.

Aerospace Science: The exploration of space. Naomi L. Mitchell and Patricia A. Roberson. Maxwell Air Force Base, AL: Air Force Junior ROTC, 1994. 1 volume. Information for secondary space science study.

Amazing Space Almanac, The. Justin Segal. Los Angeles, CA: Lowell House Juvenile, 1998. 128 pp. Presents information on the origin and nature of the universe.

Amazing Space Facts. Dinah L. Moche. Racine, WI: Western Publishing Co., 1988. 24 pp. Provides an introduction to the solar system.

Ancient Astronomy. Isaac Asimov. Milwaukee, WI: Gareth Stevens Pub., 1989. 32 pp. Discusses the beliefs of early astronomers.

Anno's Sundial. Mitsumasa Anno. New York, NY: Philomel Books, 1987. 28 pp. Discusses the earth and sun with pop-up and fold-out pages.

Apollo and the Moon Landing. Gregory Vogt. Brookfield, CT: Millbrook Press, 1991. 111 pp. Discusses the moon landing.

Astronomy. Dennis B. Fradin. Chicago, IL: Children's Press, 1987. 286 pp. Provides basic information on stars, galaxies, and the universe.

Astronomy. Ian Graham. Austin, TX: Raintree Steck-Vaughn, 1995. 46 pp. An introduction to astronomy.

Astronomy. Robin Kerrod. Milwaukee, WI: Gareth Stevens Pub., 1998. 68 pp. Gives a brief introduction to astronomy.

Astronomy. Kristen Lippincott. New York, NY: Dorling Kindersley, 1994. 64 pp. Discusses the history of astronomy and identifies important astronomers.

Astronomy. Graham Peacock and Dennis Ashton. New York, NY: Thomson Learning, 1994. 32 pp. Contains suggestions for astronomy-related activities.

Astronomy Adventures. National Wildlife Federation. Philadelphia, PA: Chelsea House Publishers, 1998. 101 pp. Explores astronomy through a variety of activities and projects.

Astronomy & Space: From the big bang to the big crunch. Phillis Engelbert. Detroit, MI: UXL, 1996, 3 volumes. Provides an introduction to outer space.

Astronomy: From Copernicus to the space telescope. Christopher Lampton, New York, NY: Franklin Watts, 1987. 96 pp. Explains the history and various theories in astronomy.

Astronomy Today. Dinah L. Moche. New York, NY: Random House, 1998. 96 pp. An introduction to the planets, stars, and space exploration.

The Big Dipper. Franklyn Mansfield Branley. New York, NY: Harper-Collins, 1991. 32 pp. Contains basic information on how to determine position by using the North Star.

The Big Dipper and You. Edwin C. Krupp. New York, NY: Morrow Junior Books, 1989. 48 pp. Gives information about the Big Dipper and the North Star.

The Birth and Death of Stars. Isaac Asimov. Milwaukee, WI: Gareth Stevens Pub., 1989. 32 pp. Tells how stars come into being and how they come to an end.

Black Holes. Heather Couper. New York, NY: Dorling Kindersley, 1996. 45 pp. Explains how we know about black holes.

Black Holes. Paul P. Sipiera. New York, NY: Children's Press, 1997. 48 pp. Explains the nature and formation of black holes.

Black Holes and Supernovae. David E. Newton. New York, NY: Twenty-First Century Books, 1997. 64 pp. Explains unusual space phenomena.

Comets and Meteors. Isaac Asimov. Milwaukee, WI: Gareth Stevens Pub., 1990. 32 pp. Discusses characteristics and some of the more famous appearances of comets and meteors.

Comets and Meteors: Visitors from space. Jeanne Bendick. Brookfield, CT: Millbrook Press, 1991. 32 pp. Contains answers to many questions that children commonly ask about comets and meteors.

Comets, Stardust, and Supernovas. Edward Willett. Austin, TX: Raintree Steck-Vaughn, 2000. 48 pp. An introduction to different aspects of outer space.

Cosmic Light Shows. Bobbie Kalman. New York, NY: Crabtree Pub., 1999. 32 pp. Introduces astronomical phenomena visible from earth such as comets, eclipses, and auroras.

Cosmic Science: Over 40 gravity-defying, earth-orbiting, space-cruising activities for kids. Jim Wiese. New York, NY: John Wiley & Sons, 1997. 120 pp. Gives instructions for activities that explore gravity and other aspects of outer space.

Could You Ever Fly to the Stars? David Darling. New York, NY; Dillon Press, 1990. 59 pp. Discusses rockets, spacecraft, and the stars most likely for future destinations.

The Day We Walked on the Moon: A photo history of space exploration. George Sullivan. New York, NY: Scholastic, Inc. 1990. 72 pp. Discusses astronauts and their training.

Deep Space Astronomy. Gregory Vogt. Brookfield, CT: Twenty-First Century Books, 1999. 79 pp. Explains where various objects are located in the universe.

Destination: Moon. James Irwin with Al Janssen. Portland, OR: Multnomah, 1989. 50 pp. Explains the training of an astronaut.

Did You Ever Wonder About Things You See in the Sky? Vera Vullo. New York, NY: Benchmark Books, 2000. 32 pp. Describes such things as the sun, moon, stars, and weather phenomena.

Don't Know Much About Space. Kenneth C. Davis. New York, NY: HarperCollins Publishers, 2001. 143 pp. Provides information in a question and answer format.

Dorling Kindersley Guide to Space. Peter Bond. New York, NY: Dorling Kindersley, 1999. 64 pp. Includes photographs from NASA.

Do Stars Have Points?: Questions and answers about stars and planets. Melvin Berger. New York, NY: Scholastic Reference, 1998. 48 pp. Uses a question and answer format to provide information about the solar system.

Earth and Universe. Storm Dunlop. Milwaukee, WI: Gareth Stevens Pub., 1997. 48 pp. Gives information about winds, storms, mountains, and earthquakes on Earth and discusses similar phenomena throughout the solar system.

Earth in Space, The. Peter D. Riley. New York, NY: Franklin Watts, 1999. 32 pp. Discusses Earth's place in the solar system.

Earth's Moon, The. Isaac Asimov. Milwaukee, WI: Gareth Stevens Pub., 1988, 32 pp. Gives many facts about the moon.

Edwin Hubble. Fiona Macdonald. Chicago, IL: Heinemann Library, 2001. 48 pp. A biography of Edwin Hubble and his contributions to astronomy.

Exploring the Universe: Science Activities for Kids. Anthony D. Fredericks. Golden, CO: Fulcrum Resources, 2000. 120 pp. Includes hands-on activities and projects related to a study of the universe.

Exploring the World of Astronomy. George Burns. New York, NY: Franklin Watts, 1995. 48 pp. Discusses astronomy and suggests simple experiments and projects.

Exploring Venus and Mercury. David Baker. Vero Beach, FL: Rourke Enterprises, 1989. 47 pp. Chronicles the NASA space explorations.

Exploring with a Telescope. Glenn F. Chaple, Jr. New York, NY: Franklin Watts, 1988. 142 pp. Discusses the parts of telescopes, how they work, and how they should be cared for.

Exploring Your Solar System. Elizabeth Rathbun. Washington, DC: National Geographic Society, 1989. 96 pp. Provides a guided tour of the nine planets and discusses the Milky Way Galaxy.

The Far Planets. Donna Bailey. Austin, TX: Steck-Vaughn Library, 1991. 48 pp. Discusses the five known planets outside the orbit of Mars.

The Galaxies: Cities of stars. David J. Darling. New York, NY: Dillon Press, 1985. 63 pp. Explains the different types of galaxies and how they formed.

Glow in the Dark Constellations: A field guide for young stargazers. C. E. Thompson. New York, NY: Grosset & Dunlap, 1989. 28 pp. Provides a useful resource to take outdoors at night when you are trying to spot constellations.

The Glow-in-the-Dark Night Sky Book. Clint Hatchett. New York, NY: Random House, 1988. 20 pp. Provides star charts to consult at night.

The Golden Book of Space Exploration. Dinah L. Moche. Racine, WI: Western Publishing Co., 1990. 45 pp. Traces the development of space travel.

The Golden Book of Stars and Planets. Judith Herbst. Racine, WI: Western Publishing Co., 1988. 45 pp. Gives introductory information on stars and planets.

Halley's Comet: What we've learned. Gregory Vogt. New York, NY: Franklin Watts, 1987. 95 pp. Discusses the research carried out on Halley's Comet in 1986.

How Did We Find Out about Neptune? Isaac Asimov. New York, NY: Walker & Company, 1990. 64 pp. Provides information about the planet Neptune.

How Did We Find Out about Pluto? Isaac Asimov. New York, NY: Walker & Company, 1991. 64 pp. Introduction to the planet Pluto.

How? More experiments for the young scientist. Dave Prochnow. Philadelphia, PA: Chelsea House Pub., 1999. 152 pp. Gives 43 experiments in various fields including astronomy.

How the Universe Works. Heather Couper. Pleasantville, NY: Reader's Digest Assn., 1994. 160 pp. Gives directions for astronomy experiments.

How Was the Universe Born? Isaac Asimov. Milwaukee, WI: Gareth Stevens Pub., 1988. 32 pp. Discusses the origin of the universe.

Hubble Space Telescope: Exploring the Universe. Michael D. Cole. Springfield, NJ: Enslow Publishers, 1999. 48 pp. Discusses the initiation of the Hubble and later repair and service missions.

I Can Be an Astronomer. Paul P. Sipiera. Chicago, IL: Children's Press, 1986. 30 pp. Discusses the work that astronomers do.

Janice Van Cleave's Constellations for Every Kid: Easy activities that make learning science fun. Janice Pratt VanCleave. New York, NY: John Wiley & Sons, 1997. 247 pp. Suggests exciting projects for science fairs.

Journey to the Planets. Patricia Lauber. New York, NY: Crown Publishers, 1990. 90 pp. Highlights the most prominent features of each of the planets.

Junk in Space. Richard Mauer. New York, NY: Simon & Schuster, 1989. 48 pp. Discusses space garbage.

Kingfisher Facts and Records Book of Space, The. Clive Gifford. New York, NY: Kingfisher, 2001. 61 pp. Interesting facts about space.

Looking at Stars. Donna Bailey. Austin, TX: Steck-Vaughn Library, 1991. 48 pp. Discusses various aspects of the stars.

Making and Enjoying Telescopes: 6 complete projects and a stargazer's guide. Robert Miller and Kenneth Wilson. New York, NY: Sterling Pub. Co., 1997. 160 pp. A useful guide for backyard astronomers.

Mars. Larry Dane Brimner. New York, NY: Children's Press, 1998. 47 pp. Gives simple facts about the Red Planet.

Mars: Our mysterious neighbor. Isaac Asimov. Milwaukee, WI: Gareth Stevens, Pub., 1988. 32 pp. Discusses the characteristics of the planet Mars.

Modern Astronomy. Isaac Asimov. Milwaukee, WI: Gareth Stevens, Pub., 1996. 32 pp. Discusses instruments used in studying the sky such as computers, the space telescope, radio telescope, and binoculars.

*The Moon. Heather Cooper and Nigel Henbest. New York, NY: Franklin Watts, 1986. 32 pp. Provides an introduction to the moon.

The Moon. David Hughes. New York, NY: Facts on File, 1989. 45 pp. Gives latest data about the moon.

Moons and Rings: Companions to the planets. Jeanne Bendick. Brookfield, CT: Millbrook Press, 1991. 32 pp. Provides answers to common questions that children have about moons and rings.

*The Moon Seems to Change. Franklyn Mansfield Branley. New York, NY: Thomas Y. Crowell, 1987. 29 pp. Discusses the phases of the moon.

Moonwalk: The first trip to the moon. Judy Donnelly. New York, NY: Random House, 1989. 47 pp. Discusses the July 1969, moon landing.

My Picture Book of the Planets. Nancy E. Krulik. New York, NY: Scholastic, Inc., 1991. 30 pp. Describes the nine planets and includes close-up color NASA photos.

Mysteries of Space: Opposing viewpoints. Michael Rasmussen. San Deigo, CA: Greenhaven, 1994. 128 pp. Different view on the universe.

The Mystery of Black Holes. Chris Oxlade. Des Plaines, IL: Heinemann Library, 2000. 32 pp. Explores black holes and why they exist.

National Audubon Society First Field Guide. Night Sky. Gary Mechler. New York, NY: Scholastic, 1999. 159 pp. A useful field guide to the night sky.

The Near Planets. Donna Bailey. Austin, TX: Steck-Vaughn Library, 1991. 48 pp. Discusses the four planets closest to the sun.

Nebulae: The birth and death of stars. Necia H. Apfel. New York, NY: Lothrop, Lee & Shepard Books, 1988. 48 pp. Discusses how nebulae are formed.

The New Book of Space. Robin Scagell. Brookfield, CT: Copper Beech Books, 1997. 31 pp. Discusses recent developments in space exploration and astronomy.

New York Public Library Amazing Space: A book of answers for kids. Ann Campbell. New York, NY: John Wiley & Sons, 1997. 186 pp. Contains basic information about space.

Our Earth and the Solar System. Ken Graun. Tucson, AZ: Ken Press, 2001. 36 pp. Information about the planets in the solar system.

Our Future in Space. Don Berliner. Minneapolis, MN: Lerner Publications Co., 1991. 71 pp. Discusses current space research and future space projects.

Our Solar System. Isaac Asimov. Milwaukee, WI: Gareth Stevens Pub., 1988. 32 pp. Discusses the characteristics of the sun, planets, and stars.

Our Stars. Anne F. Rockwell. San Diego, CA: Silver Whistle, 1999. unpaged. Provides a simple introduction to stars, planets, and outer space.

Our Sun and the Inner Planets. Don Davis and A. Chantal. New York, NY: Facts on File, 1989. 45 pp. Tells what astronomers know about the nuclear powerhouse that dominates our solar system.

Our Universe: A guide to what's out there. Russell Stannard. New York, NY: Kingfisher, 1995. 96 pp. Provides an introduction to cosmology.

Outer Space. Roger Cleeve. Englewood Cliffs, NJ: Julian Messner, 1990. 32 pp. Discusses various phenomena in our universe.

Out in Space. Tim Wood. New York, NY: Macmillan, 1991. 29 pp. Through a journey in a spaceship, the child learns about gravity, the moon, sun, and planets.

Out of This World. Carole Stott. Cambridge, MA: Candlewick Press, 1998. 24 pp. Provides a brief introduction to the universe.

Peterson's First Guide to the Solar System. Jay M. Pasachoff. Boston, MA: Houghton Mifflin, 1990. 128 pp. Provides a basic guide to the solar system for beginners.

The Picture World of Sun and Stars. Norman S. Barrett. New York, NY: Franklin Watts, 1990. 29 pp. Discusses our solar system, different types of stars, and galaxies.

Piloted Space Flights. Isaac Asimov. Milwaukee, WI: Gareth Stevens Pub., 1990. 32 pp. Gives a history of mans' experiences in space.

The Planet Hunters: The search for other worlds. Dennis B. Fradin. New York, NY: Margaret K. McElderry Books, 1997. 148 pp. Gives information about the people who have discovered planets.

Planets: A guide to the solar system. Mark R. Chartrand. Racine, WI: Golden Press, 1990. 160 pp. Presents information about the planets.

Planets and Stars. Nicholas Booth. London, England: Grange Books 1995. 46 pp. Explores the planets and unusual moons and stars.

Power Station Sun. John Mason. New York, NY: Facts on File, 1987. 47 pp. Discusses the sun and energy.

The Princeton Review Astronomy Smart Junior: The science of the solar system and beyond. Michael Lee Bentley. New York, NY; Random House, 1997. 188 pp. Introduction to astronomy for grades 6 to 8.

Quasars, Pulsars, and Black Holes. Isaac Asimov. Milwaukee, WI: Gareth Stevens Pub., 1988. 32 pp. Discusses stars and galaxies emitting special types of radio waves.

Radio Astronomy. Alan Edward Nourse. New York, NY: Franklin Watts, 1989. 96 pp. Discusses the uses of radio astronomy.

Rainbows, Mirages, and Sundogs: The sky as a source of wonder. Roy A. Gallant. New York, NY: Macmillan, 1987. 94 pp. Discusses the various visual phenomena seen in the sky.

Saturn. Dennis B. Fradin. Chicago, IL: Children's Press, 1989. 45 pp. Discusses the main characteristics of Saturn and includes Voyager photographs.

Scholastic Encyclopedia of Space, The. Jacqueline Mitton. New York, NY: Scholastic Reference, 1998. 80 pp. Discusses the origins and nature of the universe, space travel, and the solar system.

Science for Kids: 39 easy astronomy experiments. Robert W. Wood. Blue Ridge Summit, PA: TAB Books, 1991. 139 pp. Provides information on experiments such as making a spectroscope and telescope.

Seeing Stars: McDonald Observatory: Its science and astronomers. Mark G. Mitchell. Austin, TX: Eakin Press, 1997. 100 pp. Discusses the history of this observatory in West Texas.

See the Stars: Your first guide to the night sky. Ken Croswell. Honesdale, PA: Boyds Mills Press, 2000. 32 pp. An introduction to the constellations.

*Shooting Stars. Franklyn Mansfield Branley. New York, NY: Thomas Y. Crowell, 1989. 32 pp. Explains what shooting stars are.

The Solar System. Bradford Burnham. New York, NY: Thomson Learning, 1995. 64 pp. Explores the solar system.

The Solar System. Robin Kerrod. Minneapolis, MN: Lerner Publishers, 2000. 32 pp. Introduces the solar system.

The Solar System. Jane Walker. Brookfield, CT: Millbrook Press, 1990. 32 pp. Filled with fascinating facts about the solar system.

The Solar System: An A-Z guide. Christina Wilsdon. New York, NY: Franklin Watts, 2000. 96 pp. A dictionary of terms, concepts, people and places related to the solar system, astronomy, and space.

So That's How the Moon Changes Shape. Allan Fowler. Chicago, IL: Children's Press, 1991. 31 pp. Explains how the moon appears to change shape.

Space. Donna Bailey. Austin, TX: Steck-Vaughn Library. 1990. 48 pp. Provides an introduction to space exploration.

Space. Alan Dyer. Pleasantville, NY: Reader's Digest Children's Books, 1999. 64 pp. Provides descriptions of the sun, moon, planets, constellations, nebulas, and black holes.

Space. Simon Holland. New York, NY: Dorling Kindersley, 2001. 45 pp. **An** Eye Wonder book.

Space. Bobbie Kalman. New York, NY: Crabtree Pub. Co., 1997. 32 pp. Discusses the solar system, space ships, shuttles, space stations, and life in space.

Space and Astronomy: 49 science fair projects. Robert L. Bonnet and G. Daniel Keen. Blue Ridge Summit, PA: TAB Books, 1992. 128 pp. Filled with information about possible science fair projects.

Space Explained: A beginner's guide to the universe. Robin Scagell. New York, NY: Henry Holt, 1996. 69 pp. Provides an introduction to space science.

Space Exploration. Brian Jones. Milwaukee, WI: Gareth Stevens Pub., 1990. 64 pp. Explains about space, stars, and the planets in our solar system.

Space Probes and Satellites. Heather Couper and Nigel Henbest. New York, NY: Franklin Watts, 1987. 32 pp. Discusses the development in both manned and unmanned space exploration.

Space Spotter's Guide. Isaac Asimov. Milwaukee, WI: Gareth Stevens Pub., 1988. 32 pp. gives tips on buying a telescope and how to spot the wonders of the solar system.

Space: Stars, planets and spacecraft. Sue Becklake. New York, NY: Dorling Kindersly, 1991. 64 pp. Discusses outer space.

Space Telescope. Dennis B. Fradin. Chicago, IL: Children's Press, 1989. 46 pp. Discusses existing telescopes and those that might be used in the future.

Space Telescope, The. Christopher Lampton. New York, NY: Franklin Watts, 1987. 70 pp. Discusses the history and goals of the Hubble Space telescope.

Star Guide. Franklyn Mansfield Branley. New York, NY: Thomas Y. Crowell, 1987. 51 pp. Discusses the composition and behavior of stars.

*The Starry Sky. Rose Wyler. Englewood Cliffs, NJ: Julian Messner, 1989. 32 pp. Discusses the sky, sun, stars, moon, and planets.

Stars and Planets. David Lambert. Austin, TX: Raintree Steck-Vaughn, 1994. 32 pp. Discusses planets, stars, and the solar system.

Stars & Planets. David H. Levy, Editor. Alexandra, VA: Time-Life Books, 1996. 64 pp. Gives an overview of the solar system and its parts.

Stars and Planets. Patrick Moore. New York, NY: Exeter Books, 1987. 112 pp. A basic guide to stars and planets.

The Stars: From birth to black hole. David J. Darling. New York, NY: Dillon Press, 1985. 64 pp. Explains the formation, life, and destruction of stars.

The Stars: Lights in the night sky. Jeanne Bendick. Brookfield, CT: Millbrook Press, 1991. 32 pp. Provides an introduction to the stars.

Star Tales: North American Indian stories about the stars. Retold by Gretchen Will Mayo. New York, NY: Walker & Company, 1987. 96 pp. Contains a collection of Indian legends.

Starwatch. David Baker. Vero Beach, FL: Rourke Enterprises, 1989. 48 pp. Explains how astronomers use various tools to study the universe.

The Sun. Denny Robson. New York, NY: Gloucester Press, 1991. 32 pp. Provides an introduction to the sun.

*The Sun is Always Shining Somewhere. Allan Fowler, Chicago, IL: Children's Press, 1991. 31 pp. Gives introductory information about the sun.

The Sun is a Star: Other amazing facts about the universe. Kate Petty. Brookfield, CT: Copper Beech Books, 1997. 32 pp. Provides information on stars, planets, comets, and the sun.

The Sun: Our very own star. Jeanne Bendick. Brookfield, CT: Millbrook Press, 1991. 32 pp. Contains basic information on the sun.

Sun, Stars and Planets. Tom Stacy. New York, NY: Random House, 1991. 46 pp. Provides information about the sun, stars, and planets in question and answer format.

Superstar: The supernova of 1987. Franklyn M. Branley. New York, NY: Thomas Y. Crowell, 1990. 58 pp. Explains the nature and origin of a supernova.

Telescopes and Observatories. Heather Couper and Nigel Henbest. New York, NY: Franklin Watts, 1987. 32 pp. Discusses telescopes and major observatories.

Telescopes: Searching the heavens. Deborah Hitzeroth. San Diego, CA: Lucent Books, 1991. 96 pp. Discusses early astronomers and their tools and the development of telescope technology.

They Dance in the Sky: Native American star myths. Jean Guard Monroe and Ray Al. Williamson. Boston, MA: Houghton Mifflin, 1987. 130 pp. Contains a collection of legends.

The Third Planet. Sally Ride. New York, NY: Crown, 1994. 46 pp. Astronaut Sally Ride examines Earth's relationship with the other planets.

Toys in Space: Exploring science with the astronauts. Carolyn Sumners. New York, NY: McGraw Hill, 1997 (various pagings). Explores science topics including weightlessness.

Universe. Andrew Haslam. New York, NY: Thomson Learning, 1995. 48 pp. An illustrated book of projects.

The Universe. Enrico Miotto. Austin, TX: Raintree Steck-Vaughn, 1995. 45 pp. Discusses the beginnings, development, and possible future of our universe.

Uranus: The sideways planet. Isaac Asimov. Milwaukee, WI: Gareth Stevens Pub., 1988. 32 pp. Discusses the characteristics of Uranus as revealed by Voyager 2.

Venus. Dennis B. Fradin. Chicago, IL: Children's Press, 1989. 45 pp. Explains the characteristics of the planet Venus.

Venus. Gregory Vogt. Brookfield, CT: Millbrook Press, 1994. 31 pp. Gives information on Venus as studied by U.S. and Soviet spacecraft.

Voyagers from Space: Meteors and meteorites. Patricia Lauber. New York, NY: Thomas Y. Crowell, 1989. 74 pp. Explains asteroids, comets, and meteorites.

What Is a Shooting Star? Isaac Asimov. Milwaukee, WI: Gareth Stevens Pub., 1991. 24 pp. Explains the differences between shooting stars and real stars.

When? Experiments For the Young Scientist. Robert W. Wood. Philadelphia, PA: Chelsea House Publishers, 1999. 133 pp. Contains 38 experiments in various areas of science including astronomy.

Why Does the Moon Change Shape? Isaac Asimov. Milwaukee, WI: Gareth Stevens Pub., 1991. 24 pp. Explains the changes from crescent to full moon.

Why? Experiments for the Young Scientist. Dave Procknow and Kathy Prochnow. Philadelphia, PA: Chelsea House Publishers, 1999. 142 pp. Contains 49 experiments in various fields including astronomy.

The Young Astronomer. Harry Ford. New York, NY: Dorling Kindersley, 1998. 37 pp. Introduces basic astronomy through projects including making a model of a lunar eclipse and a comet's path.

Your Guide to the Sky. Rick Shaffer. Los Angeles, CA: Lowell House, 1994. 168 pp. An amateur observer's guide.

Other Resources

The following magazines may be of interest: *Astronomy; The Astronomical Journal; Earth, Moon and Planets; The Mathematics Teacher; Science and Children; Science News; Scientific American,* and *Sky and Telescope.*

Apollo 13 Videos. Nashua, NH: Delta Education. *To the Edge and Back* is an 87-minute video and *Apollo 13* is a 140-minute video about the struggle of the Apollo 13 crew.

Comets. Franklyn Mansfield Branley. Old Greenwich, CT: Listening Library, 1987. 1 book, 32 pp. 1 sound cassette, 15 minutes. Tapekit. Gives information about comets.

Lunar Globe. Nashua, NH: Delta Educaiton. A 12" globe depicts the facets of the lunar surface. Includes plastic stand and booklet.

Planets of the Sun. Leonard Nimoy (Narrator). Los Angeles, CA: Concord Video, 1985. 1 videocassette, 46 minutes. Discusses the planets and the sun.

Solar System Model. Nashua, NH: Delta Education. Model size is 18" in length. Rotating arms help students to understand the relative position of planets and their orbits around the sun.

Star Theater. Nashua, NH: Delta Education. Allows students to project stars, planets, and constellations using a powerful little planetarium. Comes with activity guide and audio cassette. Requires batteries.

Telescope-To-Go. Nashua, NH: Delta Education. Scope assembles quickly. Comes with a sturdy table tripod contained in a durable backpack.

8

Exploring geography and cartography

Exploring geography and cartography can take many forms. An interest in a state or country might encourage a child to study its mountains and valleys. Putting together a rock collection might lead a child to want to visit a certain rock formation to collect a specimen. Setting out on a camping or fishing trip, going on a hike, or planning a biking trip can create a real sense of exploration and establish the need to know more about geography. Developing a good working knowledge of map reading is a plus in any of these activities.

There are many times when hiking, as a pleasure of its own or in conjunction with another interest, is a good pursuit for adults and children. A hike might consist of a short walk with a class of students from a school to a nearby park, a weekend backpack trip with a child and adult, or a major outing with a scout group. For anything other than a brief hike in town, considerable preplanning is necessary.

Hiking requires attention to your current physical condition, to appropriate clothing (especially shoes), to equipment, and to appropriate routes and destinations. "Easy does it" is a good motto to have when beginning a season of hiking with a child or setting out on a hike with a group of children. This advice is for the adult as well as the child! Start with relatively short distances on trails that do not have sharp gains in elevation. Some of those muscles that feel fine while you are still walking might be stiff and sore the next day if you are not in shape. Gradually you can increase the distance that you travel and can tackle more difficult trails.

Perhaps the single most important factor in a comfortable hike is your selection of shoes and socks. While sneakers might be appropriate for a short hike on a dirt trail in the woods, good boots and socks are necessary to protect feet and ankles on longer hikes or on rougher terrain. A hat, sunscreen, comfortable pants or hiking shorts, and a loose-fitting shirt are also requirements. Remember that the weather is continually changing, so it's a good idea to be able to add or remove a layer of clothing.

Equipment should include a frame-pack for long trips or a day-pack for short hikes to allow you to carry rain gear, a jacket, food, water, first-aid supplies, a compass, and maps. If a group of children is involved in a hike, a list of required supplies and attire should be sent to parents. What should not be brought along should also be stressed in your note to parents.

Finding a safe and interesting place for your hiking can present a challenge. Those who live in urban or suburban settings seem to have been driven from the paths and streets by the automobile, although a few shopping malls have included marked distances for walkers. Likewise, many urban planners are including bike paths and open space for hiking. There is also a movement in our country to establish a network of trails and paths.

Don't overlook the interesting sights that can be seen on a walk in a town or city. There may be maps of historic sites to visit, a trip to the docks to consider, or an "old town" section that will be fascinating to explore. Walking on cement is especially tiring, and you will need to pace yourself so as to not get worn out. Remember, young children have a shorter stride than an adult and may tire more quickly.

Determining your walking speed

Finding out the speed at which a child walks and the length of his or her normal stride is interesting and will let you estimate how long it will take to cover a trail.

Measure the distance between two points and convert that distance into inches. Then count the number of strides a child uses to cover that distance. Divide the inches by the number of strides, and you will learn the length of the child's normal stride.

If you time the child, you will have a rough idea of how far the child will walk during a given time period, if he or she continues at the same stride and pace.

You might plan a hike in connection with another interest or class activity; for example, spotting birds or wildflowers. Maybe you want to go to an area to take photographs. Perhaps your hike will lead you to identify trees or minerals. You may want to do some fishing or do some beach combing. These and many more activities are compatible with hiking.

Should you live in the right section of the country, you may be close to a really big hiking trail that is completed or still under construction. The best known trail is the Appalachian Trail, which extends 2,000 miles from Mt. Katahdin, Maine, to Springer Mountain, Georgia. The Pacific Crest Trail stretches 2,300 miles from the Washington–Canadian border to the California–Mexican border. The Continental Divide Trail is planned to stretch from the Montana–Canadian border to Silver City, New Mexico. The Lewis and Clark Trail will stretch 4,600 miles from St. Louis, Missouri, to the mouth of the Columbia River. The Potomac Heritage Trail passes 825 miles from the mouth of the Potomac River to its sources in Pennsylvania and West Virginia. Long Trail in Vermont is a 250-mile trail.

Whenever you are out in the woods, there is a possibility of being lost. Remember to plan ahead of time in detail exactly what to do if someone gets separated from the group. Knowing how to read maps and use a compass will help you get oriented.

Testing your sense of direction

Some people believe they have a perfect sense of direction, but they may be wrong. The following experiment can help you test your sense of direction.

To test one's sense of direction, try the following in a park or playing field where you can walk for 50 yards on relatively flat, grassy ground.

Place a handkerchief on the ground 50 paces away. Put a good blindfold over the eyes of the person you are testing. Ask the person to walk 50 paces directly to the handkerchief. How close did the person come? Give the person three tries and mark each attempt.

Although children need to be given instructions on what to do if they get lost, it is of course most desirable not to get lost in the first place! One way to avoid being lost is to learn to use a compass. This is not as easy as it might seem. North and magnetic north are not the same. You can buy a compass that can be adjusted for declination, which is the value in degrees between magnetic north and true north.

Using a compass

The following experiment will help you sharpen your skills in using a compass. First align your compass with the needle pointing to magnetic north. Then, select a bearing such as 45 degrees, northeast. To follow a chosen bearing, sight along an imaginary line running from the center of your compass across the 45-degree mark to some prominent and easily recognizable natural feature, such as a tree or cliff. Try to keep it in sight as you move toward it. To return, sight another object, which is 180 degrees in the opposite direction, or 225 degrees, southwest. Then proceed toward the new object.

Once you have learned to use a compass, you can rely on it. But remember that its needle can be thrown off if it is near a large mineral iron ore deposit or even by a steel axe that you are carrying.

You can buy topographic maps of most areas. Using such a map along with a compass is a much better way to navigate. (Remember to orient your compass using the arrows on the map that indicate both magnetic north and true north.)

Wherever you live, there may be a local hiking club or at least one that is not far away. Checking with these club members may enable you and an interested child to join in their activities and hikes. Many groups publish a newsletter with a schedule of planned activities. Some of these clubs secure permission to hike in areas that might not be open to individual hikers. Members of the club might also be willing and available to visit a class of students and discuss various aspects of hiking.

As in hiking, biking also requires you to put "safety first." A child (or adult) on a bicycle must always wear a well-fitting, approved helmet while on a bicycle trip. Although bicycles come in many styles and types, it is essential that the bike that is being used be the right size for the child riding it.

In addition to the helmet, appropriate shoes and a long-sleeved shirt or sunscreen should also be worn to prevent discomfort. Carrying a first-aid kit, a supply of water, and minimum equipment for simple on-the-road repairs should be included on any bicycle expedition.

If you are a newcomer to biking, one of the best sources of information may be your local bike shop. Knowledgeable store personnel can put you in touch with local cycling groups and share maps of bike paths and routes.

Using a bicycle odometer

If you are interested in keeping track of the distance you travel on a bike trip and your speed, you can use an odometer or cyclocomputer. These give you a very good idea of your speed and distance. The following experiment will help you learn to use your bicycle odometer.

Your bike shop will have a number of odometers or cyclocomputers. Depending on the model you get, you will be able to get speed, average speed, maximum speed, elapsed time, trip distance, and other pertinent information.

Attach an odometer to your child's bike. Have the child keep a cycling diary in which he or she records bike trips. Include the data from the odometer. If this is continued over a period of time, the child should see an increase in speed and endurance.

Whether you are considering short walks, long hikes, or bike trips, map reading skills are important. Depending on the child's age and understanding of geography, skills in map-making and map-reading will vary considerably. An adult can do a great deal to build these skills.

One way to demonstrate that geography is a way of thinking and observing is to help build a vocabulary and precise mental images of places and directions for your child. For example, try saying, "We are going south to Texas to visit Grandma," rather than saying "We are going down to Texas to visit Grandma." Use words such as desert, glacier, climate, and so forth when describing areas. This will build up a language for geography.

Even very young children can learn to read a map. You might go for a neighborhood walk and then show the child a street map of your town, showing her the streets you have walked together. You might point out where friends or relatives live. Older children may be interested in topographic maps of an area in which they are planning a hike. Topographic maps are created and sold by the United States Geological Survey.

Playing the party map game

Middle grade students might find this an interesting challenge as a party game. Have children divide themselves into groups of two or three. Give each group a copy of the same state map. Ask them to write down the names of the cities that they'd visit and the highways that they'd travel to get from point A to point B, from point C to point D, and from point E to point F.

Choose destinations that have several different routes leading to them. Ask the teams to find the fastest and the shortest routes.

You might want to offer a prize to the team that can solve the map challenge first.

Students also need to learn some skills about reading a globe. Help a child or a class of students examine a globe and find the lines of longitude (lines that run from the North Pole to the South Pole, from 0 degrees, through Greenwich, England—the prime meridian, to 180 degrees east and around the globe back to 0 degrees again). Since the sun moves over 15 degrees of the earth's surface every hour, for each 15 degrees west of Greenwich, the time is set back one hour.

Determining time

Finding out what time it is in different parts of the world is an interesting activity. The following experiment can help you "determine time" around the globe.

Use a plastic globe with a slick surface. Have the child or group of students find the line 15 degrees west of Greenwich, England. Tape a colored skinny strip of paper with the numeral "1" on it to this line. Then tape a strip of paper with the numeral "2" on it to the line that is 30 degrees west of Greenwich.

Continue taping strips of paper every 15 degrees around the globe. Number "12" should be on the 180-degree line. This line is the International Date Line. It is 12 hours behind Greenwich time. If you cross this line going west, you lose a day. Traveling east, you gain a day.

When you pass the International Date Line, number the line 15 degrees past it with a number "1." Continue numbering every 15 degrees until you get back to Greenwich, England, and put your number "12" there.

Now by locating a city or country, and checking the strips of paper taped to your globe, you can add or subtract to find what time it is there.

Making a map is quite a different experience from reading one. You might want to begin your class or your child's study of geography by making a map of one room in your house or school. Trying to draw it correctly to size will be a challenge. Older children might pace off or do some rough measurements and try to draw their maps to scale.

Looking at a road map will quickly lead to a discussion of map symbols. You will need to spend some time examining and understanding symbols, which may indicate campgrounds, parks, and schools; size of print or color designations that indicate the population of a city or the type of a road; and other specifics of a map. When such symbols and details are learned, help your child put the new knowledge to use by creating his or her own map.

Mapping an imaginary island

Help the child make a map of an imaginary island. In a school setting, two students might choose to work as partners on this project. Symbols should be used to indicate the location of mountains, major cities or towns, railroad tracks, national forests, and other important items. There should be a key that also indicates the scale of miles.

RAILROAD

SCHOOL

CITY

MOUNTAINS

NATIONAL FOREST

ROAD

10 MILES

SCALE OF MILES

This map can be as simple or complex as the child has interest in making it. The important outcomes are demonstrating an understanding of using a map key or legend and determining a scale of miles.

Few explorations offer as much fun to adults and curious kids alike as a camping and/or fishing trip. To be successful, considerable preplanning is required, including preparing for a lot of "what ifs." For example, what if it rains? What if we don't catch any fish to eat? What if all the campsites are taken in one desirable location? What if someone falls in the water or gets lost?

Experienced campers have already learned about some of the mishaps that can befall a camper when car camping or backpacking and have planned how to avoid them or work around them. If you're a beginner, the one thing you can count on is the unexpected!

Realize that weather is ever changing and plan to have enough of different kinds of clothing so that you and your curious child or class of students will be comfortable. Shivering around the campfire in wet shoes or getting a bad sunburn from exposed skin in mountain sunshine can lead to a lot of discomfort.

Plan on extra food. It's amazing how appetites seem to increase with activity in the open air—and don't count on having plenty of fresh trout to cook. If you're backpacking, weight and quantity of food are a major consideration, but don't skimp. If you are car camping, it's better to cart back home some canned and packaged goods that you didn't use than it is to find yourselves hungry and out-of-sorts on the trip.

Unless you know that drinking water is available, you also need to provide plenty of liquids for drinking. Be sure not to drink any water unless you are certain that it is safe. If you are backpacking, you will need to take along a filter or tablets to make the water safe for drinking.

When going on a camping/fishing trip, the only thing better than Plan A is Plan A backed up by Plan B. You may find that a road has been closed or that a favorite area is suddenly filled with people on a family reunion. Having an alternative in mind that is almost equally as good as the most desirable destination is a great idea!

If you don't camp often, you may want to do a dry run at home or at school to be sure that you really can quickly set up your tent. Tents vary greatly—from the spacious cabin tent you may use for car camping to a small two-person tent carried in a backpack. Ropes, tarps, stakes, poles, and ground covers are all a part of the process.

The printed directions that come with a new tent don't always seem to correspond with the number of interlocking poles, ropes, and canvas that you find sitting in front of you at a campsite as storm clouds gather above and hungry children simultaneously demand to be fed. A quick practice at home or school will allow you to set up your tent confidently in a minimum amount of time.

Even though you may be sleeping in a tent, take time to enjoy a good look at the stars (see Chapter 7 "Exploring Astronomy"). Away from the lights of a city, the sky can be especially beautiful. You can probably find a few favorite constellations. Sitting around a campfire is also a great time to recite some of the constellation stories and legends.

Telling star stories

Why not make up your own story about the stars? Pick out a group of stars that seem to make a picture in the sky. Think of a story that might explain what you see.

For example, you may see a cluster of stars that resemble a bird with its wings outspread. Perhaps the bird was a seagull that guided one of the Greek gods to shore when he was lost one night on a wind-tossed sea. The grateful god then put the helpful bird up in the sky so that it could guide other lost and weary travelers at night.

Each person on your camping outing might find a star cluster, make up a story, and then share it with the others.

A folding table, a fly to cover the cooking/eating area, and simple, dependable lanterns and stoves will help you enjoy your car camping experience. You may find that everything at your campground in the woods is dry and there is plenty of firewood readily available for your campfire. There may be tables and benches and a metal or cement barbecue area for a cooking pit. But if some of these ideal conditions are lacking, having a back-up could save the day.

You need warm sleeping bags, flashlights with "new" batteries, a mosquito repellent, and sunscreen lotions. Another must is a well-supplied first aid kit.

Plan for emergencies. If you are going to be near water, be sure to review water safety. Children also need to be advised of what to do if they
believe they are lost. Supply them with a whistle to blow should they become lost or hurt and need to alert others to come to their rescue. Taking
along a big scale map of the area and a compass is an excellent idea. Taking a compass reading and getting oriented right after arriving in camp is
time well spent.

Using a wristwatch as a compass

Between the hours of six in the morning and six at night, you can use a wrist-
watch much as you would a compass to roughly tell direction.

Point the hour hand at the sun while holding the watch face-up, flat in
your hand. Halfway between the hour hand and the 12 lies south in the
northern hemisphere.) If you are on daylight saving time, south is half-way
between the hour hand and the 1.)

If you are going to fish, you need to be sure that all of your equipment
is ready. This includes a check of your boat (if you are using one), rods,
reels, lines, hooks, lures, flies, bait, and other needed tackle. Be sure that you
are familiar with fishing license requirements and the various regulations in
the area so that you can obey them.

If you are hiking into a fishing area, be sure to wear good hiking boots.
If you are going to be in a boat, sneakers or soft-soled shoes are important.
A pair of sunglasses and a wide-brimmed hat are good items to have in a
boat for protection from sun and glare off the water.

Knowing a variety of simple knots used in fishing is a plus. At home you
and your curious child, or at school, your classroom of students, can practice
such knots as a blood or barrel knot for tying monofilament, clinch knot,
square knot, figure eight knot, and other simple knots.

After all this preplanning, you are ready to go off on your exploration
and enjoy yourselves! For your first adventure, you might want to plan a one-
night trip. You'll learn a lot from this experience. Then you might want to try
a longer trip.

One of the joys while out on a camping/fishing trip is observing birds
and animals (see Chapter 5 "Exploring Ethology"). You should not try to
touch wildlife, however, because animals can become frightened and bite,
and they may carry diseases. But you might toss them a nut and watch them
from a distance.

If you are lucky enough to see wildlife, you may want to sketch what
you find and see, and add these drawings to your notebook along with the
date, time, and location of the sighting (see Chapter 13 "Exploring Science
through Art").

Learning to "freeze"

Some animals have learned to "freeze" when they sense an enemy. Learning to "freeze" is a good skill for a camper in the woods who has spotted a bird or animal. Staying very still may encourage the creature not to run away; thus, it may continue with its activities.

Some animals are curious and you might be able to lure them out into the open. For example, tapping on the trunk of a dead tree that has a hole in it where you suspect birds or animals may be hiding might cause them to come to an opening and look out. Similarly, lightly tapping two stones together might cause a squirrel or chipmunk to come watch what you are doing.

After packing all your things back up after a successful camping/fishing trip, remember that you have one more responsibility—to leave your campsite neat and clean. Be sure that any fire you have made is completely out. This is an excellent time to help a child or class learn about responsibility for the environment.

Whether you go for a short hike from school, ride along a city bike path, take a major hike in the mountains, or go off on a camping or fishing trip, there will be an opportunity to use map skills and to observe many things along the way. Other chapters in this book that may be of particular interest include Chapter 4 "Exploring Botany," Chapter 5 "Exploring Ethology," Chapter 6 "Exploring Geology and Paleontology," Chapter 9 "Exploring the Watery World," Chapter 10, "Exploring the Ocean," and Chapter 13 "Exploring Science through Art."

Resource Books

Alaska, the Great Land. Lynn M. Stone. Vero Beach, FL: Rourke Book Co., 1994. 24 pp. Gives an introduction to the geography of Alaska.

The Animal Atlas. Barbara Taylor. New York, NY: Alfred A. Knopf, 1992. 64 pp. Shows the different habitats and animals that live in them.

Animals in Rivers and Lakes. Moira Butterfield. Austin, TX: Raintree Steck-Vaughn, 2000. 32 pp. Introduces wildlife such as the kingfisher and bullfrog.

Anybody's Bike Book: An original manual of bicycle repairs. Tom Cuthbertson. Berkeley, CA: Ten Speed Press, 1990. 215 pp. Provides a manual for help in making bicycle repairs.

The Arctic Land. Bobbie Kalman. New York, NY: Crabtree Pub. Co., 1988. 57 pp. Discusses the arctic regions of the world.

As the Crow Flies: A first book of maps. Gail Hartman. New York, NY: Bradbury Press, 1991. 32 pp. Provides a look at different geographic areas from the perspectives of an eagle, rabbit, crow, horse, and gull.

Atlas of Countries. Claude Delafosse. New York, NY: Scholastic, 1996. unpaged. Uses transparent overlays to introduce continents and their physical features.

Atlas of Plants. Claude Delafosse. New York, NY: Cartwheel Books, 1996. 36 pp. Uses overlays to introduce over 50 plants from around the world.

The Atlas of Space. Jack Challoner. Brookfield, CT: Copper Beach Books, 2001. 80 pp. Gives an introduction to space science.

Atlas of Space Exploration. Tim Furniss. Milwaukee, WI: Gareth Stevens Pub., 2000. 96 pp. Examines the history of humans' interest in space exploration.

Atlas of Today: The world behind the news. Jon Snow. New York, NY: Warwick Press, 1987. 61 pp. A good tool for use in discussing world events.

Backpacking. Jimmy Holmes. Minneapolis, MN: Lerner Publishers, 1992. 48 pp. Introduces backpacking and includes a section on map reading.

Bicycle Racing. Nancy J. Nielson. Mankato, MN: Crestwood House, 1988. 48 pp. Discusses racing strategy and different types of bikes used in racing.

Bicycling Magazine's Complete Guide to Bicycle Maintenance and Repair. Editors of *Bicycling*. Emmaus, PA: Rodale Press (distributed by St. Martin's Press), 1990. 310 pp. Provides a complete bicycle repair guide.

Bikes. Anne Rockwell. New York, NY: Dutton, 1987. 24 pp. Discusses different bikes such as the unicycle, tandem bike, racing bike, trail bike, and exercise bike.

*Bike Trip. Betsy and Giulio Maestro. New York, NY: HarperCollins, 1992. 32 pp. Describes a family on a bike trip.

BMX Bikes. Norman S. Barrett. New York, NY: Franklin Watts, 1987. 32 pp. Describes bikes, riding techniques, and bicycle motorcross racing.

BMX Freestyle. Larry Dane Brimner. New York, NY: Franklin Watts, 1987. 72 pp. Offers an introduction to stunts and routines performed on motorcross bicycles.

BMXs. Paul Estrem. Mankato, MN: Crestwood House, 1987. 47 pp. Provides an introduction to the sport of bicycle motorcross.

Camping and Orienteering. Michael Jay. New York, NY: Warwick Press, 1990. 40 pp. Offers a guide to planning a camping trip with tips on reading maps.

Camping and Walking. David Watkins and Meike Dalal. Tulsa, OK: EDC Pub. 1989. 128 pp. Discusses camping, hiking, and walking.

Camping Basics. Wayne Armstrong. Englewood Cliffs, NJ: Prentice-Hall. 1985. 48 pp. Describes skills and equipment needed to camp safely.

Camping in the Temple of the Sun. Deborah Gould. New York, NY: Bradbury Press, 1992. 32 pp. Describes the fun and mishaps on a family's first camping trip.

*Camping Out: A book of action words. Betsy Maestro and Giulio Maestro. New York, NY: Crown Publishers, 1985. 32 pp. Provides labeled illustrations of backpacking, fishing, and hiking.

Children Just Like Me. Barnabas Kindersley and Anabel Kindersley. New York, NY: Dorling Kindersley, 1995. 79 pp. Discusses the cultures of young people around the world.

Children's Atlas of World Wildlife. Elizabeth G. Fagan. Chicago, IL: Rand McNally. 1990. 93 pp. A zoogeography.

Children's Pictorial Atlas of the World. Alison Cooper and Anne McRae. Hauppauge, NY: Barron's Educational Series, 1998. 43 pp. A simple world atlas.

The Children's Space Atlas: A voyage of discovery for young astronauts. Robin Kerrod. Brookfield, CT: Millbrook Press, 1992. 95 pp. Discusses gathering information and mapping the solar system and space.

Christopher Columbus, How He Did It. Charlotte Yue and David Yue. Boston, MA: Houghton Mifflin, 1992. 136 pp. Looks at the discoveries and explorations of Columbus.

Click It. Computer Fun Geography. Lisa Trumbauer. Brookfield, CT: Millbrook Press, 1999. 32 pp. Explores various aspects of geography and explains how to use a compass. For grades 2-4.

Colorado Cycling Guide. Jean and Hartley Alley. Boulder, CO: Pruett Publishing Co., 1990. 377 pp. Contains route maps, city maps, sources of food and lodging, and information on clubs, publications, and source materials for bicyclists.

The Continents: Puzzles for learning world geography. Jeanne S. Cheyney. Glenview, IL: GoodYear Books, 1994. 168 pp. Contains more than 100 puzzles and word games.

Cool Geography: Miles of maps, wild adventures, fun activities, facts from around the world, and more! Jane Glicksman. New York, NY: Price, Stern, Sloan, 1998. 96 pp. Goes around the world describing countries and people.

Cycling. Donna Bailey. Austin, TX: Steck-Vaughn Library, 1991. 32 pp. Tells a story of a boy who learns to ride a bike and fix a tire. Also gives highlights of the Tour de France.

Desert of Ice: Life and work in Antarctica. W. John Hackwell. New York, NY: Scribner, 1991. 40 pp. Discusses the life and type of research done at an Antarctic base.

Deserts. Jane Parker. New York, NY: Franklin Watts, 1998. 32 pp. Provides an overview of the world's desert regions.

Deserts. Philip Steele. Minneapolis, MN: Carolrhoda Books, 1996. 32 pp. Describes the arid zones of the world.

The Doubleday Children's Atlas. Jane Olliver (Editor). Garden City, NY: Doubleday, 1987. 93 pp. Using over 100 color photos, introduces countries of the world.

The Doubleday Picture Atlas. Wendy Roebuck. New York, NY: Doubleday, 1988. 61 pp. Provides maps, background information, and discusses geographical features of countries of the world.

Eastern Great Lakes: Indiana, Michigan, Ohio. Thomas C. Aylesworth and Virginia L. Aylesworth. New York, NY: Chelsea House Publishers, 1991. 64 pp. Discusses the geography, history, and cultural aspects of Indiana, Michigan, and Ohio. Includes maps.

Encyclopedia of World Geography. Peter Haggett (Editor). New York, NY: Marshall Cavendish, 1994. 24 volumes. A presentation of world geography.

Everything Is Somewhere: The geography quiz book. Jack McClintock and David Helgren. New York, NY: Morrow Junior Books, 1986. 160 pp. Contains 30 quizzes about countries.

Everything You Need to Know About Geography Homework. Anne Zeman and Kate Kelly. New York, NY: Scholastic Reference, 1997. 133 pp. For ages nine and up.

Explor-a-maze. Robert Snedden. Brookfield, CT: Millbrook Press, 1998. 42 pp. Follows the journeys of ten famous explorers including Leif Erickson and Marco Polo.

Explorer. Rupert Matthews. New York, NY: Alfred Knopf, 1991. 63 pp. Highlights the lives of various explorers and their discoveries.

Explorers & Discoverers: From Alexander the Great to Sally Ride. Peggy Saari. New York, NY: UXL, 1995. 5 volumes. Tells about famous discoverers.

Explorers and Mapmakers. Peter Ryan. New York, NY: Dutton, 1990. 48 pp. Discusses early explorers and their maps.

The Explorer's Handbook: How to become an intrepid voyager. Marilyn Tolhurst. New York, NY: Dutton Children's Books, 1998. 29 pp. Includes instructions for making a compass and a survival kit.

Exploring the World. Fiona Macdonald and Gerald Wood. New York, NY: Peter Bedrick Books, 1996. 48 pp. Looks at the first explorers to travel around the world.

The Facts on File Children's Atlas. David and Jill Wright. New York, NY: Facts on File, 1987. 96 pp. Provides a useful children's atlas.

Facts on File Stars & Planets Atlas. Ian Redpath. New York, NY: Facts on File, 1997. 80 pp. An introduction to stars and planets.

Finding Your Way. Jennifer Dewey. Brookfield, CT: Millbrook Press, 2001. 63 pp. Explains orienteering.

Fish in a Flash!: A personal guide to spin fishing. Jim Aronsky. New York, NY: Bradbury Press, 1991. 63 pp. Offers an introduction to fishing with spin lures.

Fishing. Bruno Broughton. New York, NY: Bookwright Press, 1991. 32 pp. Describes techniques of fishing and safety features.

Fishing with Cap'n Bob and Matey: An encyclopedia for kids of all ages. Lew Hackler. Colonial Heights, VA: Seascape Enterprises, 1990. 32 pp. Consists of a glossary of boating terms for beginners.

Fishing with Small Fry: How to hook your kids on fishing. Bob Ellsburg. Portland, OR: Flying Pencil Pub., 1991. 119 pp. Describes how to introduce children to fishing.

Food from the Sea. Daniel Rogers. New York, NY: Bookwright Press, 1991. 32 pp. Discusses fish, types of fishing, and fish farming.

Freshwater Fishing. Katherine Jarman. Morristown, NJ: Silver Burdett Press, 1988. 63 pp. Discusses the history, equipment, tactics, and recent developments in freshwater fishing.

Fun on the Run: Travel games and songs. Joanna Cole and Stephanie Calmenson with Michael Street. New York, NY: Morrow Junior Books, 1999. 126 pp. A collection of games.

Geo Challenge: 180 daily geography brain teasers for kids! Arnold B. Cheyney. Glenview, IL: GoodYear Books, 1996. 180 pp. For students aged 9–11.

Geography From A to Z: A picture glossary. Jack Knowlton. New York, NY: Crowell, 1988. 47 pp. Explains specific geography terms such as archipelago.

Globes. Paul Sipiers. Chicago, IL: Children's Press, 1991. 45 pp. Explains the usefulness of globes.

The Great Atlas of Discovery. Neil Grant. New York, NY: Alfred Knopf, 1992. 64 pp. Shows routes of exploration from 6000 BC to the present time.

The Great Dinosaur Atlas. William Lindsay. Englewood Cliffs, NJ: Julian Messner, 1991. 64 pp. Provides a guide to the prehistoric world of dinosaurs. With maps.

The Great Plains: Montana, Nebraska, North Dakota. Thomas G. Aylesworth and Virginia L. Aylesworth. New York, NY: Chelsea House Publishers, 1988. 64 pp. Discusses the geography, history, and cultural aspects of Montana, Nebraska, and North Dakota. Includes maps.

The Great World Atlas. The American Map Corporation. Tucson, AZ: Zephyr Press, 1989. 384 pp. Includes a section on the Nature of Our Planet and the Nature of Our Universe.

Greg LeMond: Premier cyclist. A. P. Porter, Minneapolis, MN: Lerner Publications Co., 1990. 64 pp. Tells of the training and courage needed by Greg LeMond, the first American to win the Tour de France.

Help Is on the Way for Maps and Globes. Marilyn Berry. Chicago, IL: Children's Press, 1985. 46 pp. Helps in map skills development.

Hiking and Climbing. Jeremy Evans. New York, NY: Crestwood House, 1992. 48 pp. This guide includes directions on how to use special equipment.

Historical Atlas of Colorado. Thomas J. Noel. Norman, OK: University of Oklahoma Press, 1994. 60 pp. Traces locations from pre-historic Indian cultures to the present.

How Maps Are Made. Martyn Bramwell. Minneapolis, MN: Lerner Publications, 1998. 48 pp. Gives instructions for making maps.

How to Make and Repair Your Own Fishing Tackle: An illustrated step-by-step guide for the fisherman and hobbyist. Jim Mayes, New York, NY: Dodd, Mead, 1986. 172 pp. Tells how to make and fix fishing tackle.

How to Teach with Topographic Maps. Dana Van Burgh. Arlington, VA: National Science Teachers' Association, 1994. 23 pp. Teaches map reading.

Hudson River: An adventure from the mountains to the sea. Peter Lourie. Honesdale, PA: Caroline House (distributed by St. Martin's Press),. 1992. 47 pp. Offers an account of a 315-mile canoe trip down the Hudson River with color photos and maps.

I Can Ride a Bike. Sheila Fraser. New York, NY: Barron's 1991. 21 pp. Tells of a young girl who overcomes her fear of riding a bike.

Illustrated Atlas of World History. Simon Adams, John Brequebec and Ann Kramer. New York, NY: Random House, 1992. 160 pp. Has sections on the ancient world and on exploration and empire.

Illustrated World Atlas. David Wright and Jill Wright. New York, NY: Warwick Press, 1987. 64 pp. Provides an illustrated atlas of the world.

In the Water—On the Water. Dorothy Chlad. Chicago, IL: Children's Press, 1988. 31 pp. Gives pointers to readers on water safety.

Janice VanCleave's Geography for Every Kid: Easy activities that make learning geography fun. Janice Pratt VanCleave. New York, NY: John Wiley & Sons, 1993. 211 pp. Introduces basic concepts of geography.

Junior Worldmark Encyclopedia of the Nations. Timothy Gall and Susan Gall (Editors). New York, NY: UXL, 1996, 9 volumes. Discusses countries in the United Nations.

Just Camping Out. Mercer Mayer. Racine, WI: Western Publishing Co., 1989. 23 pp. Presents a Golden picture book about camping.

Kids' Book of Fishing, The. Michael J. Rosen. New York, NY: Workman Pub., 1991. 96 pp. Discusses a variety of basic techniques and equipment for the beginning fisherman.

Kids Learn America! Bringing geography to life with people, places & history. Patricia Gordon and Reed C. Snow. Charlotte, VT: Williamson Pub. Co., 1999. 176 pp. For ages 7–12, this provides a survey of the geography of the states and territories of the U.S.

Kids Outdoors: Skills and knowledge for outdoor adventurers. Victoria Logue, Frank Logue, and Mark Carroll. Camden, ME: Ragged Mountain Press, 1996. 139 pp. Discusses the equipment and skills needed to enjoy hiking.

Know Your Hometown History: Projects and activities. Abigail Jungreis. New York, NY: Franklin Watts, 1992. 61 pp. Includes directions for making a contour map and a model of your town.

Learn How to Fly Fish in One Day: Quickest way to start tying flies, casting flies, and catching fish. S. Nemes. Harrisburg, PA: Stackpole Books, 1986. 124 pp. Provides information about all aspects of fly fishing.

Let's Go Fishing. Jan Wahl. Racine, WI: Western Publishing Co., 1987. 24 pp. Presents a big, little Golden book on fishing.

Mapping Our World. Martyn Bramwell. Minneapolis, MN: Lerner Publications Co., 1998. 48 pp. Shows various kinds of maps and describes aspects of the earth.

Maps. Andrew Haslam. Chicago, IL: World Book, 1996. 47 pp. Explores mapmaking and what maps tell us.

Maps and Globes. Sabrina Crewe. New York, NY: Children's Press, 1997. 32 pp. An introduction to maps and globes and how to use them.

Maps and Mapmaking. Fran Sammis. New York, NY: Marshall Cavendish, 2000. 64 pp. Tells the history and importance of maps.

Let's Go Fishing! A book for beginners. Gerald D. Schmidt. Niwot, CO: Roberts Rinehard, Inc. 1990. 85 pp. Offers an introduction to fishing.

Mapping the World. Sylvia A. Johnson. New York, NY: Atheneum Books, 1999. 32 pp. Provides a history of mapmaking.

Maps and Globes. Jack Knowlton. New York, NY: Thomas Y. Crowell, 1985. 42 pp. Provides a brief history of mapmaking and instructions on how to read maps and globes.

Maps and Globes. David Lambert. New York, NY: Bookwright Press, 1987. 32 pp. gives an introduction to maps and globes.

Maps and Mapmaking: Facts, things to make, activities. Anita Ganeri. New York, NY: Franklin Watts, 1995. 32 pp. Discusses cartography.

Maps and Symbols. Angela Royston. Austin, TX: Raintree Steck-Vaughn, 1999. 32 pp. An introduction to maps and how to read them.

Maps: Getting from here to there. Harvey Weiss. Boston, MA: Houghton Mifflin, 1991. 64 pp. Explains such things as map symbols, latitude, longitude, and special purpose maps.

Maps: Plotting places on the globe. Paula Bryant Pratt. San Diego, CA: Lucent Books, 1995. 96 pp. Provides an introduction to cartography.

Measuring and Maps. Keith Lye. New York, NY: Gloucester Press, 1991. 32 pp. Explores the science of geography and globes, maps, symbols, and suggested projects.

Mexico From A to Z. Bobbie Kalman. New York, NY: Crabtree Pub. Co., 1999. 32 pp. Provides an alphabetical introduction to the geography and culture of Mexico.

Mountain Biking. Tim Wood. New York, NY: Franklin Watts, 1989. 32 pp. Provides an introduction to mountain biking.

My America: A poetry atlas of the United States. Lee Bennett Hopkins (Editor). New York, NY: Simon & Schuster Books for Young Readers, 2000. 83 pp. This collection of poems is evocative of seven geographical regions of the United States.

My First Atlas. Pamela Mayo. Newmarket, Eng.: Brimax Books, 1989. 45 pp. An introductory atlas for children aged 4-7.

My Summer Vacation. Sumiko. New York, NY: Random House, 1990. 30 pp. Describes a little girl's camping trip.

Northern New England: Maine, New Hampshire, Vermont. Thomas G. Aylesworth and Virginia L. Aylesworth. New York, NY: Chelsea House Publishers, 1991. 64 pp. Discusses the geography, history, and cultural aspects of Maine, New Hampshire, and Vermont. Includes maps.

Olympia National Park. Ruth Radlaver. Chicago, IL: Children's Press, 1988. 48 pp. Describes the physical features, plants, animals, and camping accommodations in Olympia National Park.

Passport to Australia. Susan Pepper. New York, NY: Franklin Watts, 1987. 48 pp. Surveys the geography, people, and natural resources of Australia.

Passport to Spain. Keith Lye. New York, NY: Franklin Watts, 1987. 48 pp. Surveys the geography, people, and natural resources of Spain.

The People Atlas. Philip Steele. New York, NY: Oxford University Press, 1991. 64 pp. Explores the people of the world through text and map spreads.

Peoples of the Rain Forest. Robert Low. New York, NY: PowerKids Press, 1996. 24 pp. Discusses life in the rain forests of the world.

Picture Atlas of the World. Roy Woodcock. New York, NY: Derrydale Books (distributed by Crown Publishers), 1987. 96 pp. Offers a picture atlas.

The Picture World of BMX. R. J. Stephen. New York, NY: Franklin Watts, 1989. 29 pp. Describes BMX bikes, equipment, skills, tricks, and races.

Planet Earth. Joanne Jessop. Austin, TX: Raintree Steck-Vaughn, 1994. 32 pp. An introduction to physical geography.

Pocket Guide to Bicycle Maintenance and Repair. Greg LeMond. New York, NY: G. P. Putnam's Sons, 1990. 119 pp. Provides a handy guide to bike maintenance and repair.

Puzzle Maps U.S.A. Nancy L. Clouse. New York, NY: Henry Holt, 1990. 32 pp. Provides a series of simple puzzle maps of all 50 states.

Rand McNally Children's Atlas of the United States. Rand McNally. Chicago, IL: Rand McNally and Co., 1989. 109 pp. A simple atlas of the United States.

Riddle King's Camp Riddles, The. Mike Thaler. New York, NY: Random House, 1989. 32 pp. Contains riddles about camping.

Rivers and Lakes. Rose Pipes. Austin, TX: Raintree Steck-Vaughn, 1998. 32 pp. Introduces famous lakes and rivers of the world such as Lake Titicaca and the Ganges River.

Rivers and Lakes. Sarah Levette. Brookfield, CT: Copper Beech Books, 1999. 32 pp. Explores the world of rivers and lakes.

Roadside Bicycle Repairs: The simple guide to fixing your bike. Rob Van der Plas. New York, NY: Talman Co., 1990. 126 pp. Explains how to repair your bicycle.

Safety First—Bicycle. Cynthia Fitterer Klingel. Mankato, MN: Creative Education, 1986. 27 pp. Discusses bicycle safety.

Science for Kids: 39 easy geography activities. Robert W. Wood. Blue Ridge Summit, PA: TAB Books, 1992. 141 pp. Provides an introduction to the science of geography through activities.

Scholastic Atlas of Exploration. Dinah Starkey. New York, NY: Scholastic Reference, 1994. 64 pp. Discusses famous voyages and geographic discoveries.

Seas and Coasts. Patience Coster. New York, NY: Children's Press, 1997. 32 pp. Discusses the geographic features of oceans and coastlines.

Sierra Club Wayfinding Book, The. Vicki McVey. Boston, MA: Little Brown, 1988. 88 pp. Explains how humans get around using their senses, landmarks, signs, and maps.

Somewhere in the World Right Now. Stacey Schuett. New York, NY: Knopf, 1995. unpaged. Describes what is happening in different places around the world at a particular time.

The South: Alabama, Florida, Mississippi. Thomas C. Aylesworth and Virginia L. Aylesworth. New York, NY: Chelsea House Publishers, 1988. 64 pp. Discusses geography, history, and cultural aspects of Alabama, Florida, and Mississippi. Includes maps.

The Southwest: Colorado, New Mexico, Texas. Thomas G. Aylesworth and Virginia L. Aylesworth. New York, NY: Chelsea House Publishers, 1992. 64 pp. Discusses the geography, history, and cultural aspects of Colorado, New Mexico, and Texas. Includes maps.

The Story of Maps and Navigation. Anita Ganeri. New York, NY: Oxford University Press, 1997. 30 pp. Gives an introduction to maps and how they are used.

The Student Bible Atlas. Tim Dowley. Minneapolis, MN: Augsburg, 1996. unpaged. Puts into context geographical places mentioned in the Bible.

Take a Hike! The Sierra Club kids' guide to hiking and backpacking. Lynne Foster: Boston, MA: Little, Brown, 1991. 176 pp. Tells how to prepare for and enjoy hikes and backpack trips.

A Ticket to Canada. Janice Hamilton. Minneapolis, MN: Carolrhoda Books, 1999. 48 pp. Gives information on the people, geography, history, and culture of Canada.

The Travels of Vasco de Gama. Jeanne Mattern. Austin, TX: Steadwell Books, 2001. 48 pp. Discusses exploration.

*The Treasure Hunt: A story about geography and maps. Liza Alexander. Racine, WI: Western Publishing Co., 1990. 32 pp. Describes how Big Bird and Elmo of Sesame Street television go on a treasure hunt using a map.

United States Atlas for Young People. Kathie Billingslea Smith. Mahwah, NJ: Troll Associates, 1991. 128 pp. Provides a map for each state and U.S. Possession.

United States in Pictures. Geography Department of Lerner Pub. Co. Minneapolis, MN: Lerner Publishers, 1995. 64 pp. A visual geography book.

Upper Atlantic: New Jersey, New York. Thomas G. Aylesworth and Virginia L. Aylesworth. New York, NY: Chelsea House Publishers, 1990. 64 pp. Discusses the geography, history, and cultural aspects of New Jersey and New York. Includes maps.

The Warwick Atlas of World History. Jane Olliver (Editor). New York, NY: Warwick Press, 1988. 93 pp. Provides an atlas of history.

The West: Arizona, Nevada, Utah. Thomas C. Aylesworth and Virginia L. Aylesworth. New York, NY: Chelsea House Publishers, 1992. 64 pp. Discusses the geography, history, and various cultural aspects of Arizona, Nevada, and Utah. Includes maps.

Western Great Lakes: Illinois, Iowa, Minnesota, Wisconsin. Thomas G. Aylesworth and Virginia L. Aylesworth. New York, NY: Chelsea House Publishers. 1992. 64 pp. Discusses the geography, history, and cultural aspects of Illinois, Iowa, Minnesota, and Wisconsin. Includes maps.

What's Inside Lakes? Jane Kelly Kosek. New York, NY: PowerKids Press, 1999. 24 pp.
Discusses life of lakes such as fish, snails, algae, and otters.
Wheels!: The kids' bike book. Megan Stine. Boston, MA: Little, Brown, 1990. 83 pp. Explains how to choose a bike, equipment, accessories, and gives instruction for riding.
Young People's Atlas of the United States, The. James Harrison and Eleanor VanZandt. New York, NY: Kingfisher, 1996. 128 pp. An illustrated atlas of the United States.
Yukon. Lyn Hancock. Minneapolis, MN: Lerner Publications, 1996. 72 pp. Introduces the Yukon Territory.

Other Resources

To secure information about hiking clubs in your area, you may wish to write to the Bureau of Outdoor Recreation, Washington, DC, 20240 or the Department of Conservation in your state capital.

A resource to consult about maps and geography education is the National council for Geographic Education, Western Illinois University, Macomb, IL.

The following magazines often contain interesting articles on hiking and biking: *Bicycling, Women's Sports and Fitness, Backpacker, Outside, Sport's Afield, Boys' Life,* and *Mountaineer.* For articles on camping and fishing you might want to read: *Boating, Camping Magazine, Country Journal, Field and Stream, Motor Boating, Motor Boating and Sailing, Outdoor Life, Sierra, Sports Afield, Trailer Life,* and *Travel-Holiday.*

The ABCs of Compass and Map. Presented by John Street. Riverton, WY: Brunton, U.S.A., 1989. 1 videocassette, 25 minutes. Provides activities to develop the basics of compass and map skills.
Basic Fly Casting. Doug Swisher. St. Paul, MN: Scientific Anglers/3M, 1987. 1 videocassette, 63 minutes. A short course in fly casting.
Bicycle Repair. Tom Cuthbertson. Charlotte, NC: Do It Yourself Video Corp., 1985. 1 videocassette, 60 minutes. Explains step-by-step roadside bicycle repair.
Bicycle Repair Made Easy. Los Angeles, CA: Increase Video, 1986. 1 videocassette. Explains bicycle maintenance and repair.
Bicycle Safety Camp. Broad Street Productions (Producer). Los Angeles, CA: David Levine & Assoc., Inc. 1 videocassette, 25 minutes. For children ages 6–12, shows cycling safety.
*Campfire Sing-Along. F. Olsen. Allen, TX: Lyons Corp., 1990. 1 videocassette, 45 minutes. Barney, the dinosaur, introduces the backyard gang to the fun of camping out.
Contour Model Kit. Nashua, NH: Delta Education. For grades 5–8, demonstrates how contours indicate levels of elevation on maps.
Geo-Safari. Tucson, AZ: Zephyr Press, 1989. Electronic machine, user's guide, and full-color maps. Requires four D-cell batteries. Students learn basic map skills.
GeoSafari Talking Globe. Nashua, NH: Delta Education. Available for for grades K–3 and for grades 3–8. Teaches about geography basics including continents, countries, bodies of water, mountains, rivers, and more.

Landform Discovery Pack. Nashua, NH: Delta Education. For grades 5–12. Pack features eight 3D models of various landforms. Includes teacher's guide and student workbooks.

Map and Globe Terms. Beth Kirk and Purves Harley, Jr. Marina del Rey, CA: Tell Me Why Sales Company, 1991. 1 videocassette, 15 minutes. Explains the meanings of map and globe terms.

Map Skills. Beth Kirk and Purves Harley, Jr. Marina del Rey, CA: Tell Me Why Sales Company, 1991. 1 videocassette, 15 minutes. A geography tutorial on map skills.

Sleep Out. Carol Carrick and Donald Carrick. Boston, MA: Book and Cassette Favorites, 1988. 1 book, 30 pp. 1 sound cassette, 15 minutes. Tapekit on camping.

Tying Western Trout Flies. Jack Dennis. Jackson Hole, WY: Snake River Books, 1986. 1 videorecording, 120 minutes. How to select animal hair and the tools to use in tying flies.

Types of Maps and Map Projections. Beth Kirk and Purves Harley, Jr. Marina del Rey, CA: Tell Me Why Sales Company, 1991. 1 videocassette, 15 minutes. Discusses types of maps and map projections.

Where in the world? Tucson, AZ: Zephyr Press, 1986. World awareness games with four levels of challenge. Teaches geographic, cultural, and economic facts.

9
Exploring the watery world

Most kids love water and are fascinated by life in and around it. Exploring the watery world with a single child or with a class of students can be exciting. It also poses some special safety concerns, so if you are making a watery world exploration with a group of students, be sure to have one adult for every five children. Outline very carefully and be sure everyone understands procedures before you begin your outing.

Wherever you live, you can probably visit a pond, lake, or stream. If you live in the country or the mountains, you may be able to plan a hiking, biking, fishing, or camping trip along with your visit to a favorite stream. If you live in a city, you may need to content yourself with a visit to a lake in a park or even a trip to see a large aquarium.

On your explorations, you are sure to see a variety of interesting water plants, fish, insects, and animals that will probably arouse the children's curiosity and lead to further investigations. If you have time, space, and interest, your observations, reading, and research may lead you and your curious kids to want to keep some pets from the pond.

If you are going to collect specimens, it's wise to make some preparations ahead of time—you will certainly need some kind of containers. Since not all water creatures live happily together, it may be a good idea to have several medium-size containers rather than a single large one. Some of your containers may be kept open, while others will need a screen or glass top.

Whatever kind of container you use should have a wide top opening so that it will let in enough oxygen. You can use a gallon jar, a plastic vegetable crisper, a pottery casserole dish, an enamel bucket or dishpan, a plastic dishpan, or an aquarium tank. It is not a good idea to use metal containers because they may make the water poisonous to fish and other creatures.

Keeping pond specimens

To make preparations to house your pond specimens, first thoroughly clean the containers that you are going to use. In cleaning your containers, be sure not to use soap. Use fresh, hot water and a rubber scraper or a copper pad if it is needed to remove scum from an old tank.

Spread a layer of sand or fine gravel about 2 inches deep over the bottom. Have the sand or gravel higher in the back than in the front so that you can siphon out any dirt that collects. (If you are going to keep your pond creatures long, it is wise to invest in an aquarium and to place an under-gravel filter in the bottom, beneath the aquarium sand. This filter can be attached by a plastic tube to an air pump, and helps keep your aquarium water clean. If you are only going to keep your pond specimens for a few hours or days and then return them to the pond, a temporary container should work just fine.)

When you pour water into your container, put a piece of clean paper over the sand or gravel before pouring to keep the water from getting cloudy. When you are done pouring, remove the paper. Wait at least 24 hours after pouring the water to allow any chlorine to escape before adding plants or animals.

You may collect a pail of pond water to use in your aquarium. This water may be used right away for plants and animals.

If you are going to keep air-breathing pond creatures, provide a clean stone with a flat top for them to crawl out of the water and rest upon. You may also want to use a screen, a mosquito net, or glass to cover the top. If you use glass, put a small piece of cork on top of each of the corners of your aquarium to rest the glass on. This will create an air space.

Now, you're ready to house your pond specimens!

When you and your class or your curious child go out to collect snails, fish, or plants for your pond aquarium, take along pails or other containers, a cloth net, and a metal strainer. Wear old sneakers that you can wade in. Be sure to always practice water safety.

PAPER

SAND

GLASS TANK

SCREEN LID

MESH NET FOR TADPOLES

CLOTH NET FOR FISH

PLANTS IN WATER

Collecting snails, fish, and tadpoles

To collect snails, take a kitchen strainer and tape a stick onto it so that you have a longer handle. Poke along the shallow edge of a lake, pond, or stream. Scoop up your find in the strainer and put it in a bucket of pond water to carry home.

To catch fish, you will need a cloth net that you can buy or make. Look for small fish in ponds, along the shallow edges of a lake, or in brooks. (Fish that live in swift rivers or streams usually cannot live in a container unless you have a good system to aerate the water.) Sweep your net down through the water toward your feet while wading. Carry your find home in your bucket of pond water.

While you are on your exploration, you can also look for some aquatic plants to carry home. When you dig up the aquatic plants, try not to disturb the roots. Floating plants may be taken without roots. Keep the plants wet until you get them home.

Rinse the plants with fresh water before planting them in your aquarium. Let the roots of the plant spread out as you lower it in the water. Use your fingers or a fork to do the planting and then cover the roots with the sand from the bottom of your aquarium.

Even if you decide that you do not want to collect specimens and try to maintain a pond aquarium at home, you can still learn a lot by visiting ponds, lakes, and streams. It is handy to carry a notebook to jot down what you observe, noting the place, date, and time of your discoveries. You may want to bring along materials so that the child can sketch some of the fish, birds, insects, animals, or plants and include these sketches in his or her notes.

Using a microscope to study water

Taking a water sample and studying a drop of water under a microscope can be a most interesting activity. A bucket, securely tied to a string, can be used to drop from a bridge, boat, or bank to collect a sample of the pond or lake water.

Although the drop of water may appear to be clear, under a microscope the child may find it teeming with tiny water plants and animals. Magnification of 20X to 200X is most useful for this purpose.

Encourage your curious child to draw what is observed under the microscope and to add these drawings to his or her field notes as to where and when you collected the water sample.

Collecting snail shells

Another interesting item for a curious child to collect is a snail shell. The following experiment will explain how to do so.

If you visit a freshwater area where it is permitted, collecting snail shells for study can be fascinating. These mollusk shells are made chiefly of calcium-containing minerals. Aquatic mollusks are more commonly found in "hard water" areas.

You might hope to find water snails (pulmonates) that breathe air when they float up to the surface of the water and open their breathing hole to take in air. The great pond snail, ram's horn snail, and bladder snail are three that you might find.

Other snails (prosobranchs) breathe by absorbing oxygen from the water through their gills. You might also find valve, river, and spire snails.

In ponds and streams, you will discover many different types of water plants. It is interesting to note the differences between water plants and land plants. Among the details you and your curious child or class of students will note about underwater plants are: they do not need thick stems to support them, they have large air spaces inside their leaves to keep them floating in the water, and they take in water and dissolved gases and nutrients over their whole surface. Land plants, however, take in water only through their roots and release it only through their leaves—called transpiration. The following experiment will help your curious child understand this phenomenon.

Displaying transpiration

To show transpiration in action, tie a plastic lunch bag around a shoot on a potted plant. Make a tight seal. After a few hours, check the plastic bag. There will be drops of water inside it.

Showing how plants make food

Another interesting phenomenon that the curious child can observe is a plant making food.

Cut a shoot of Canadian pondweed and put it in a clean pickle jar. The plant will give off oxygen when it makes food in sunlight.

If you put the jar with the pondweed in a sunny spot, you will be able to observe bubbles of oxygen. If you then move the jar of the pondweed out of the sunlight, the bubbles will cease to rise.

A visit to a fish shop or to a large aquarium can be a very interesting trip even if you do not plan to keep fish at home. You will be able to see many different types of fish, plants, and other water life. You can observe egg layers, live bearers, and bubble-nest builders and will probably see tropical fish of every color of the rainbow. In addition, you may see frogs, turtles, snails, salamanders, and newts.

As a result, you may decide to set up a tropical aquarium. Your pet shop probably has simple starter kits for beginners. The basic needs are similar to those discussed in setting up a pond aquarium: a clean tank, an undergravel filter, an air pump, and a heater, plus aquarium gravel and plants.

Your specialty pet shop will be helpful in suggesting fish that are compatible with one another and that are the right size for the tank that you will be using. After you have maintained your aquarium for a while, some shops will even take your too-large fish or baby fish in trade for other fish or aquarium supplies.

Although you will probably not find as many live animal specimens to take home, a visit to the river can be equally as exciting as your trips to ponds, lakes, and small streams. Depending on the season of the year and the part of the country you are in, you might see a barred owl, an egret, a snake, a garfish, crayfish, a turtle, lichens and mosses, warblers, an otter, ferns, or wildflowers. And you will certainly find a lot of interesting rocks on the river bottom, too.

Many of the resource books that follow should be of help in your watery world explorations. You might also want to read the section on water birds in Chapter 5 "Exploring Ethology" and the section on saltwater aquariums in Chapter 10 "Exploring the Ocean." Chapter 4 "Exploring Botany" and Chapter 8 "Exploring Geography and Cartography" might also be of interest on the topic.

Resource Books

All Along the River. Allan Fowler. Chicago, IL: Children's Press, 1994. 31 pp. A Rookie read-about science book.

America's Top Ten Rivers. Jenny E. Tesar. Woodbridge, CT: Blackbirch Press, 1998. 24 pp. Explores ten U.S. rivers including the Yukon and the Rio Grande.

Animal Homes: Water. Shirley Greenway. Brookfield, CT: Newington Press, 1991. 24 pp. Discusses aquatic animals in seas, lakes, rivers, and ponds.

The Aquarium Book. George Ancona. New York, NY: Clarion Books, 1991. 47 pp. Uses text and photos to explore four major aquariums.

Be an Expert Naturalist. John Stidworthy. New York, NY: Gloucester Press, 1991. 32 pp. Examines various environments including a pond, seashore, and woodland.

The Big Rivers: The Missouri, the Mississippi, and the Ohio. Bruce Hiscock. New York, NY: Atheneum Books for Young Readers, 1997. unpaged. Discusses conditions that lead to severe flooding.

By Lakes & Rivers. Tessa Paul. New York, NY: Crabtree Pub. Co., 1997. 32 pp. Discusses the tracks of otter, beaver, frogs, minks, and heron.

The Call of the Running Tide: A portrait of an island family. Nancy Price Graff. Boston, MA: Little, Brown, 1992. 77 pp. Describes a fishing family on Swan's Island off the coast of Maine.

Crocodile. Joyce Pope. Austin, TX: Raintree Steck-Vaughn, 2001. 48 pp. Follows a young crocodile's life in Africa's rivers and lakes.

Disappearing Lake: Nature's magic in Denali National Park. Debbie S. Miller. New York, NY: Walker and Co., 1997. unpaged. Describes a vernal lake in Denali National Park and the creatures that make their homes in and around it.

*Ducklings and Polliwogs. Anne F. Rockwell. New York, NY: Maxwell MacMillan International, 1994, unpaged. Shows the changes at a pond during each season of the year.

Environmental Awareness Activities for Librarians and Teachers: 20 interdisciplinary units for use in grades 2-8. Martha Seif Simpson. Jefferson, NC: McFarland, 1991. 275 pp. Contains sections on ponds, wetlands, rivers, and lakes.

Exploring Parks with Ranger Dockett. Alice K. Flanagan. New York, Children's Press, 1997. 32 pp. Shows the work of an urban park ranger tending ponds and fountains.

Discovering Pond Life. Colin S. Milkins. New York, NY: Bookwright Press, 1990. 47 pp. Describes the physical characteristics of the plant and animal life of a pond.

Down A River. Carole Telford. Des Plaines, IL: Heinemann Interactive Library, 1998. 32 pp. Stresses the importance of conservation.

A Drop of Water: A book of science and wonder. Walter Wick. New York, NY: Scholastic, 1997. 40 pp. Discusses the characteristics and uses of water.

First Look at Rivers. Susan Baker. Milwaukee, WI: Gareth Stevens Children's Books, 1991. 32 pp. Explains how rivers begin and how they benefit people.

Fish. Donna Bailey. Austin, TX: Steck-Vaughn Library, 1990. 48 pp. Discusses various sea animals.

Follow the Water from Brook to Ocean. Arthur Doros. New York, NY: HarperCollins, 1991. 32 pp. Follows the path of water in a brook to the ocean.

Food from the Sea. Daniel Rogers. New York, NY: Bookwright Press, 1991. 32 pp. Discusses fish, types of fishing, and fish farming.

A Freshwater Pond. Adam Hebbert. New York, NY: Crabtree Publications Co., 1999. 32 pp. Discusses different kinds of plant and animal life that can be found in freshwater ponds.

Goldfish: Everything about aquariums, varieties, care, nutrition, diseases, and breeding. Marshall Ostrow. New York, NY: Barron's, 1985. 88 pp. Gives information on how to set up and maintain an aquarium of goldfish.

*Good Morning, Pond. Alyssa Satin Capucilli. New York, NY: Hyperion Books for Children, 1994. unpaged. Follows creatures of a pond as they go through their morning rituals.

Great Experiments with H₂O. Noel Fiarotta and Phyllis Fiarotta. New York, NY: Sterling Pub. Co., 1996. 80 pp. Provides basic facts and suggests simple experiments.

The Great Lakes. Sharon Katz. New York, NY: Benchmark Books, 1999. 64 pp. Describes the formation of the Great Lakes and lifeforms that are part of this ecosystem.

The Hidden Life of the Pond. David M. Schwartz. New York, NY: Crown Publishers, 1988. 40 pp. Explores the animals, plants, and insects of a pond through photos and text.

Howell Beginner's Guide to Garden Ponds. Brian Robinson. New York, NY: Howell Book House, 1985. 52 pp. Explains how to set up a garden pond.

Insects in the Pond. Hidetoma Oda. Milwaukee, WI: Raintree Childrens Books, 1986. 32 pp. Explains a pond's ecosystem and shows diving beetles, water scorpions, and dragonflies.

Inside the Aquarium. Wendy Wax. Chicago, IL: Contemporary Books, 1989. 32 pp. Tells a story of how a girl observes the work in a large, metropolitan aquarium.

In the Water—On the Water. Dorothy Chlad. Chicago, IL: Children's Press, 1988. 31 pp. gives pointers to readers on water safety.

A Kid's Guide to Staying Safe Around Water. Maribeth Boelts. New York, NY: PowerKids Press, 1997. 24 pp. Gives advice for keeping safe around pools, lakes, and oceans.

Lake. Lionel Bender. New York, NY: Franklin Watts, 1989. 32 pp. Discusses lake ecology.

Lake and Pond. April Pulley Sayre. New York, NY: Twenty-First Century Books, 1996. 78 pp. Discusses lake and pond biomes.

Lake Erie. Harry Beckett. Vero Beach, FL: Rourke Corporation, 1999. 32 pp. Discusses the geography and history of Lake Erie.

Lake Huron. Harry Beckett. Vero Beach, FL: Rourke Corporation, 1999. 32 pp. Discusses the geography and history of Lake Huron.

Lake Michigan. Harry Beckett. Vero Beach, FL: Rourke Corporation, 1999. 32 pp. Discusses the geography and history of Lake Michigan.

Lake Ontario. Harry Beckett. Vero Beach, FL: Rourke Corp., 1999. 32 pp. Discusses the history and geography of Lake Ontario.

Lakes. Catherine Chambers. Chicago, IL: Heinemann Library, 2000. 32 pp. Explores the world of lakes.

Lake Superior. Harry Beckett. Vero Beach, FL: Rourke Corp., 1999. 32 pp. Discusses the history and geography of Lake Superior.

Let's Explore a River. Jane R. McCauley. Washington, DC: National Geographic Society, 1988. Explores the plants and animals along a river during a canoe trip, as seen by a father and his three children.

Life in a Pond. Allan Fowler. New York, NY: Children's Press, 1996. 31 pp. Gives an introduction to plants and animals found in and around ponds.

Life in a Pond. Janet Halfmann. Mankato, MN: Creative Education, 2000. 25 pp. Describes various pond creatures such as water striders and tadpoles and suggests activities.

Life in the Water. Editors of Time-Life. Alexandria, VA: Time-Life Books, 1989. 87 pp. Discusses, in a question/answer format, such topics as sharks, crabs, fish, frogs, and barnacles.

The Living Pond. Nigel Hester. New York, NY: Franklin Watts, 1990. 32 pp. Explores plants and animals in a pond habitat.

The Living River. Nigel Hester. New York, NY: Franklin Watts, 1991. 32 pp. Shows the network of animals, insects, fish, and plants that cohabit rivers.

Mississippi River: A journey down the father of waters. Peter Lourie. Honesdale, PA: Boyds Mills Press, 2000. 48 pp. Explores the Mississippi River.

My Camera: At the aquarium. Janet Perry Marshall. Boston, MA: Little, Brown, 1989. 32 pp. Sea animals are seen slightly askew, the readers guess what the animal is, and then there is a clear view of the creature.

My First Visit to the Aquarium. G. Sales and J.M. Parramon. New York, NY: Barron's 1990. 31 pp. Tells the story of a teacher who takes her class to visit an aquarium and learns about marine animals.

My Summer Vacation. Sumiko. New York, NY: Random House, 1990. 30 pp. Describes a little girl's camping trip.

Nature Hide & Seek. John Norris Wood. New York, NY: Knopf, 1993. unpaged. Provides information on freshwater creatures found in lakes and rivers of the world.

Olympia National Park. Ruth Radlaver. Chicago, IL: Children's Press, 1988. 48 pp. Describes the physical features, plants, animals, and camping accommodations in Olympia National Park.

Pond & River. Steve Parker. New York, NY: Alfred A. Knopf, 1988. 64 pp. Discusses plants, animals, fish, and waterfowl that might be found in ponds and rivers.

Pond Life. Terry Jennings. Chicago, IL: Children's Press, 1989. 34 pp. Provides an introduction to pond life, including study questions, activities, and experiments.

Ponds & Streams. John Stidworthy. Mahwah, NJ: Troll Associates, 1990. 31 pp. Discusses the characteristics of various animals that live in or around ponds and streams.

Pond Watching with Ann Morgan. Michael Elsohn Ross. Minneapolis, MN: Carolrhoda Books, 2000. 48 pp. Tells of the life and work of Ann Haven Morgan and includes suggestions for student activities.

Protecting Our Rivers and Lakes. Rosa Cosla-Pau. New York, NY: Chelsey House Publishers, 1994. 31 pp. Discusses water quality management.

Puddles and Ponds. Rose Wyler. Englewood Cliffs, NJ: Julian Messner, 1990. 32 pp. Contains suggestions for experiments about plants and animals that live in and around ponds and other small bodies of water.

Raindrops. Larry Dane Brimner. New York, NY: Children's Press, 1999. A Rookie reader that follows a drop of water down a creek, stream, and river to the ocean.

River. Debby Atwell. Boston, MA: Houghton Mifflin, 1999. 31 pp. Discusses pollution and depletion of water resources.

Rivers. Donna Bailey. Austin, TX: Steck-Vaughn Library, 1990, 48 pp. Discusses aspects of rivers and lakes.

Rivers. Catherine Chambers. Chicago, IL: Heinemann Library, 2000. 32 pp. Explores how rivers are formed, what organisms live there, and how rivers are used.

Rivers. Randy Frahm. Mankato, MN: Creative Education, 1998. 31 pp. Explores various types of rivers.

Rivers. Terry J. Jennings. Parsippany, NJ: Silver Burdett Press, 1998. 32 pp. Discusses the water cycle and ecosystems of rivers.

Rivers. Jane Parker. New York, NY: Franklin Watts, 1998. 32 pp. Discusses five of the most famous rivers of the world.

Rivers and Lakes. David Cumming. New York, NY: Thomson Learning, 1995. 48 pp. Describes plant and animal life and effects of pollution.

Rivers and Lakes. Neil Morris. New York, NY: Crabtree Pub., 1998. 32 pp. Examines rivers and lakes of the worlds.

Rivers and lakes. Helena Ramsay. New York, NY: Children's Press, 1997. 32 pp. Explains how rivers and lakes are formed and how people use them.

Rivers and Seas. Pam Robson. Brookfield, CT: Copper Beech Books, 2001. 32 pp. Contains directions for several water experiments.

Rivers and Streams. Jenny Vaughan. Austin, TX: Raintree Steck-Vaughn, 1998. 32 pp. Gives basic information on how rivers form and on the animals that inhabit them.

Rivers and Valleys. Philip Arthur. Minneapolis, MN: Carolrhoda Books, 1996. 32 pp. Provides information on such related topics as waterfalls, dams, and flooding.

Rivers in the Rain Forest. Saviour Pirotta. Austin, TX: Raintree Steck-Vaughn, 1999. 32 pp. Gives a description of the water cycle and of water plants and animals.

Rivers, Lakes, and Ponds. Eric Braun. Austin, TX: Steadwell Books, 2002. 32 pp. Discusses rivers, lakes, and ponds and the plant and animal life within them.

River Story. Meredith Hooper. Cambridge, MA: Candlewick Press, 2000. 29 pp. Follows a river from its source to the sea.

The River. David Bellamy. New York, NY: C.N. Potter (distributed by Crown), 1988. 26 pp. Shows how plants and animals co-exist in a river and what happens during a man-made catastrophe.

The River. Laura Bour and Gallemard Jeunesse. New York, NY: Scholastic, 1993. p.cm. Transparent overlays show plants and animal life found along rivers.

Riverkeeper. George Ancona. New York, NY: Macmillan, 1990. 48 pp. Examines, through text and photos, the duties of John Cronin, riverkeeper of the Hudson River.

Science Experiments with Water. Sally Nankivell-Aston and Dorothy Jackson. New York, NY: Franklin Watts, 2000. 32 pp. Explores the properties of water.

Science for Fun Experiments. Gary Gibson. Brookfield, CT: Copper Beech Books, 1996. 224 pp. Suggests experiments in areas such as water, magnetism, and electricity.

Science in Seconds at the Beach: Exciting experiments you can do in ten minutes or less: with activities for ponds, lakes, and rivers. Jean Potter. New York, NY: John Wiley & Sons, 1998. 122 pp. Experiments for the watery world.

Science Project Ideas About Rain. Robert Gardner. Springfield, NJ: Enslow Publishers, 1997. 96 pp. Filled with ideas for science experiments.

Science Projects About the Environment and Ecology. Robert Gardner. Springfield, NJ: Enslow Publishers, 1999. 112 pp. Presents projects and experiments involving water.

Squirts and Spurts: Science Fun with Water. Vicki Cobb. Brookfield, CT: Millbrook Press, 2000. 48 pp. Explains the physics of water pressure.

Taking Care of Your Fish. Joyce Pope. New York, NY: Franklin Watts, 1987. 32 pp. Offers important facts about aquarium fishes.

To Climb A Waterfall. Jean Craighead George. New York, NY: Philomel Books, 1995. unpaged. Explains where to rest and what to look for while climbing a waterfall.

Tropical Fish. Pam Jameson. Vero Beach, FL: Rourke Enterprises, 1989. 32 pp. Contains instructions for set up, selection, and care of tropical fish in an aquarium.

Water & Boats. Jan Richards. Brookfield, CT: Copper Beech Books, 1999. 31 pp. Simple experiments demonstrate the properties of water.

Water and Other Liquids. Robert C. Mebane. New York, NY: Twenty-First Century Books, 1995. 64 pp. Suggests science experiments using everyday materials.

Water Dance. Thomas Locker. San Diego, CA: Harcourt Brace & Co., 1997, unpaged. Provides information on the water cycle.

Water: The Source of Life: Glaciers, springs, oceans, tide pools, lakes, swamps, rivers, and oases. Jennifer Riggs. New York, NY: Scholastic, 1995. 47 pp. Uses overlays to present information.

Waterways to the Great Lakes. Harry Beckett. Vero Beach, FL: Rourke Corporation, 1999. 32 pp. Describes the wildlife and bodies of water of the Saint-Lawrence–Great Lake Waterway.

Wetlands. Michael Allaby. Danbury, CT: Grolier Educational, 1999. 64 pp. Describes wetlands and defines their important features.

Woods, Ponds, & Fields. Ellen Doris. Danbury, CT: Grolier Educational, 1996. 72 pp. Contains ideas for projects and experiments.

Yosemite National Park. David Petersen. Chicago, IL: Children's Press, 1993. 45 pp. Discusses waterfalls, glaciers, and other features of the park.

Other Resources

The following magazines may contain articles of interest on camping and fishing: *Boating, Camping Magazine, Country Journal, Field and Stream, Motor Boating, Motor Boating and Sailing, Outdoor Life, Sierra, Sports Afield, Trailer Life,* and *Travel-Holiday*.

Places that you may wish to write for information include: American Fisheries Society, 5410 Grosvenor Lane, Suite 100, Bethesda, MD 20814-2199; National Wetlands Conservation Project, c/o Nature Conservancy, 1800 North Kent Street, Suite 800, Arlington, VA 222-0; and the U.S. Fish and Wildlife Service Publications Unit, 1717 H Street, NW., Room 148, Washington, DC 20240.

All About Water Ecosystems. Wynnewood, PA: Schlessinger Media, 2001. 1 videocassette. 23 minutes. For grades K–4, explores fresh water and marine ecosystems.

All About the Water Cycle. Wynnewood, PA: Schlessinger Media, 2000. 1 videocassette, 23 minutes. Discusses evaporation, condensation, and precipitation for primary and intermediate grade students.

Babies of the Pond. Bill Grunkmeyer (Producer). Sheridan, WY: Grunko Films, 1988. 1 videocassette, 45 minutes. Offers hints on pond ecology.

Box Turtle at Long Pond. William T. George. Norwalk, CT: Soundprints, 1989. 1 book, 26 pp. 1 sound cassette, 10 minutes. Examines the busy day of a box turtle.

Island Ecosystem. Nashua, NH: Delta Education. Allows students to create a complete terrarium–aquarium community. Water conditioner, seed, soil, and guide are included.

Trip to the Aquarium, A. East Aurora, NY: Fisher-Price, 1987. 1 videocassette, 30 minutes. Shows an aquarium visit.

10
Exploring the ocean

It's hard to imagine living on our planet and not being interested in oceans. Three-quarters of the Earth's surface is covered by water. If you and your classroom of students or your curious child live near an ocean, trips to the shore are probably a common part of your life. For others who are landlocked, only rare vacations take the family to beaches and coasts, but the interest in oceans may still be high from reading, television programs, and videos. If you are planning a trip with children to the ocean, be sure to have one adult for every five children in your group.

One of the fascinating things about exploring oceans is that there is still so much to learn about them and the life within them. We've sent astronauts to walk on the moon, but no one has stepped on the deepest spot in the ocean floor—35,000 feet below the surface.

With new scientific advances in technology and equipment, more and more ocean exploration is taking place. Scientists study currents, tides, waves, and the fish, animals, and plants that live in the oceans and seas.

Scientific ocean exploration often makes the news. Perhaps a sunken treasure is located or an underwater lab sets records for the length of time humans have spent beneath the water. At other times we read or hear reports that contain disturbing information about the pollution that is taking place in our ocean waters. There have been gigantic oil spills that foul the waters, spoil resort beaches, and destroy fish and marine animals. Sometimes factories and cities spill waste into the waters.

At yet other times, some sea creature, such as Humphrey the Wrong-Way Whale, captures the interest of the public and is featured in headlines and on television programs. Any such event may provoke interest in curious kids and provide a natural springboard to studying more about some aspect of the ocean that is of immediate interest.

Examining the different substances in salt water

One of the first things a curious child may ask about ocean water is how is it different from fresh water. What's in ocean water? The following experiment will help examine the differences.

Put a small amount of seawater into an enamel saucepan on a burner. Carefully boil the water away, turn the flame off, and allow the pan to cool.

Wet an ordinary steel sewing needle with tap water and run the needle in the salt that is left at the bottom of the pan. Using a pot holder and tongs, carefully hold the salt-covered needle in the blue flame of a gas burner. The heated salt will give off colors depending upon the different minerals contained in it. Sodium, for example, gives off a yellow color (two-thirds of the ocean salt is sodium chloride). Potassium will give off a purple color, calcium will be orange, and copper will give off a green color.

Through this simple experiment of seeing colors, you will learn something about the different substances that are in salt water.

Showing how objects float

Another simple experiment will show how objects float differently in salty water than in fresh water.

Take a wide-mouthed jar and fill it with fresh water. Take a test tube and put some weights in it such as small nuts and bolts. Push some plastic clay into the test tube to hold the weights in place. Cork the test tube tightly and float it in the water. (Add enough weight so that about half of the test tube is below the water.) Mark the water level of the test tube with a marking crayon.

Now remove your test tube and add salt to the water. Stir. Replace the test tube in the salty water. Mark the water level on the test tube now. The test tube floats higher in the salty water than it did in the fresh water.

Salty water is heavier and denser than fresh water, and a dense liquid supports a floating object more easily than a less dense liquid.

Turning saltwater into fresh water

Knowing that saltwater is denser than fresh water and is filled with many different substances may cause a class of students or a curious child to ask if you can turn saltwater into fresh drinking water—and, of course, you can! The following experiment will show you how.

Get two, disposable aluminum baking pans. Paint the inside of the smaller pan black. Punch a hole in a bottom corner of the larger pan. Place the smaller black pan, filled with salt water, inside the larger empty aluminum pan that has a hole poked in a bottom corner.

At each end of the aluminum pans, bend a coat hanger to form a triangular shape. Use clear plastic wrap to form a tent supported by the coat hangers, covering the aluminum pans.

Place your tented pans on a block of wood in the bright sun. The block of wood should be high enough so that you can place a glass to collect water right under the hole you punched in the large aluminum pan.

The black pan will absorb the rays of sun and become warm. As the pan warms the water, the water evaporates and becomes water vapor. The vapor condenses back into water, drips down the plastic into the larger aluminum pan and out through the hole in the pan into a glass.

The water in the glass will not be salty.

The curious child or the group in the class who have questions about how huge airplanes can fly in the sky will probably also have questions about how huge ocean liners, filled with passengers and cargo, can stay afloat in the water. A few simple materials in your kitchen sink can help explain this mystery.

Determining an object's floatability

This experiment will help your curious child understand that a floating object has enough volume (or size) to displace its own weight in water.

Fill a large mixing bowl half full of water. Use aluminum foil to shape a small boat about 4 inches long and 2 inches wide. Put the boat in the water and watch it float. One by one, add 12 paper clips to the boat for cargo and notice that the boat still floats.

Now squish the aluminum boat with the paper clips in it into a lump. Drop the lump into the water. Even though the foil and clips still weigh exactly the same as before, the crumpled boat sinks because its size and shape have changed.

The next best thing to visiting the shore or a large marine aquarium to observe marine animals is to set up a saltwater aquarium in your home. This takes considerable time and effort and should not be undertaken lightly. Reference books will be helpful, but someone who already maintains such an aquarium or someone from a local pet shop/fish supply shop who is knowledgeable and friendly will be of utmost value.

Setting up a saltwater aquarium

Setting up and maintaining a saltwater aquarium is a challenge, but when successful, the results are exciting.

You need a 10-gallon, all glass aquarium with a cover, an undergravel filter, 10 pounds of aquarium gravel, and an air pump. First wash thoroughly with fresh water (no soap) your tank, filter, and gravel. Place the filter in the bottom of the tank, attach a flexible plastic air tube to the filter and to the air pump, and cover the filter with 3 inches of gravel.

You can collect natural seawater to put in your tank if you live near the ocean, choosing a clean place to collect it. Gather the water in clean plastic bags and filter it to remove any dirt. You can make artificial seawater by buying 3 pounds of marine salt and mixing it with 10 gallons of water.

Once the aquarium is set up, every few days add fresh water (not salt water) to replace the water than has evaporated. Put in an aquarium thermometer so that you can maintain a constant temperature. Also use a hydrometer so that you can keep the salinity constant. Place your aquarium where it is not in direct sunlight or near a heater or drafts. Cover the aquarium to keep out dirt. Let the water sit for three weeks before adding any plants or marine animals.

Once your aquarium is established, you can begin adding your plants and animals.

Maintaining plants and animals in a saltwater aquarium

Selecting and maintaining plants and animals in your saltwater aquarium takes careful thought. Discuss this with your local aquarium or pet shop dealer. Certain plants and animals can be purchased that will not harm one another and that can adjust to minor temperature fluctuations.

If you live near the ocean, and collecting specimens is not prohibited in your area, you might be able to collect your own creatures by using nets and containers and searching tide pools.

Once you have marine animals, float them in a plastic bag containing their original water in your tank, allowing time for water temperatures to adjust, before letting them into the tank. Watch new animals closely. If they appear to be sick or if they die, remove them immediately.

Most sea animals can be fed live brine shrimp and very small bits of lean meat. Feed your fish a small amount once a day, removing uneaten scraps of food from the water.

There are numerous books available about specific sea creatures, tides, currents, and other topics that relate to the ocean. Once you and your class or your curious child begin your study of the ocean, one topic may very well lead to another. Other sections of this book, especially Chapter 9 "Exploring the Watery World," might prove helpful.

Resource Books

Across the Big Blue Sea: An ocean wildlife book. Jakki Wood. Washington, D.C.: National Geographic Society, 1998. unpaged. Follows a little red boat as it meets many different sea animals.

Album of Whales. Tom McGowan. New York, NY: Checkerboard Press, 1987. 61 pp. Provides an introduction to various types of whales, dolphins, and porpoises.

Animals in the Oceans. Moira Butterfield, Austin, TX: Raintree Steck-Vaughn, 2000. 32 pp. Discusses such creatures as jellyfish, whales, and manta rays.

Animals of the Seashore. Hidetoma Oda. Milwaukee, WI: Raintree Children's Books, 1986. 32 pp. Describes the lifecycle of crabs, sea anemones, and sea snails.

Animals of the Oceans. Stephen Savage. Austin, TX: Raintree Steck-Vaughn, 1997. 32 pp. Describes oceans and the creatures that live in them.

The Arctic. Pat Hargreaves (Editor). Morristown, NJ: Silver Burdett Press, 1987. 66 pp. Offers an introduction to the Arctic Ocean.

The Atlantic. Pat Hargreaves (Editor). Morristown, NJ: Silver Burdett Press, 1987. 66 pp. gives an introduction to the Atlantic Ocean.

The Atlantic Gray Whale. Jan Mell. Mankato, MN: Crestwood House, 1989. 48 pp. Describes ancient and modern whaling.

The Atlantic Ocean. Susan Heinrichs. Chicago, IL: Childrens Press, 1986. 47 pp. Describes features of the Atlantic Ocean and discusses its inhabitants.

Baby Whale. Lynn Wilson. New York, NY: Platt & Munk, 1991. 30 pp. Tells about a baby whale.

Beneath Blue Waters: Meetings with remarkable deep-sea creatures. New York, NY: Viking, 1996. 64 pp. Gives information on mysterious sea creatures.

Beneath the Oceans. Penny Clarke. New York, NY: Franklin Watts, 1997. 39 pp. Tells of the importance of oceans.

Big Ocean Creatures. Mary Gibbin. New York, NY: Ladybird, 1996. 25 pp. Provides information on marine animals.

Bill Nye the Science Guy's Big Blue Ocean. New York, NY: Hyperion Books for Children, 1999. 48 pp. Discusses ocean ecology.

Blue Whales. Sarah Palmer. Vero Beach, FL: Rourke Enterprises, 1988. 23 pp. Describes the blue whale.

The Bottlenose Dolphin. William R. Sanford and Carl R. Green. Mankato, MN: Crestwood House, 1987. 47 pp. Discusses the physical characteristics and the lifecycle of bottlenose dolphins.

Can the Whales Be Saved?: Questions about the natural world and the threats to its survival answered by the natural history museum. Philip Whitfield. New York, NY: Viking Kestrel, 1989. 96 pp. Discusses the balance of nature in a question/answer format.

The Continental Shelf: An underwater frontier. Alice Gilbreath. New York, NY: Dillon Press, 1986. 103 pp. Describes the shelves under the world's oceans at the shoreline.

Corals. Lola M. Shaefer. Mankato, MN: Pebble Books, 1999. 24 pp. Text and photos introduce the physical characteristics and behavior of corals.

Corals: The sea's great builders. Cousteau Society. New York, NY: Books for Young Readers, 1992. 28 pp. Describes how corals grow, eat, and nourish other animals.

Crabs. Donna Bailey and Christine Butterworth. Austin, TX: Steck-Vaughn Library, 1991. 32 pp. Describes the different kinds of crabs, and their use of claws and legs to catch food, walk, and swim.

Crabs. Lola M. Shaefer. Mankato, MN: Pebble Books, 1999. 24 pp. Text and photos introduce the physical characteristics and behavior of crabs.

Creeps from the Deep. L. R. Taylor. San Francisco, CA: Chronicle Books, 1997. 45 pp. Provides text and photos of exotic sea creatures.

Danger—Icebergs! Roma Gans. New York, NY: Thomas Y. Crowell, 1987. 31 pp. Explains how icebergs are formed and how they move in oceans.

Deep-Sea Explorer: The story of Robert Ballard. Rick Archbold. Boston, MA: Houghton Mifflin, 1996. 165 pp. A biography of Robert Ballard that includes diagrams of ocean depths.

Deep-Sea Vents: Living worlds without sun. John Frederick Waters. New York, NY: Cobblehill Books, 1994. 48 pp. Discusses what has been found around openings in the ocean floor where heated water escapes.

Discovering Crabs and Lobsters. Jill Bailey. New York, NY: Bookwright Press, 1987. 46 pp. Describes the habitat, food, and behaviors of crabs and lobsters.

Discovering Jellyfish. Miranda MacQuitty. New York, NY: Bookwright Press, 1989. 47 pp. Discusses jellyfish, sea anemones, coral, and hydras.

Discovering Otters. Martin Banks. New York, NY: Bookwright Press, 1988. 46 pp. Provides an introduction to sea and freshwater otters.

Dive!: My adventure undersea. Sylvia A. Earle. Washington, DC: National Geographic Society, 1998. p.cm. Relates undersea adventures including living in an underwater laboratory.

Dolphin Adventure: A true story. Wayne Grover. New York, NY: Greenwillow Books, 1990. 47 pp. Tells about a diver who gains the trust of a dolphin.

Dolphins. Judith Hodge. Hauppauge, NY: Barron's Educational Series, 1997. 32 pp. Discusses the physical characteristics, behavior, and lifecycle of the dolphin.

Dolphins. Sarah Palmer. Vero Beach, FL: Rourke Enterprises, 1989. 24 pp. Discusses dolphins, their habits, and behaviors in simple understandable terms.

Down, Down, Down in the Ocean. Sandra Markle. New York, NY: Walker, 1999. 32 pp. Discusses an ecosystem off the coast of California.

The Earth is Mostly Ocean. Allan Fowler. Chicago, IL: Children's Press, 1995. 31 pp. A Rookie read-about science book.

Easy Answers to First Science Questions about Oceans. Q. L. Pearce. New York, NY: Smithmark Publishers, 1991. 31 pp. Offers information on marine science.

The Everything Kids' Nature Book: Create clouds, make waves, defy gravity, and much more! Kathiann M. Kowalski. Hollbrook, MA: Adams Media Corp., 2000, 132 pp. Explores different habitats, including oceans.

Exploring the Deep, Dark Sea. Gail Gibbons. Boston, Little, Brown, 1999. 30 pp. Explores various aspects of the oceans.

Exploring the Oceans: Science activities for kids. Anthony D. Fredericks. Golden, CO: Fulcrum Resources, 1998. 118 pp. Describes the importance of oceans to life and the threats that oceans currently face.

Fin Whales. Sarah Palmer. Vero Beach, FL: Rourke Enterprises, 1988. 23 pp. Describes the most common fin whales.

Floating and Sinking. Karen Bryant-Mole. Des Plaines, IL: Heinemann Interactive Library, 1998. 24 pp. Explains why things float or sink.

Follow that Fin!: Studying Dolphin Behavior. Amy Samuels. Austin, TX: Raintree Steck-Vaughn, 2000. 48 pp. Discusses the bottlenose dolphin of Shark Bay, Australia.
Follow the Water from Brook to Ocean. Arthur Doros. New York, NY: HarperCollins, 1991. 32 pp. Explains how water travels from brooks to reach the ocean.
Footsteps in the Ocean: Careers in diving. Denise V. Lang. New York, NY: Dutton, 1987. 143 pp. Discusses sport and commercial diving and scientific and military research.
Freshwater Giants: Hippopotamus, River Dolphins, and Manatees. Phyllis J. Perry. Franklin Watts, 1999. 64 pp. Gives information about huge animals that make their home in fresh rather than salt water.
Gentle Giant Octopus. Karen Wallace. Cambridge, MA: Candlewick Press, 1998. 29 pp. Discusses the physical characteristics and behavior of the giant octopus.
Golden Book of Sharks and Whales, The. Kathleen N. Daly. Racine, WI: Western Publishing Co., 1989. 45 pp. Discusses the habitat and behavior of sharks and whales.
Gray Whales. Sarah Palmer. Vero Beach, FL: Rourke Enterprises, 1988. 23 pp. Gives a discussion of gray whales.
The Great Barrier Reef: A treasure in the sea. Alice Gilbreath. New York, NY: Dillon Press, 1986. 103 pp. Describes the construction of the barrier reef and the life among it.
Great Whales, The Gentle Giants. Patricia Lauber. New York, NY: Henry Holt, 1991. 64 pp. Describes the characteristics and behaviors of different kinds of whales and the threats they face.
Hermit Crabs. Sylvia A. Johnson. Minneapolis, MN: Lerner Publications Co., 1989. 47 pp. Introduces the reader to the hermit crab.
Hidden Treasures of the Sea. Washington, DC: National Geographic Society, 1988. 104 pp. Provides an introduction to nautical archeology.
Homes in the Sea: From the shore to the deep. Jean H. Sibbald. New York, NY: Dillon Press, 1986. 95 pp. Provides an introduction to sea animals.
How to Be an Ocean Scientist in Your Own Home. Seymour Simon. New York, NY: J. B. Lippincott, 1988. 136 pp. Contains a collection of experiments to reveal the different characteristics of oceans.
Humpback Whale. Michael Bright. New York, NY: Gloucester Press, 1990. 32 pp. Discusses the characteristics, feeding habits, and migration routes of whales.
Humpback Whales. Dorothy Palmer. Vero Beach, FL: Rourke Enterprises, 1988. 23 pp. Discusses humpback whales.
Humphrey, The Wrong Way Whale. Kathryn A. Golner and Carole Garbung Vogel. New York, NY: Dillon Press, 1987. 127 pp. Tells the story of a whale off the coast of California.
Incredible Facts about the Ocean. W. Wright Robinson. New York, NY: Dillon Press, 1986. 3 vols. Provides facts about oceans in a question and answer format.
The Indian Ocean. Pat Hargreaves (Editor). Morristown, NJ: Silver Burdett Press, 1987. 65 pp. Introduces the reader to the Indian Ocean.
The Indian Ocean. Susan Heinrichs. Chicago, IL: Children's Press, 1986. 45 pp. Discusses ocean features such as plants, animals, and volcanic action.
In the Ocean. Dawn Apperley. Boston, Little Brown, 1996. 12 pp. A pop-up book revealing ocean life.

I Wonder Why the Sea is Salty and Other Questions About the Ocean. Anita Ganeri. New York, NY: Kingfisher, 1995. 32 pp. Humorous questions and answers with accurate illustrations.

Jacques Cousteau: Man of the oceans. Carol Greene. Chicago, IL: Children's Press, 1990. 45 pp. Provides a simple biography of Jacques Cousteau.

Jane Goodall's Animal World: Sea otters. Ruth Ashby. New York, NY: Atheneum, 1990. 30 pp. Offers an introduction to sea otters.

Janice VanCleave's Oceans for Every Kid: Easy activities that make learning science fun. Janice Pratt VanCleave. New York, NY: John Wiley, 1996. 245 pp. Activities include studying the topology of the ocean floor and the properties of seawater.

Jellyfish to Insects: Projects with science. William Hemsley. New York, NY: Gloucester Press, 1991. 32 pp. Contains experiments and projects for investigating the lifecycle and behavior of the main groups of invertebrates.

Killer Whales. Sarah Palmer. Vero Beach, FL: Rourke Enterprises, 1988. 24 pp. Discusses the physical characteristics, habits, and environment of killer whales.

The Killer Whales. Lynn M. Stone. Mankato, MN: Crestwood House, 1987. 47 pp. Describes the physical characteristics, habitat, and behavior of killer whales.

The Kingfisher Young People's Book of the Oceans. David Lambert. New York, NY: Kingfisher, 1997. 95 pp. Discusses oceans, tides, and sea life.

The Life Cycle of a Crab. Jill Bailey. New York, NY: Bookwright Press, 1990. 32 pp. Describes the physical characteristics, habitat, food, and reproduction of crabs.

*Life in the Oceans. Lucy Baker. New York, NY: Franklin Watts, 1990. 31 pp. Examines plants, animals, and minerals in the ocean.

Life in the Oceans. Norbert Wu. Boston, MA: Little Brown, 1991. 96 pp. Offers an introduction to life in the ocean from microscopic plants to sharks.

Life in the Sea. Jennifer Coldrey. New York, NY: Bookwright Press, 1991. 32 pp. Provides an introduction to fish, reptiles, birds, mammals, and plants that live in or near oceans.

Living Fossils. Joyce Pope. Austin, TX: Steck-Vaughn Library. 1992, 47 pp. Discusses species that have survived over millions of years such as the shark, crocodile, and horseshoe crab.

The Living Ocean. Robert A. Mattson. Hillside, NJ: Enslow Publishers., 1991. 64 pp. Describes the different kinds of organisms found in oceans.

Make a Splash! Thompson Yardley. Brookfield, CT: Millbrook Press, 1992. 40 pp. Explores oceans and threats to them.

Make Your Own Paper Ocean. Sally Walton. New York, NY: Smithmark, 1994. 32 pp. A fold-out ocean diorama.

Migration in the Sea. Liz Oram and R. Robin Baker. Austin, TX: Steck-Vaughn Library, 1992. 47 pp. Describes the migration patterns of turtles, whales, salmon, anemones, barnacles, crabs, and sea lions.

Monster Seaweeds: The story of the giant kelp. Mary Daegling. New York, NY: Dillon Press, 1986. 119 pp. Discusses the kelp that are home for countless sea creatures.

Monsters of the Deep. Norman Barrett. New York, NY: Franklin Watts, 1991. 32 pp. Offers a look at sharks, jellyfish, and octopuses.

Monster of the Deep. Stewart Ross. Brookfield, CT: Copper Beach Books, 1997. 48 pp. Discusses such creatures as the Great White shark, Lock Ness Monster, and giant squids.

My Home is the Sea: Who Am I? Valeria Tracqui. Watertown, MA: Charlesbridge Publishers, 1996. unpaged. A board book that presents 10 sea animals.

Narwhales. Sarah Palmer. Vero Beach, FL: Rourke Enterprises, 1988. 23 pp. Discusses this toothed whale.

Near the Sea: A portfolio of paintings. Jim Arnosky. New York, NY: Lothrop, Lee & Shepard Books, 1990. 28 pp. Contains paintings of a beach, rock, water, gulls, and fish.

The Night of the Sea Turtle. Lynn M. Stone. Vero Beach, FL: Rourke Enterprises, 1991. 48 pp. Explains the life and habits of loggerhead turtles.

Ocean. Ron Hiroschi. New York, NY: Bantam Books, 1991. 32 pp. Depicts ocean animals. Describes their behaviors and characteristics, and asks the reader to guess the animal.

Ocean. Miranda MacQuitty. New York, NY: Alfred Knopf, 1995. 63 pp. An Eyewitness Book on marine biology.

Ocean. Edward R. Ricciuti. New York, NY: Marshall Cavendish, 1996. 64 pp. An introduction to the oceans.

The Ocean. Anne W. Phillips. Mankato, MN: Crestwood House, 1990. 48 pp. Discusses oceans and pollution.

The Ocean Alphabet Book. Jerry Pallotta. Watertown, MA: Charlesbridge, 1986. 29 pp. Shows fish and other creatures, from A to Z.

Ocean Animals. Michael Chinery. New York, NY: Random House, 1992. 40 pp. Provides an introduction to animals of the ocean.

The Ocean Book: Aquarium and seaside activities and ideas for all ages. Center for Environmental Education. New York, NY: John Wiley & Sons, 1989. 113 pp. Contains ideas for many activities.

Ocean Environments. Renato Massa. Austin, TX: Raintree Steck-Vaughn, 1998. 56 pp. Discusses the different plant and animal life found in oceans.

The Ocean Floor. Keith Lye. New York, NY: Bookwright Press, 1991. 32 pp. Discusses the origin of oceans and the characteristics of the ocean floor.

Ocean Life. David Cook. New York, NY: Crown Publishers, 1985. 30 pp. Describes the dangers faced by the animals that live in the sea.

Ocean Life. Les Holliday. New York, NY: Crescent Books (distributed by Outlet Book Co.), 1991. 62 pp. Describes the variety of animals that live in oceans.

Ocean Mammals. Elaine Landau. New York, NY: Children's Press, 1996. 48 pp. Discusses marine mammals including dolphins, manatees, and walruses.

Ocean Parade: A counting book. Patricia MacCarthy. New York, NY: Dial Books for Young Readers, 1990. 26 pp. Contains a variety of colored fish that introduce the numbers one through twenty.

Oceans. Michael Allaby. Danbury, CT: Grolier Educational, 1999. 64 pp. Describes important features of oceans, animals that live in them, and environmental issues.

Oceans. Moira Butterfield. Pleasantville, NY: Reader's Digest Children's Publishing, 1999. 17 pp. An introduction to marine ecology.

Oceans. Susan Heinrichs. Minneapolis, MN: Compass Point Books, 2001. 48 pp. Discusses the community of plants and animals that inhabit oceans.

Oceans. Anna O'Mara. Mankato, MN: Bridgestone Books, 1996. 24 pp. Provides basic information on ridges, trenches, volcanoes, currents, and tides.

Oceans. Adele Richardson. Mankato, MN: Bridgestone Books, 2001. 24 pp. An introduction to oceans.

Oceans. Darlene R. Stills. New York, NY: Children's Press, 1999. 47 pp. Describes the physical characteristics as well as plants and animals of the ocean.

Oceans. Seymour Simon. New York, NY: Morrow Junior Books, 1990. 32 pp. Oceans are explored through text and photos.

Oceans. Philip Whitfield. New York, NY: Viking Penguin. 1991. 72 pp. Offers information on oceanography.

Oceans and Seas. Catherine Chambers. Chicago, IL: Heinemann Library, 2000. 32 pp. Tells how oceans and seas are formed and discusses the organisms that live in them.

The Oceans. Martyn Bramwell. New York, NY: Franklin Watts, 1987. 32 pp. Discusses the physical features and the marine life of the world's oceans.

The Oceans. Lisa A. Wroble. San Diego, CA: Lucent Books, 1998. 96 pp. Discusses oceans as habitats and how pollution affects them.

Oceans: Looking at beaches and coral reefs, tides and currents, sea animals and fish, seaweeds and other ocean wonders. Adrienne Mason. Toronto, Canada: KidsCan Press, 1995. 80 pp. Information on marine ecology.

Ocean Tide Pool. Arthur John L'Hommedieu. New York, NY: Children's Press, 1997. 31 pp. Explains how tide pools form and shows the plants and animals that live there.

Oceanwatch. Martyn Bramwell. New York, NY: Dorling Kindersley Pub., 2001. 60 pp. Issues around protecting our planet.

Ocean World. Tony Rice. Brookfield, CT: Millbrook Press, 1991. 64 pp. Surveys oceans and ocean life.

The Octopus. Carl R. Green and William R. Sanford. Mankato, MN: Crestwood House, 1988. 47 pp. Discusses the physical characteristics and behavior of an octopus.

Octopuses. Lola M. Shaefer. Mankato, MN: Pebble Books, 1999. 24 pp. Text and photos introduce the physical characteristics and behavior of octopuses.

*An Octopus Is Amazing. Patricia Lauber. New York, NY: Thomas Y. Crowell, 1990. 32 pp. Provides an introduction to the octopus.

Off to Sea: An inside book at a research cruise. Deborah Kovacs. Austin, TX: Raintree Steck-Vaughn, 2000. 48 pp. Shows the duties and routines on the research ship *Atlantis.*

Our Mysterious Ocean. Peter D. Riley. Westport, CT: Joshua Morris Pub., 1998. 17 pp. Deep-sea ecology.

The Pacific. Pat Hargreaves (Editor). Morristown, NJ: Silver Burdett Press, 1987. 67 pp. Introduces the reader to ocean plants and animals and island life.

The Pacific Ocean. Luciani Bottoni, Valeria Lucini, and Renato Massa. Milwaukee, WI: Raintree Children's Books, 1989. 128 pp. Discusses the plant and animal life found in the Pacific Ocean.

The Pacific Ocean. Susan Heinrichs. Chicago, IL: Children's Press, 1986. 45 pp. Gives basic information about the Pacific Ocean and the ocean floor.

Parrotfish. Lola M. Shaefer. Mankato, MN: Pebble Books, 1999. 24 pp. Text and photos introduce the physical characteristics and behavior of parrotfish.

Pioneering Ocean Depths. Sandra Markle. New York, NY: Atheneum, 1995. 48 pp Discusses underwater exploration.

The Plight of the Whales. J. J. McCoy. New York, NY: Franklin Watts, 1989. 144 pp. Discusses how whales have become endangered.

Protecting the Oceans. John Baines. Austin, TX: Steck-Vaughn Library, 1991. 48 pp. Discusses protecting oceans from pollution.

A Reef Comes to Life: Creating an undersea exhibit. Nat Segaloff and Paul Erickson. New York, NY: Franklin Watts, 1991. 40 pp. Discusses constructing a coral reef environment for a museum exhibit.

River in the Ocean: The story of the Gulf Stream. Alice Gilbreath. New York, NY: Dillon Press, 1986. 95 pp. Discusses the warm river flowing in the Atlantic Ocean.

Science in Seconds at the Beach, with Activities for Ponds, Lakes, and Rivers: Exciting experiments you can do in ten minutes or less. Jean Potter. New York, NY: John Wiley & Sons, 1998. 122 pp. Contains directions for a variety of simple experiments.

The Sea. Brian Williams. New York, NY: Warwick Press, 1991. 48 pp. Provides an introduction to the wealth of the sea.

Sea Anemones. Lola M. Shaefer. Mankato, MN: Pebble Books, 1999. 24 pp. Text and photos introduce the physical characteristics and behavior of sea anemones.

Sea Creatures on the Move. Jean H. Bibbald. New York, NY: Dillon Press, 1990. 95 pp. Offers a collection of ocean poems.

Sea Horses. Lola M. Shaefer. Mankato, MN: Pebble Books, 1999. 24 pp. Text and photos introduce the physical characteristics and behavior of sea horses.

The Sea is calling me: Poems. Selected by Lee Bennett Hopkins. San Diego, CA: Harcourt Brace Jovanovich, 1986. 32 pp. Offers a collection of ocean poems.

Seals. Eric S. Grace. Boston, MA: Little, Brown, 1991. 62 pp. Describes the physical characteristics, habits, and habitat of seals.

Seals and Sea Lions. Vassili Papastavrou. New York, NY: Bookwright Press, 1992. 32 pp. Describes different species of pinnipeds.

Seals, Sea Lions and Walruses. Victoria Sherrow. New York, NY: Franklin Watts, 1991. 64 pp. Describes the habits and habitats of seals, sea lions, and walruses.

Sea Stars. Lola M. Shaefer. Mankato, MN: Pebble Books, 1999. 24 pp. Text and photos introduce the physical characteristics and behavior of sea stars.

Sea Mammals: The warm-blooded ocean explorers. Jean H. Sibbald. New York, NY: Dillon Press, 1988. 95 pp. Contains information on four groups of sea mammals.

Sea Otter Rescue: The aftermath of an oil spill. Roland Smith. New York, NY: Dutton, 1990. 64 pp. Describes rescue operations after the 1989 *Valdez* oil spill in Alaska.

*Sea Otters. Sarah Palmer. Vero Beach, FL: Rourke Enterprises, 1989. 24 pp. Offers an introduction to sea otters.

Seas and Coasts. Patience Coster. New York, NY: Children's Press, 1997. 32pp. Discusses features of oceans and their coastlines.

Seas and Oceans. Felicity Brooks. Tulsa, OK: EDC Publishing, 1993. 32 pp. A basic introduction to seas and oceans.

Seas and Oceans. David Lambert. Austin, TX: Raintree Steck-Vaughn, 1994. 32 pp. Provides an introduction to the world's oceans.

Seas and Oceans. Clint Twist. New York, NY: Dillon Press, 1991. 45 pp. Discusses diverse ocean life.

Sea Searcher's Handbook: Activities from the Monterey Bay Aquarium. Pam Armstrong (Editor). Monterey, CA: The Monterey Bay Aquarium, 1996. 224 pp. Discusses kelp forest, wetlands, and the open ocean.

Seashore Life. Ellen Doris. Danbury, CT: Grolier Educational, 1996. 72 pp. Contains ideas for projects exploring the seashore.

Sea Urchins. Lola M. Shaefer. Mankato, MN: Pebble Books, 1999. 24 pp. Text and photos introduce the physical characteristics and behavior of sea urchins.

Seawater: A delicate balance, A. Lee Meyerson. Hillside, NJ: Enslow Publishers., 1988. 64 pp. Discusses the saltiness of oceans.

The Sea World Book of Whales. Eve Bunting. San Diego, CA: Harcourt Brace Jovanovich, 1987. 96 pp. Gives the physical characteristics and habits of various species.

Sharks. Susan Brocker. Hauppauge, NY: Barron's Educational Series, 1997. 32 pp. Discusses the physical characteristics, behavior, and lifecycle of sharks.

Sharks. Gilda Berger. New York, NY: Doubleday. 1987. 41 pp. Describes 20 major types of sharks.

Sharks. Gail Gibbons. New York, NY: Holiday House, 1992. 32 pp. Discusses different kinds of sharks and their behavior.

Sharks and Other creatures of the Deep. Philip Steele. New York, NY: Dorling Kindersley, 1991. 64 pp. Describes a number of strange and intimidating creatures of the sea.

Sharks: The super fish. Helen Roney Sattler. New York, NY: Lothrop, Lee & Shepard Books, 1986. 96 pp. Discusses shark behaviors and gives tips for swimmers.

Signs of the Apes, Songs of the Whales: Adventure in human-animal communication. George and Linda Harrar. New York, NY: Simon & Schuster, 1989. 48 pp. Describes experiments in which apes and dolphins have been taught aspects of human language.

The Six Bridges of Humphrey the Whale. Toni Knapp. Colorado Springs, CO: Rock-rimmon Press, 1989. 44 pp. Tells how a young humpback whale swims into the San Francisco Bay and winds up in the Sacramento River Delta.

Something's Fishy! Jokes about sea creatures. Rick Walton and Ann Walton. Minneapolis, MN: Lerner Publications Co., 1987. 32 pp. Contains jokes and riddles about the sea.

Somewhere in the Ocean. Jennifer Ward. Flagstaff, AZ: Rising Moon, 2000. 30 pp. A counting book in rhyme showing marine animals.

The Story of Three Whales. Giles Whittell. Milwaukee, WI: Gareth Stevens Pub., 1989. 28 pp. Describes how an international team tries to save three whales trapped in ice off the coast of Alaska.

Strange Eating Habits of Sea Creatures. Jean H. Sibbold. New York, NY: Dillon Press, 1985. 111 pp. Describes what and how sea creatures eat.

Stranger than Fiction: Sea monsters. Melvin Berger. New York, NY: Avon Books, 1991. 86 pp. Discusses the killer whale, electric eel, and giant squid.

Super Science Projects about Oceans. Allan B. Cobb. New York, NY: Rosen Publishing Group's Rosen Central, 2000. 48 pp. Includes projects that demonstrate facts about oceans, such as buoyancy and density.

A Swim Through the Sea. Kristin Joy Pratt. Nevada City, CA: Dawn Publications, 1994. unpaged. Letters of the alphabet introduce such favorites as angelfish, dolphins, and the octopus.

That's for Shore: Riddles from the beach. June Swanson. Minneapolis, MN: Lerner Publishing Co., 1991. 32 pp. Contains riddles about the beach.

They Swim the Seas: The Mystery of Animal Migration. Seymour Simon. San Diego, CA: Harcourt Brace, 1998. unpaged. Discusses marine plants and animals.

This Is the Sea That Feeds Us. Robert F. Baldwin. Nevada City, CA: Dawn Publications, 1998. unpaged. Discusses food chains and marine ecology.

Those Amazing Eels. Cheryl M. Halton. New York, NY: Dillon Press, 1990. 94 pp. Discusses the physiology, habits, and uses of eels.

Threatened Oceans. Jenny Tesar. New York, NY: Facts on File, 1991. 112 pp. Explains how fishing, dumping, oil spills, and humans endanger a marine environment.

Tidal Waves and Other Ocean Wonders. Querida Lee Pearce. Englewood Cliffs, NJ: Julian Messner, 1989. 64 pp. Describes the biological and geological wonders found in the ocean depths.

Tidepools. Diana Barnhart and Vicki Leon. San Luis Obispo, CA: Blake Publishing, 1989. 39 pp. Discusses tide pool ecology.

Tidepools: The bright world of the rocky shoreline. Diana Barnhart. Parsippany, NY: Silver Burdett, 1995. 43 pp. Discusses tide pool ecology.

To the Bottom of the Sea: The Exploration of exotic life, the Titanic, and other secrets of the oceans. George M. Sullivan. Brookfield, CT: Twenty-First Century Books, 1999. 80 pp. Examines the past and present of undersea exploration.

The Truth About Great White Sharks. Mary M. Carullo. San Francisco, CA: Chronicle Books, 2000. 48 pp. A book about sharks.

The Twelve Days of Summer. Elizabeth Lee O'Donnell. New York, NY: Morrow Junior Books, 1991. 30 pp. A counting verse in which a girl sees things at the beach such as one purple sea anemone.

The Ultimate Ocean Book: A unique introduction to the world under water in fabulous, full- color pop-ups. Maria Mudd-Ruth. New York, NY: Artists & Writers Guild Books, 1995. unpaged. Marine animals.

Undersea Archaeology. Christopher Lampton. New York, NY: Franklin Watts, 1988. 96 pp. Describes the use of technology to retrieve artifacts from the ocean floor.

Undersea Technology. Mark Lambert. New York, NY: Bookwright Press, 1990. 47 pp. Examines submarines, mining, oil production, and underwater exploration.

Under the Sea. Lindsay Knight. Alexandria, VA: Time-Life Books, 1995. 64 pp. Presents the immense variety of sea life.

Under the Sea. Brian Williams. New York, NY: Random House, 1989. 24 pp. Offers an illustrated introduction to the sea.

Under the Sea. Jenny Wood. New York, NY: Macmillan, 1991. 29 pp. Reveals the secrets of sharks, whales, and a coral reef during a submarine voyage.

Under the Sea: Book and Activity Kit. Liane B. Onish (Adaptor). New York, NY: Scholastic, 1996, 32 pp. Underwater exploration for ages 6 and up.

Underwater Life: The oceans. Dean Morris. Milwaukee, WI: Raintree Children's Books, 1988. 47 pp. Discusses plants and animals of the deep sea.

Walk by the Seashore, A. Caroline Arnold. Morristown, NJ: Silver Burdett Press, 1990. 32 pp. Shows sand, waves, plants, and animals at the shore through a child's eyes.

Watching Whales. John F. Waters. New York, NY: Cobblehill Books/Dutton, 1991. 42 pp. Tells about the natural life of whales.

Waves, Tides, and Currents. Daniel Rogers. New York, NY: Bookwright Press, 1991. 32 pp. Tells how waves, tides, and currents are created and the effect on climate and shorelines.

Way Down Deep: Strange ocean creatures. Patricia Demuth. New York, NY: Grosset & Dunlap, 1995. 48 pp. Simple oceanography for grades 1 to 3.

Whale. Jill Bailey. New York, NY: Gallery Books, 1991. 47 pp. Walter Coleman takes six tourists on a boat to a lagoon to see the birth of gray whales.

Whales. Gilda Berger. New York, NY: Doubleday, 1987. 41 pp. Describes 20 species of whales.

Whales. Gail Gibbons. New York, NY: Holiday House, 1991. 30 pp. Introduces the different kinds of whales.

Whales. Judith Hodge. Hauppauge, NY: Barron's Educational Series, 1997. 32 pp. Discusses the physical characteristics, behavior, and lifecycle of whales.

Whales. Anthony R. Martin. New York, NY: Crescent Books (distributed by Outlet Book Co.), 1990. 64 pp. Provides an introduction to whales.

Whales. Louise Martin. Vero Beach, FL: Rourke Enterprises, 1988. 24 pp. Describes 12 species of whales and efforts of the World Wildlife Fund.

Whales. Malcolm Penny. New York, NY: Bookwright, 1990. 32 pp. Introduces different types of whales.

Whales and Dolphins. Vassili Papastavrou. New York, NY: Bookwright Press, 1991. 32 pp. Tells about different kinds of whales.

Whales: And other marine mammals. George S. Fichter. Racine, WI: Golden Press, 1990. 160 pp. Discusses whales, dolphins, porpoises, manatees, dugongs, sea lions, walruses, seals, otters, and polar bears.

Whales of the World. June Behrens. Chicago, IL: Children's Press, 1987. 44 pp. Describes such creatures as the right whale, bottlenose dolphin, and humpback whale.

Whales, The Nomads of the Sea. Helen Roney Sattler. New York, NY: Lothrop, Lee & Shepard Books, 1987. 126 pp. Describes the physical characteristics and habits of whales and dolphins.

Whales: Whale magic for kids. Tom Wolpert. Milwaukee, WI: Gareth Stevens Pub., 1990. 48 pp. Discusses different kinds of whales.

What Makes an Ocean Wave? Questions and answers about oceans and ocean life. Melvin Berger and Gilda Berger. New York, NY: Scholastic, 2001. 48 pp. Gives information about topics such as waves, tides, and marine creatures.

What's Inside? Shells. Angela Royston. New York, NY: Dorling Kindersley (distributed by Houghton Mifflin). 1991. 17 pp. Offers a first guide to the wonders of life inside shells.

What is a Fish? Barbara R. Stratton. New York, NY: Franklin Watts, 1991. 33 pp. Discusses the common characteristics of fish.

Women Explorers of the Oceans: Ann Davison, Eugenie Clark, Sylvia Earle, Naomi James, Tania Aebi. Margo McLoone. Mankato, MN: Capstone Press, 2000. 48 pp. Discusses the lives and accomplishments of these women explorers.

The World's Oceans. Cass R. Sandak. New York, NY: Franklin Watts, 1987. 32 pp. Explains how inventions have extended the scope of ocean exploration.

The World of a Jellyfish. David Shale and Jennifer Coldrey. Milwaukee, WI: Gareth Stevens Pub., 1987. 32 pp. Discusses the characteristics, habits, and environment of jellyfish.

The World of Fishes. Hiroshi Takeuchi. Milwaukee, WI: Raintree Publishers, 1986. 32 pp. Discusses the behavior patterns of unusual ocean fish in the deep sea or near coral reefs.

Other Resources

A bimonthly magazine of interest might be *Dolphin Log,* Los Angeles, CA: published by the Cousteau Society, Inc.

Amazing Underwater Animals. New York, NY: Dorling Kindersley Vision and Partridge Films in association with The Disney Channel, 1998. 1 videocassette, 30 min. The animals shown include sharks and an ink-spraying octopus.

The Big A: Telling a story in art. Lincoln, NE: Great Plains National Instructional Television Library, 1987. 1 videocassette, 15 minutes. Shows a field trip to Sea Monster House to discuss the stories and designs in Northwest Coastal Indian arts.

Gift of the Whales. Jan C. Nickman (Producer). Seattle, WA: Miramar Images, 1989. 1 videocassette, 30 minutes. Tells the story of a young boy and his relationship with whales near his village.

Hands on Explorations: Shells. Nashua, NH: Delta Education. This mini-kit contains 3 pounds of shells, a *Peterson Shell Guide,* and 10 magnifying lenses.

Humphrey the Lost Whale: A true story. Wendy Tokuda and Richard Hall. Lincoln, NE: The Library, 1989. 1 videocassette, 30 minutes. Explains how a migrating humpback whale ended up 64 miles inland.

Jellies and Other Ocean Drifters. Robin Burnett. Monterey, CA: Monterey Bay Aquarium Foundation, 1996. 1 videocassette, 35 minutes. Shows several varieties of jellies including long-tentacled jellies and comb jellies.

Marine Ecosystems. Wynnewood, PA: Schlessinger Media, 2001. 1 videocassette, 23 minutes. A discussion of the diversity and population of marine ecosystems for grades 5 to 8.

Night-Hunting Lobster, The. Bill Martin, Jr., with John Archambault. Chicago, IL: Encyclopedia Britannica Educational Corp., 1985. 1 book, 14 pp. 1 sound cassette, 10 minutes. A read-along tape kit.

Oceans DSM II Kit. Nashua, NH: Delta Education. For grades 5-6. Comes with 172 page teacher's guide and 12 step-by-step activities with materials for 32 students. Includes topics such as hydrometers to measure the density of saltwater samples, mapping a section of ocean floor, and modeling ocean waves and currents.

The Singing Whales. Bill Martin Jr., with John Archambault. Chicago, IL: Encyclopedia Britannica Educational Corp., 1985. 1 book. 14 pp. 1 sound cassette, 10 minutes. A fun-filled tape kit with music.

11

Exploring science through your senses

Although scientists often use very sophisticated equipment, it is also true that people take in scientific information through their senses. Exploring science through the senses comes about very naturally because you and your curious child or classroom of students are experiencing sensations all the time. We respond to stimuli that are separate from us, and we are constantly using our specialized sense organs: eyes, ears, tongue, nose, and skin.

All of our sense organs have one thing in common—nerve cells. These cells, called receptors, respond to stimuli and carry messages to the brain. For example, eyes are sensitive to light; sound is usually sensed by ears, although some vibrations are sensed by the skin; your nose and mouth are sensitive to chemicals; and the skin responds to temperature, pressure, pain, and helps you to recognize many of the things that you touch. Finally, past experience helps you decide how to respond to the stimuli and sensations that you receive.

Often we take this sensory information for granted, but now and then, something will happen that causes a curious child to stop and think about it. For example, some friends, relatives, or classmates may wear glasses or contact lenses, while others simply put on sunglasses when they go out to drive, ski, or go to the beach. The child may raise questions about these various lenses, why they are worn, and what they do.

Similarly, a friend, relative, or classmate might have a hearing loss and wear a hearing aid. The child might have questions about how this aid works and what it does. The child might comment on the smoothness of a piece of silk or the fender of a new car, or may make an accurate guess at what's cooking for dinner by the smells that are arising in the kitchen. All of these are opportunities for exploring the senses. The following experiment can show how smell affects a person's sense of taste.

Showing how smell affects taste

To show how the sense of taste and smell are interrelated, blindfold a child and have him hold his nostrils closed by pinching them between finger and thumb.

Then put a small piece of food on the child's tongue and have him taste it without chewing and then guess what it is.

If you use small pieces of apple, pear, raw potato, and onion, the child will probably make some mistakes in the guesses. It is the odors that make these foods taste different.

Demonstrating the sense of touch

To demonstrate the sense of touch for your curious child, simply conduct the following experiment.

There is a simple guessing game you can play with a child to demonstrate her sense of touch. Get an ordinary paper bag and put about 20 different items into it. (None of these items should be sharp or pointed—they might cause injury.)

Include many shapes, sizes, and weights. For example, you might include: a plastic spoon, a paper clip, a thimble, a lemon, a pencil, a marble, a clothespin, and a hard-boiled egg.

Have the child reach in the bag without looking inside. Give the child a couple of minutes to feel. Then put the bag aside and have the child name as many items as she was able to identify. Older children may write the items in a list. Young children can simply tell you.

Remove all the identified items and let the child have one more try at feeling the unidentified items. How many of the 20 items could be identified simply by the sense of touch?

Although our senses can help us in identifying objects and making sense of our world, these same senses can sometimes trick us. Our perceptions come from stimuli of the physical world, sensations, and our experience in interpreting data. Although we believe our perceptions to be accurate, we can be deceived. This is when some interesting questions arise.

Confusing your sense of touch

One simple experiment that shows you can be deceived by the sense of touch can be carried out by taking a hairpin or paper clip and spreading apart the two legs into a V-shape.

Touch various parts of the body (e.g., back, hand, leg) with both tips of the V. Vary the distance between the two points that are touching. It may help to close your eyes while you are carrying out this experiment.

On some parts of the body, you will feel two distinct spots where the points of the V are touching. In other parts of the body, although two points are touching, you will feel only one.

Determining an object's temperature

Another simple experiment involving our sense of touch uses temperature to trick us.

Using three pans of water, fill one pan with water at room temperature, a second with ice water, and a third with comfortably hot tap water.

Have the child put one hand in the ice water and another in the hot water for 30 seconds. Then have the child put both hands in the water that is room temperature. Ask if the room temperature water is hot or cold.

The water at room temperature will feel warm to the hand that had been in ice water and cool to the hand that had been in hot water.

Creating sound effects

Exploring the sense of hearing can also be interesting. If the child likes storytelling or dramatics, sound effects will be a natural entry into exploring sounds.

First choose a suitable story for recording into a tape recorder. It should be one that has a fair number of possible sound effects (e.g., wind, rain, thunder, crackling fire, foghorn, slamming or creaking doors, gun shot, galloping hoof beats, splashing water).

The story can be original or an old favorite such as *The Three Billy Goats Gruff,* who tramp across a bridge.

Try various ways of making the sound effects, (e.g., breathe into the microphone, crumple paper, blow across a pop bottle, rattle rice in a box, hit the floor with a ruler). Select the best.

Record the story and the sound effects. Try it out on an audience to see how well you did.

Your eyes can play tricks on you, too. When driving along the highway in the summer, you may have experienced a mirage that looks like a pool of water ahead of you on the hot highway. The water seemed to vanish when you came closer. Mirages like this are caused by the way light is reflected inside rising masses of hot air.

Demonstrating an optical illusion

To demonstrate a simple optical illusion, take a sheet of paper and roll it into a tube. Have the child hold the tube to one eye, keep both eyes open, and focus on an object about 15 feet away.

Now hold a small book right next to the tube in front of the eye that is not looking through the tube. Continue to focus on the distant object.

You may have to move the book a little, either closer or more distant, to get it into just the right position, but suddenly it will look as though you are looking at the distant object right through a hole in the book!

This happens because your eyes are set apart from one another, and when you focus on a distant object, near objects are slightly out of focus, and the image from one eye overlaps improperly from the image in the other eye.

Take advantage of the events that arise in everyday living to further explore your various senses. The resources that follow should help you find materials in areas that are of interest to your class or your curious child.

Resource Books

All About Your Senses. Donna Bailey. Austin, TX: Steck-Vaughn Library, 1991. 48 pp. Explains the functions of the five senses.

*Amazing Animal Senses. Ron Van der Meer. Boston, MA: Joy Street Books, 1990. 12 pp. Provides facts about animal senses and includes animation glasses, action flaps, and scratch and sniff patches.

Animals and Their World. Sally Morgan. New York, NY: Kingfisher, 1996. 32 pp. Explains how animals use their senses and suggests related activities.

Animal Senses. Jim Flegg with Eric Hosking and David Hosking. Brookfield, CT: Newington Press, 1991. 32 pp. Discusses animal senses, locomotion, and behavior.

Animal Senses: How animals see, hear, taste, smell and feel. Pamela Hickman. Toronto, Canada: Kids Can Press, 1998. 40 pp. Gives information on the senses of animals.

Animal Vision. Tony Seddon. New York, NY: Facts on File, 1988. 61 pp. Provides an overview of how different animals see and how eyes function.

Beyond Your Senses: The new world of sensors. Hal Hellman. New York, NY: Lodestar Books, 1997. 87 pp. Explains how sensors work and operate devices.

Discovering Sign Language. Laura Green and Eva Barash Dicker. Washington, DC: Kendall Green Publications, 1988. 89 pp. Explains about the development of sign language.

The Ear and Hearing. Steve Parker. New York, NY: Franklin Watts, 1991. 40 pp. Explains the anatomy of the ear.

Ears Are for Hearing. Paul Showers. New York, NY: Thomas Y. Crowell, 1990. 31 pp. Explains about the process of hearing.

*Ears, Eyes and Noses. Rachel Wright. New York, NY: Franklin Watts, 1989. 32 pp. Discusses the appearance and functions of ears, eyes, and noses in several animals, insects, and fish.

Eating and Tasting. Henry Arthur Pluckrose. Austin, TX: Raintree Steck-Vaughn, 1998. 30 pp. Explains how we use our senses to enjoy food.

Experiment with Senses. Monica Byles. Minneapolis, MN: Lerner Publishers, 1994. 32 pp. Suggests simple experiments involving the 5 senses.

Exploring Matter with Toys: Using and understanding the senses. Mickey Sarquis. New York, NY: Learning Triangle/McGraw Hill, 1997. 206 pp. For grades 1–4, presents hands-on activities to demonstrate how the senses work.

The Eye and Seeing. Steve Parker. New York, NY: Franklin Watts, 1989. 48 pp. Introduces the reader to the sense of sight.

Eyes. Brian Ward. New York, NY: Franklin Watts.1990. 32 pp. Explains the construction of the eye and tells how vision problems can be corrected.

*Eyes. Judith Worthy. New York, NY: Doubleday, 1989. 32 pp. Describes in verse the eyes of several animals.

Feel and Touch! Julian Rowe and Molly Perham. Chicago, IL: Children's Press, 1993. 32 pp. Explains how we feel hot–cold and rough–smooth.

Feeling Things. Allan Fowler. Chicago, IL: Children's Press, 1991. 31 pp. Discusses the sense of touch.

Feeling Your Way: Discover Your Sense of Touch. Vicki Cobb. Brookfield, CT: Millbrook Press, 2001. unpaged. Introduces the sense of touch.

Fingers and Feelers. Henry Arthur Pluckrose. New York, NY: Franklin Watts. 1990. 32 pp. Examines the sense of touch in the animal kingdom, including humans.

*First Delights: A book about the five senses. Tasha Tudor. New York, NY: Platt & Munk, 1988. 48 pp. Offers an introduction to the senses.

The Five Senses. Jacqueline Dineen. Morristown, NJ: Silver Burdett Press, 1988. 48 pp. Provides an introduction to the five senses.

*5 Senses: Ready-to-go activities, games, literature selections, poetry, and everything you need for a complete theme unit. Tracey West. New York, NY: Scholastic Professional Books, 1997. 48 pp. A unit on the senses designed for grades K–1.

Follow Your Nose: Discover your sense of smell. Vicki Cobb. Brookfield, CT: Millbrook Press, 2000. unpaged. Explores the sense of smell through simple experiments.

*Fun With My 5 Senses: Activities to build learning readiness. Sarah A. Williamson. Charlotte, VT: Williamson Pub. Co., 1998. 141 pp. Presents activities for exploring the five senses.

Getting Started in Science Fairs: From planning to judging. Phyllis J. Perry. Blue Ridge Summit, PA: TAB Books, McGraw Hill, 1995. 183 pp. Contains examples of science fair projects in many different categories, including some involving the senses.

Glasses and Contact Lenses: Your guide to eyes, eyewear and eye care. Alvin and Virginia B. Silverstein. New York, NY: J. B. Lippincott, 1989. 135 pp. Explains the structure of the eyes and how to correct various visual problems.

Heads. Ron and Nancy Goor. New York, NY: Atheneum, 1988. 64 pp. Compares and contrasts the characteristics of eyes, ears, nose, and mouth in a variety of animals.

Head to Toe Science: Over 40 eye-popping, spine-tingling, heart-pounding activities that teach kids about the human body. Jim Wiese. New York, NY: John Wiley & Sons, 2000. 120 pp. Contains suggestions for activities and experiments.

Hearing. Kathie Billingslea and Victoria Crenson. Mahwah, NJ: Troll Associates, 1988. 24 pp. Provides information on hearing in a question/answer format.

Hearing. Sharon Gordon. New York, NY: Children's Press, 2001. 31 pp. A Rookie read-about health book.

Hearing. Sue Hurwitz. New York, NY: Franklin Watts, 1998. 24 pp. Explains how the ear works.

Hearing. Laurence P. Pringle. New York, NY: Benchmark Books, 2000. 32 pp. Discusses the parts of an ear and how they function.

Hearing. Maria Rius, J.M. Parramon, and J. J. Puig. New York, NY: Barron's 1985. 31 pp. Explores the sense of hearing.

Hearing. Mandy Suhr. Minneapolis, MN: Carolrhoda Books, 1994. 32 pp. Explores the sense of hearing.

Hearing Loss. Karen N. Mango. New York, NY: Franklin Watts, 1991. 144 pp. Discusses hearing loss and deafness.

Hearing Sounds. Sally Hewitt. New York, NY: Children's Press, 1998. 30 pp. Suggests a variety of activities involving sounds.

Hearing Things. Allan Fowler. Chicago, IL: Children's Press, 1991. 31 pp. Discusses the sense of hearing.

Highlights Big Book of Science Secrets, The: 101 amazing experiments. Highlights Staff. Honesdale, PA: Boyds Mills Press, 1997. Topics explored include the senses.

Hot and Cold. Henry Pluckrose. New York, NY: Franklin Watts, 1986. 32 pp. Explains how we sense hot and cold.

How Do Our Eyes See? Carol Ballard. Austin, TX: Raintree Steck-Vaughn, 1998. 32 pp. Explores such topics as light, dark, color, and wearing glasses.

How to Really Fool Yourself: Illusions for all your senses. Vicki Cobb. New York, NY: John Wiley & Sons, 1998. 128 pp. Provides demonstrations with explanations.

Human Body. Kathleen Weidner Zoehfeld. New York, NY: Scholastic, 2000. 32 pp. Provides a simple explanation of the five senses.

I Can Tell by Touching. Carolyn Otto. New York, NY: HarperCollins, 1994. 32 pp. Explains how the sense of touch helps us identify everyday objects.

Intuition. Sue Hurwitz. New York, NY: Power Kids Press, 1997. 24 pp. Defines intuition, the sixth sense, and explains how it works.

Learning a Lesson: How you see, think and remember. Steve Parker. New York, NY: Franklin Watts, 1991. 32 pp. Explores the functions of the brain and nervous system and discusses how sensory experiences and information are processed.

Lenses! Take a Closer Look. Siegfried Aust. Minneapolis, MN: Lerner Publications Co., 1991. 31 pp. Looks at different lenses including a magnifying glass, telescope, microscope, and eyeglasses.

Let's Take a Walk in The City. Karen O'Connor. Elgin, IL: Child's World (distributed by Children's Press), 1986. 30 pp. Tells a story of how Tony uses his five senses as he takes a walk in the city.

Let's Take a Walk in the Zoo. Jane Belk Moncure. Elgin, IL: Child's World, 1986. 32 pp. Tells a story of how Laura uses her five senses as she enjoys a visit to the zoo.

Let's Take a Walk on the Beach. Karen O'Connor. Elgin, IL: Child's World (distributed by Children's Press), 1986. 31 pp. Tells a story of how a child uses his five senses as he walks along the beach.

Living with Deafness. Barbara Taylor. New York, NY: Franklin Watts, 1989. 32 pp. Discusses various forms of deafness, their causes, and treatment.

Look At Your Eyes. Paul Showers. New York, NY: HarperTrophy, 1992. 32 pp. Describes the parts of the eye and how they work.

Looking and Seeing. Henry Arthur Pluckrose. Austin, TX: Raintree Steck-Vaughn, 1998. 24 pp. Presents basic concepts about seeing.

Looking at Senses. David Suzuki with Barbara Hehner. New York, NY: John Wiley & Sons, 1991. 96 pp. Discusses sight, hearing, taste, touch, and ESP.

Magic and Perception: The art and science of fooling the senses. Robert Friedhoffer. New York, NY: Franklin Watts, 1996. 109 pp. Step-by-step directions for staging tricks that fool the senses.

Magic School Bus Explores the Senses, The. Joanna Cole. New York, NY: Scholastic Press, 1999. 47 pp. Mrs. Frizzle and her class explore the senses.

Making Sense: Animal perception and communication. Bruce Brooks. New York, NY: Farrar, Straus, Giroux, 1993. 73 pp. Discusses animal senses and how they are used.

*My Five Senses. Aliki. New York, NY: Thomas Y. Crowell, 1989. 31 pp. Explains ways we use our five senses.

My Five Senses. Margaret Miller. New York, NY: Simon & Schuster Books, 1994. Unpaged. Provides an introduction to the five senses.

Nerves to Senses. Steve Parker. New York, NY: Gloucester Press, 1991. 32 pp. Explains how bodies respond to stimuli of the nervous system and outlines some related projects.

*Night Sounds, Morning Colors. Rosemary Wells. New York, NY: Dial Books for Young Readers, 1994. unpaged. Explores senses through experiences associated with seasons.

101 Questions Your Brain Has Asked about Itself but Couldn't Answer–Until Now. Faith Hickman Brynie. Brookfield, CT: Millbrook Press, 1998. 176 pp. Explains how the brain functions and discusses memory and the senses.

Out of Sight. Seymour Simon. New York, SeaStar Books, 2000. unpaged. Discusses objects so small that microscopes, telescopes, or x-rays are needed for viewing.

Riddles about the Senses. Jacqueline A. Ball. Morristown, NJ: Silver Burdett Press, 1989. 30 pp. Contains rhyming riddles.

The Science Book of the Senses. Neil Ardley. San Diego, CA: Harcourt Brace Jovanovich, 1992. 29 pp. Gives instructions for simple experiments that show how the five senses work.

Seeing. Sharon Gordon. New York, NY: Children's Press, 2001. 31 pp. A Rookie read-about health book.

Seeing. Kathie Billingslea Smith and Victoria Crenson. Mahwah, NJ: Troll Associates, 1988. 24 pp. Answers questions about the eye and how people and animals see.

Seeing. Alvin Silverstein. Brookfield, CT: Twenty-First Century Books, 2001, 64 pp. Discusses vision.

Seeing in Special Ways: Children living with blindness. Thomas Bergman, Milwaukee, WI: Gareth Stevens Pub., 1989. 54 pp. Explains how other senses compensate for lost sight, as told through interviews with partially-sighted children.

Seeing Is Believing: Activities to show you how people think and see. Patrick R. Green. Parsippany, NJ: Julian Messner, 1996. 46 pp. Contains self-tests and puzzles.

Seeing Things. Allan Fowler. Chicago, IL: Children's Press, 1991. 31 pp. Discusses parts of the eye and explains how eyes work.

Sense-abilities: Fun ways to explore the senses. Michelle O'Brien-Palmer. Chicago, IL: Chicago Review Press, 1998. 166 pp. Suggests activities that delve into the senses.

Senses. Steve Parker. Brookfield, CT: Copper Beech Books, 1997. 31 pp. Discusses senses and sensations.

Senses. Anna Sandeman. Brookfield, CT: Copper Beech Books, 1995. 30 pp. Introduces senses and sensations.

The Senses. Mary Kittredge. New York, NY: Chelsea House Publishers, 1990. 111 pp. Explains the structure and functions of our sensory organs.

The Senses. Tracy Maurer. Vero Beach, FL: Rourke Corp., 1999. 24 pp. Provides an introduction to the five senses and how they work.

*The Senses: A lift-the-flap body book. Angela Royston. Hauppauge, NY: Barrons, 1993. 21 pp. Identifies five senses and explains how they work.

Senses: How we connect with the world. Francesca Baines. Danbury, CT: Grolier Educational, 1998. 48 pp. Discusses senses and sensations.

Sense Suspense: A guessing game for the five senses. Bruce McMillan. New York, NY: Scholastic, 1994. unpaged. Explores our five senses.

The Sierra Club Wayfinding Book. Vicki McVey. Boston, MA: Little, Brown, 1988. 88 pp. Explains how humans develop systems using their senses and includes suggestions for student activities.

Sight. Sue Hurwitz, New York, NY: Franklin Watts, 1998. 24 pp. Explains how the sense of sight works.

Sight. Laurence P. Pringle. New York, NY: Benchmark Books, 2000. 32 pp. Discusses the parts of the eye and how they work.

Sight. Maria Rius, J. M. Parramon and J. J. Puig. Chicago, IL: Children's Press, 1987. 32 pp. Explores the sense of sight.

Sight. Mandy Suhr. Minneapolis, MN: Carolrhoda Books, 1994. 32 pp. Explores the sense of sight.

Smell. Sue Hurwitz. New York, NY: Franklin Watts, 1998. 24 pp. Explains how the nose works.

Smell. Laurence P. Pringle. New York, NY: Benchmark Books, 2000. 32 pp. Explores the nose and how it functions.

Smell. Maria Rius, J. M. Parramon, and J. J. Puig. Chicago, IL: Children's Press, 1987. 31 pp. Explores the sense of smell.

Smell. Mandy Suhr. Minneapolis, MN: Carolrhoda Books, 1994. 32 pp. Explores the sense of smell.

Smell: The Subtle Sense. Alvin Silverstein. New York, NY: Morrow Junior Books, 1993. 90 pp. Presents the complex nature of the sense of smell.

Smelling. Kathie Billingslea Smith and Victoria Crenson. Mahwah, NJ: Troll Associates. 1988. 24 pp. Explores the sense of smell using a question and answer format.

Smelling. Sharon Gordon. New York, NY: Children's Press, 2001. 31 pp. A Rookie read-about health book.

Smelling Things. Allan Fowler. Chicago, IL: Children's Press, 1991. 31 pp. Explores the sense of smell through text and photos.

Sound and Hearing. John Farndon. New York, NY: Benchmark Books, 2001. 32 pp. Suggests experiments that explore the nature of sound.

Sounds. Terry J. Jennings. Chicago, IL: Children's Press, 1989. 34 pp. Provides an introduction to sounds and how they travel.

Stop, Look & Listen: Using your senses from head to toe. Sarah A. Williamson. Charlotte, VT: Williamson Pub. Co., 1996. 141 pp. Contains directions for over 70 activities.

Taste. Sue Hurwitz. New York, NY: Franklin Watts, 1998. 24 pp. Explains how the sense of taste works.

Taste. Laurence P. Pringle. New York, NY: Benchmark Books, 2000. 32 pp. Explains the parts of a mouth and how they function.

Taste. Maria Rius, J.M. Parramon, and J. J. Puig. New York, NY: Barron's, 1985. 31 pp. Contains an explanation of the sense of taste.

Taste. Mandy Suhr. Minneapolis, MN: Carolrhoda Books, 1994. 32 pp. Explores the sense of taste.

Tasting. Sharon Gordon. New York, NY: Children's Press, 2001. 31 pp. A Rookie read-about health book.

Tasting. Kathie Billingslea Smith and Victoria Crenson. Mahwah, NJ: Troll Associates, 1988. 24 pp. Discusses the sense of taste using a question and answer format.

Tasting Things. Allan Fowler. Chicago, IL: Children's Press, 1991. 31 pp. Provides a simple introduction to the sense of taste.

Teach Me about Listening. Joy Wilt Berry. Chicago, IL: Children's Press, 1988. 35 pp. Offers an introduction to the sense of hearing.

Teach Me about Smelling. Joy Wilt Berry. Chicago, IL: Children's Press, 1988. 34 pp. Explores the sense of smell.

Teach Me about Tasting. Joy Wilt Berry. Chicago, IL: Children's Press, 1988. 34 pp. Provides an introduction to the sense of taste.

Teach Me about Touching. Joy Wilt Berry. Chicago, IL: Children's Press, 1988. 35 pp. Offers an introduction to the sense of touch.

Tongues and Tasters. Henry Pluckrose. New York, NY: Franklin Watts, 1990. 32 pp. Explores the sense of taste in the animal kingdom, including humans.

Too Fast to See. Kim Taylor. New York, NY: Delacorte, 1991. 24 pp. Explains about motion perception.

Too Slow to See. Kim Taylor. New York, NY: Delacorte, 1991. 24 pp. Discusses motion perception.

Touch. Sue Hurwitz. New York, NY: Franklin Watts, 1998. 24 pp. Discusses skin and nerve endings.

Touch. Laurence P. Pringle. New York, NY: Benchmark Books, 1999. 32 pp. Explores the sense of touch.

Touch. Maria Rius, J. M. Parramon, and J. J. Puig. New York, NY: Barron's, 1985. 29 pp. Discusses touch and includes a detailed diagram of a section of skin.

Touch. Mandy Suhr. Minneapolis, MN: Carolrhoda Books, 1994. 32 pp. Explores the sense of touch.

Touching. Kathie Billingslea Smith and Victoria Crenson. Mahwah, NJ: Troll Associates, 1988. 23 pp. Explores the sense of touch.

Touching. Lillian Wright. Austin, TX: Raintree Steck-Vaughn, 1994. 32 pp. An introduction to the sense of touch.

Touching a Nerve: How to touch, sense and feel. Steve Parker. New York, NY: Franklin Watts, 1992. 32 pp. Discusses the sense of touch.

Touch, Taste and Smell. Steve Parker. New York, NY: Franklin Watts, 1989. 40 pp. Explores touch, taste, smell, and the bodily processes that contribute to these senses.

Touch the Poem: Poems. Arnold Adoff. New York, NY: Blue Sky Press, 2000. unpaged. A collection of poems about the sense of touch.

Touch—What do you feel? Nicholas Wood. Mahwah, NJ: Troll Associates, 1991. 32 pp. Explores the world of touch and how it works.

You Can't Smell a Flower With Your Ear: All about your senses. Joanna Cole. New York, NY: Grosset & Dunlap, 1994. 48 pp. Explores each of the senses.

You Smell: And taste and feel and see and hear. Mary Murphy. New York, NY: Dorling Kindersley, 1997. unpaged. Follows the use of the senses from taste at breakfast to hearing a bedtime story at night.

Weird, Wacky Science. Sandra Markle. New York, NY: Hyperion Paperbacks for Children, 1998. 70 pp. Presents general science facts and suggests experiments.

What Happens When You Listen? Joy Richardson. Milwaukee, WI: Gareth Stevens Pub., 1986. 32 pp. Explains how ears turn sounds into messages to the brain.

What Happens When You Look? Joy Richardson. Milwaukee, WI: Gareth Stevens Pub., 1986. 32 pp. Explains how eyes send visual information to the brain.

What's that I feel? Kate Petty and Lisa Kopper. New York, NY: Franklin Watts, 1987. 22 pp. Explores the sense of touch.

While You're Waiting for the Food to Come: A tabletop science activity book: experiments and tricks that can be done at a restaurant, the dining room table, or wherever food is served. Eric Paul Muller. New York, NY: Orchard Books, 1999. 84 pp. Explores gravity, water, and the senses.

Your Amazing Senses: 36 games, puzzles and tricks that show how your senses work. Ron and Atie van der Meer. New York, NY: Aladdin Books, 1987. 12 pp. Explores the senses and provides entertainment with the book's moveable parts.

You Won't Believe Your Eyes! Catherine O'Neill. Washington, DC: National Geographic Society, 1987. 104 pp. Explains visual illusions and the working of the eye–brain system.

Other Resources

All About the Senses. Wynnewood, PA: Schlessingr Media, 2001. 1 videocassette, 23 minutes. Discusses senses and sensations for students in grades K-4.

Ear, Eye, and Nose. Nashua, NH: Delta Education. For grades 4 and up. Durable plastic models with corresponding anatomy cards.

The Human Body Cluster. Nashua, NH: Delta Education, Inc. These titles investigate the human body systems, how they work together. Includes one on Smell, Taste, and Touch and another on Vision & Hearing.

Human Machine. David Hanson. New York, NY: Dorling Kindersley Vision, 1997. 1 videocassette, 35 minutes. Explores vital organs of humans and the instruments of the senses.

We Learn about the World. Melville, NY: Video Knowledge, Inc., 1986. 1 videocassette. Explores the senses through the investigation of size, shape, and color.

12

Exploring science through writing

Much science information is communicated through writing. A classroom of students or a curious child may go to the library to find what has already been written on a topic of interest. As children learn through observations and experimentation, they may record their own findings in journals, make charts, or prepare science papers. Writing is an important tool for a scientist.

Writing can also be a means of sharing feelings and giving pleasure to writer and reader alike. Beautiful essays and poems on a variety of nature topics are in our rich heritage of literature.

Exploring poetry can begin with the youngest children. There are many delightful finger plays and nursery rhymes that tiny tots love. Often these old favorites, half-forgotten, are stored in the back of an adult's memory and can easily be refreshed by reading some of the resource books listed at the end of this chapter.

Older children may have preferences for the types of poetry that they read or have had read to them. For example, some children like nature poems, others prefer humorous ones, while still others love to read poems about bears, cats, or other favorite animals. Some enjoy reading about the weather, the seashore, or the mountains, whereas others prefer the imaginative and fantastic.

The enjoyment that comes from listening to or reading poems sometimes leads to the desire to write.

Writing a lune

Lunes are an easy type of poem for many children to write. These poems are short and unrhymed, and unlike Haiku, do not require the counting of syllables. Lunes are three line poems, in any mood, on any topic, with three words in lines one and three, and five words in line two. For example:

Tiny raindrops fall
On the dusty street, washing
It sparkling clean.

Telling a science acrostic

An acrostic poem can tell some essentials about a science subject of interest. The following activity is an example of how an acrostic poem can be used in science.

Have the child or individuals in a class write one word vertically down the paper. Then write a line of poetry for each letter in the word. The lines need not rhyme, and they can be of any length, but they should have something to do with the subject of the poem. For example:

CRYSTAL
Clear and many-faceted
Readily made from sugar or salt
Yet looking like diamonds
Sparkling on a string
Taken from the heart of a geode
At last glittering out in the light
Letting everyone admire one of
Science's great beauties.

Using a science
"I remember" poem

An "I Remember" poem can also be used as a means of recollecting stages of science observations. The following experiment is an example of how an "I remember" poem can be used in science.

Have the child write three or more lines on a topic, with each line beginning with the phrase, I remember . . .. For example:

I remember gathering the seed in a long, dark brown pod in the park.
I remember thinking that the pods looked like those Jack might have traded his cow for in the old *Jack and the Beanstalk* story.
I remember tearing the pods apart and pulling out the dark brown seeds.
I remember planting eight seeds in a terra-cotta flower pot, and patting the soil down gently on top of each one.
I remember when the first seed broke through the earth. It was pale white, bent over, and looked like a lima bean.
I remember when the "bean" split and a tiny shoot climbed toward the sun.
I remember when the shoot grew little leaves, a miniature of the tree in the park where I had found the dark brown pod.

Many poetry books have beautiful illustrations, and there are numerous children's picture books on science topics that are written in verse.

Whether you simply enjoy reading poems together or whether you and your class or your curious child decide to write some to share your love of nature and interest in science with a relative or friend, you have happy times in store as you explore poetry together.

Science reports can be very exciting. Unfortunately, many of them do not turn out that way. Children need guidance to prepare an effective report. If a classroom of students or a single child is interested in sharing some science information, it is important to discuss ways to write interesting reports. (Chapter 14 "Exploring Science in the Library" will provide helpful hints about researching and writing reports.)

Too often a child comes home to an adult and says, "I have to write something about spiders or insects." The child then goes to the library and finds a book or goes to an encyclopedia and locates an article on the topic. Or the child may turn to a computer search engine to see what can be found on a topic. The child ends up copying the information from one spot to another and not much is learned in the process.

Clearly, to write an interesting report, one of the first requirements is that the child cares about the topic and wants to learn more about it. Even if a "generic topic" such as spiders and insects has been given for an assignment, at least the child has some choice and can decide whether to write about a tarantula or a mosquito!

A good way to approach a writing assignment is to formulate some questions. For example, if a child wants to write about a tarantula, the child might list the following questions: Where do tarantulas live? Are there different types? How big do they grow? What do they eat? Are they helpful in any way? Are they harmful in any way? Are they known for being great jumpers? Armed with a list of questions in which the child is interested, the research to prepare the science paper becomes exciting.

Next, the child needs to know that information can come from many sources. Reading about tarantulas in the encyclopedia may prove helpful, but there are sites on the Internet that will have pictures and information, too. There are also books on the topic. Maybe there are some magazine articles on the subject. A newspaper may have carried an article about a tarantula or perhaps a local pet shop carries tarantulas, and the pet shop owner is willing to be interviewed. Help the child explore different avenues of getting information.

Conducting the 'Appearance of the Pipe Cleaners from Outer Space' trick

Creative writing can easily be merged with science activities and experiments. One such activity is conducting The Appearance of the Pipe Cleaners from Outer Space trick.

It takes some time and thought to set up this activity. Choose pipe cleaners of three different colors. Make some arbitrary decisions such as: White pipe cleaners are always found in pairs and are never found on the ground. In the outdoor science area you have selected, put several pair of white pipe cleaners up in bushes, on top of a fence, hanging from a sturdy plant, and other such places. Always put two of them together.

Red pipe cleaners are loners and are always found on the ground. Place a variety of red pipe cleaners on the ground throughout the area, on rocks, in the grass, at the base of a tree, and so forth.

Blue pipe cleaners are found singly, in pairs, and in groups, but are always in shady places. Place a number of blue pipe cleaners in the area both on the ground and above it, but always in shady places.

Explain to the child or to the class that the pipe cleaners arrived from outer space during the night and are to be found in a certain area near the school room or near the house. The task is to learn as much about them as possible by observing.

Have the child or children take a note tablet and pencil to the area where they will observe and make notes. Ask them not to touch or move any of the pipe cleaners.

Singly, or in groups, have the children write what they know about the pipe cleaners based on their observations. (Children may come up with some observations that the adult didn't think of when setting up the area. These are valid, too.)

Observing a tree

Another way of getting students to use their observation skills is to ask them to choose a favorite tree and to make observations over a period of a month.

Have your curious child (or a class of students) select a tree that can be observed easily at different times of the day over a period of a month. Ask that children make at least four observations and that they write in their notebooks the date, time of observation, and everything that they noticed in and around the tree.

Sights and sounds such as blowing wind, leaf color change, budding leaves, blossoms, insects, birds, squirrels, and so forth may appear in these notations.

Writing a short story about a tree

Next, ask the child or students to use creative writing skills. Suppose that the tree they have been studying for a month could suddenly tell them a story. What would it say?

Have the child or children refer back to the notes they have taken during their observations of a single tree. Tell them they may add other details to their creative story that they may not have observed.

Have each child write a short story, in the first person, told by the tree. Ask them to imagine how a tree might "feel" to have a bird's nest in it, to have a squirrel running up and down its trunk, to have a girl climb to its top, to have a woodpecker peck at it, to have its leaves turn colors or its blossoms, fruits, or pine cones grow.

During the science/writing activities you may also need to take time to teach some specific writing skills. Making an outline, taking notes, keeping track of information for a bibliography, and learning to conduct an interview and to quote people correctly can all come into use during science writing. Chapter 14 "Exploring Science in the Library" has additional helpful hints.

Resource Books

*All Join In. Quentin Blake. Boston, MA: Little, Brown, 1991. 30 pp. Contains six 'noisy' poems.

Always Wondering: Some favorite poems of Aileen Fisher. Aileen Fisher. New York, NY: HarperCollins, 1991. 86 pp. Contains favorite poems.

*The Animal Fair: Animal verses. Compiled by Jill Bennett. New York, NY: Viking Penguin, 1990. 32 pp. Includes verses about many animals including a zoo party, the kangaroo, and the crocodile.

Anna's Summer Song. Mary Steele. New York, NY: Greenwillow Books, 1988. 30 pp. Contains a collection of poems about plants.

*Bear Hugs. Kathleen Hague. New York, NY: Henry Holt, 1989. 24 pp. Contains a collection of poems about teddy bears.

Beasts by the Bunches. A. Mifflin Lowe. New York, NY: Doubleday, 1987. 46 pp. Contains an illustrated collection of poems about animal groups such as a gaggle of geese.

Best Wishes. Cynthia Ryland. Katonah, NY: R. C. Owen, 1992. 32 pp. A writer explains how she weaves the writing process into her daily activities.

Birds, Beasts and Fishes: A selection of animal poems. Selected by Anne Carter. New York, NY: Macmillan, 1991. 64 pp. Contains poems from around the world with illustrations.

Bird Watch: A book of poetry. Jane Yolen. New York, NY: Philomel Books, 1990. 36 pp. Contains poems about birds and their activities.

Books By Kids! Helping young children create their own books. Carthage, IL: Fearon Teacher Aids, 1993. 80 pp. Contains composition exercises.

A Bookworm Who Hatched. Verna Aardema. Katonah, NY: R. C. Owen Publishers, 1992. 32 pp. Explains how one writer weaves the writing process and daily activities together.

The Brook. Alfred Tennyson. Orchard Books, 1994. 25 pp. A new illustrated version of the classic poem originally published in 1855.

Bungalow Fungalow: Poems. Pegi Deltz Shea. New York, NY: Clarion Books, 1991. 31 pp. Contains 15 poems about a summer vacation at the beach.

Cats Are Cats. Compiled by Nancy Larrick. New York, NY: Philomel Books, 1988. 80 pp. Offers a collection of 43 poems about all kinds of cats.

Celebrate America: In poetry and art. Nora Panzer, Editor. New York, NY: Hyperion Books for Children, 1994. 96 pp. A collection of poetry celebrating over 200 years of American life and history.

*A Child's Garden of Verses. Robert Louis Stevenson. San Francisco, CA: Chronicle Books, 1989. 128 pp. A new edition of a favorite book with old-fashioned pictures.

A Child's Treasury of Seaside Verse. Compiled by Mark Daniel. New York, NY: Dial Books for Young Readers, 1991. 137 pp. Contains a collection of poems by 19th and 20th century British and American poets about the sea.

*The Christmas Fox and Other Winter Poems. John Bush. New York, NY: Dial Books for Young Readers, 1989. 26 pp. Contains poems about animals and the winter season.

Click it: Computer fun writing. Lisa Trumbauer. Brookfield, CT: Millbrook Press, 2000. 32 pp. Explains how to use a word processor and suggests activities to improve sentence structure.

Cockroaches, Stinkbugs, and Other Creepy Crawlies. Christine Becker. Los Angeles, CA: Lowell House Juvenile, 1996. 64 pp. Gives drawing tips for such subjects as a dragonfly and the hercules beetle, which could be sketched in a journal.

Coconut Kind of Day: Island Poems. Lynn Joseph. New York, NY: Lothrop, Lee & Shepard Books, 1990. 30 pp. Contains poems about the Caribbean Islands.

Come on into My Tropical Garden. Grace Nichols. New York, NY: J. B. Lippincott, 1990. 38 pp. Contains poems about the people and lands of the Caribbean.

Consider the Lemming. Jeanne Steig. New York, NY: Farrar, Straus & Giroux, Inc. 1988. 48 pp. Contains a collection of humorous poems.

The Content Connection: How to integrate thinking and writing in the content areas. Hilarie N. Staton. Glenview, IL: GoodYear Books, 1991. 144 pp. Designed for use in grades 4 to 8.

Create Your Own Magazine. Barbara Taylor. New York, NY: Sterling Pub. Co., 1993. 46 pp. Provides tips on creating magazines.

Creative Nonfiction: How to live it and write it. Lee Gutkind. Chicago, IL: Chicago Review Press, 1996. 168 pp. Explains how to write nonfiction in an entertaining way.

The Creative Writing Handbook. Jay Amberg and Mark Larson. Glenview, IL: GoodYear Books, 1992. 143 pp. Useful guide to writing.

Crow Doesn't Need a Shadow, A: A guide to writing poetry from nature. Lorraine Ferra. Salt Lake City: Peregrine Smith Books, 1994. 127 pp. Hints on nature poetry writing.

Desktop Publishing: The art of communication. John Madama. Minneapolis, MN: Lerner Publications, Co., 1993. 64 pp. Explains the process of desktop publishing.

Dinosaur Dances. Jane Yolen. New York, NY: G. P. Putnam's Sons, 1990. 39 pp. Contains 17 whimsical poems.

Dinosaurs Forever. William Wise. New York, NY: Dial Books for Young Readers, 2000. unpaged. A collection of poems about dinosaurs.

Dinosaurs: Poems. Selected by Lee Bennett Hopkins. San Diego, CA: Harcourt Brace Jovanovich, 1987. 46 pp. Contains 18 poems about dinosaurs.

Earth Always Endures: Native American poems. Neil Philip. New York, NY: Viking, 1996. 93 pp. A collection of poems about such topics as birds, the wind, and the sky.

Earth Songs. Myra Cohn Livingston. New York, NY: Holiday House, 1986. 32 pp. Contains poems that pay tribute to earth.

Earth Verses and Water Rhymes. J. Patrick Lewis. New York, NY: Atheneum, 1991. 32 pp. Contains poems about our natural world.

*Eric Carle's Animals, Animals. Compiled by Laura Whipple. New York: Philomel Books, 1989. 87 pp. Contains illustrations around a collection of poems on wild and domestic animals by various authors.

Exciting Writing, Successful Speaking: Activities to make language come alive. Martin Kimeldorf. Minneapolis, MN: Free Spirit Pub., 1994, 208 pp. Contains useful exercises.

Four and Twenty Dinosaurs. Bernard Most. New York, NY: Harper & Row, 1990. 32 pp. Contains nursery rhymes in which dinosaurs have been substituted for the traditional main characters.

Getting Your Message Across. Kathlyn Gay. New York, NY: New Discovery Books, 1993. 128 pp. A guide to effective communication.

Grass Green Gallop, A: Poems. Patricia Hubbell. New York, NY: Atheneum, 1990. 48 pp. Contains poems about horses.

Hippopotamusn't and Other Animal Verses. A J. Patrick Lewis. New York, NY: Dial Books for Young Readers, 1990. 40 pp. Contains more than 30 funny animal poems.

The House of a Mouse: Poems. Aileen Fisher. New York, NY: Harper & Row, 1988. 31 pp. Contains poems about mice.

How to Read and Write Poems. Margaret Ryan. New York, NY: Franklin Watts, 1991. 63 pp. Explains some of the basic concepts of poetry and gives suggestions for beginning writers.

How to Write a Story. Kathleen C. Phillips. New York, NY: Franklin Watts, 1995. 159 pp. Gives basic tips for writing a story.

How to Write Poetry. Paul B. Janeczko. New York, NY: Scholastic, 1999. 117 pp. Gives practical advice for writing poetry.

How to Write Super School Reports. Elizabeth James and Carol Barkin. New York, NY: Beech Tree, 1998. 90 pp. Discusses all aspects of reports from choosing a topic to revision.

How to Write the Best Research Paper Ever. Elizabeth Blandford. Marion, IL: Pieces of Learning, 1998. 112 pp. Suggestions for report writing.

I Can Draw a Weeposaur and Other Dinosaurs: Poems. Eloise Greenfield. New York, NY: Greenwillow Books, 2001. unpaged. Contains poems and drawings of imaginary dinosaurs.

If the Owl Calls Again: A collection of owl poems. Selected by Myra Cohn Livingston. New York, NY: Margaret K. McElderry Books, 1990. 114 pp. Contains poems by different authors about owls.

I'm Going to Pet a Worm Today, and Other Poems. Constance Levy. New York, NY: Margaret K. McElderry Books, 1991. 38 pp. Contains 39 poems about everyday things.

Incredible Insects!: (And spiders, too). Analisa Suid. Palo Alto, CA: Monday Morning Books, 1996. 80 pp. Tips for reading writing, and speaking about insects.

In Fall. Rochelle Nielsen-Barsuhn, Jane Belk Moncure, and Eleanor Hammond. Elgin, IL: Child's World (distributed by Children's Press), 1985. 31 pp. Contains a collection of autumn poems.

Insectlopedia: Poems and paintings. Douglas Florian. San Diego, CA: Harcourt Brace, 1998. 47 pp. Contains 21 short poems about such creatures as the termite and the ladybug.

In Spring. Jane Belk Moncure. Elgin, IL: Child's World (distributed by Children's Press), 1985. 31 pp. Contains a collection of spring poems.

In Summer. Jane Belk Moncure and Aileen Fisher. Elgin, IL: Child's World (distributed by Children's Press), 1985. 31 pp. Contains a collection of poems about summer.

In Winter. Jane Belk Moncure. Elgin, IL: Child's World (distributed by Children's Press), 1985. 31 pp. Contains a collection of fifteen winter poems.

January Brings the Snow. Sara Coleridge. New York, NY: Simon & Schuster, 1987. 26 pp. Contains poems for each month of the year.

Jean Craighead George. Alice Cary. Santa Barbara, CA: Learning Works, 1996. 36 pp. Tells how an author combined her love of writing and wildlife into a successful career.

Joyful Noise: Poems for two voices. Paul Fleischman. New York, NY: Harper & Row, 1988. 44 pp. Contains poems about a variety of insects.

Kids Celebrate Nature Through Words and Pictures. Barbara Moran (Editor). Half Moon Bay, CA: 1996, 79 pp. Contains drawings, poems, reports, and essays created by children.

Kids Have All the Write Stuff: Inspiring your children to put pencil to paper. Sharon A. Edwards and Robert W. Maloy. New York, NY: Penguin Books, 1992. 3000 pp. Includes ideas for parent participation in encouraging writing.

Kids' How to Do (Almost) Everything Guide. Murray Suid, Editor. Palo Alto, CA: Monday Morning Books, 1998. 176 pp. A collection of how to articles by experts from several fields including writing.

Kids Write Right! What you need to be a writing powerhouse. Jan Venolia. Berkeley, CA: Tricycle Press, 2000. 156 pp. Suggestions for young writers.

Legends of Landforms. Carole Garbuny Vogel. Brookfield, CT: Millbrook Press, 1999. 96 pp. Includes stories created by native peoples to explain natural wonders.

Leonardo da Vinci. Diane Stanley. New York, NY: Morrow Junior Books, 1996. 46 pp. A biography that emphasizes the importance of the notebooks Leonardo da Vinci kept.

Letter from Phoenix Farm, A. Jane Yolen. Katonah, NY: R. C. Owen, 1992. 32 pp. A writer tells how she weaves the writing process into her daily life.

Locust Pocus: A book to bug you. Douglas Kaine McKelvey. New York, NY: Philomel, 2001. 32 pp. Rhyming verses about insects including termites, beetles, and bees.

The Lost Garden. Laurence Yep. Englewood Cliffs, NJ: J. Messner, 1991. 117 pp. An author explains about growing up and using his ethnic heritage in his writing.

*The Midnight Farm. Reeve Lindberg Brown. New York, NY: Dial Books for Young Readers, 1987. 25 pp. Contains poems about a farm at midnight.

Mockingbird Morning. Joanne Ryder. New York, NY: Four Winds Press, 1989. 32 pp. Contains poems around the theme of an early morning walk.

Mojave. Diane Siebert. New York, NY: Thomas Y. Crowell, 1988. 32 pp. Contains poems about the land and animals of the Mojave Desert.

New Moon. Writing: How to express yourself with passion. Flynn Berry (Editor). New York, NY: Crown Publishers, 2000. 86 pp. Explores outlets for writing, makes suggestions for writing improvement, and suggests places to get published.

The New York Public Library Kid's Guide to Research. Deborah Heiligman. New York, NY: Scholastic Reference, 1998. 124 pp. Guide on doing research.

On the Farm: Poems. Selected by Lee Bennett Hopkins. Boston, MA: Little, Brown, 1991. 32 pp. Contains poems about farm animals.

On the River ABC. Caroline Stutson. Niwot, CO: Roberts Rinehart Pub., 1993. 31 pp. An ant encounters an alphabet of wildlife while being swept downstream during a summer storm.

Outstanding Oceans! Annalisa Suid. Palto Alto, CA: Monday Morning Books, 1996. 80 pp. Gives ideas for reading, writing, and speaking about oceans.

Painless Research Projects. Rebecca Elliott and James Elliott. Hauppauge, NY: Barron's, 1998. 260 pp. Gives step-by-step instructions from choosing a topic for investigation to writing the final paper.

Painting the Sky: Writing poetry with children. Shelley Tucker. Glenview, IL: GoodYear Books, 1995. 148 pp. Tips on writing poetry with children.

A Paper Zoo: A collection of animal poems by modern American poets. Selected by Renee Karol Weiss. New York, NY: Macmillan, 1987. 38 pp. Contains poems by well-known American poets.

Poem-making: Ways to begin writing poetry. Myra Cohn Livingston. New York, NY: HarperCollins Publishers, 1991. 162 pp. An introduction to the mechanics and different types of poetry.

Pond Seasons. Sue Ann Alderson. Groundwest Books/Douglas & McIntyre: Distributed by Publishers Group West, 1997. 25 pp. Poetry about ponds.

The Princeton Review Writing Smart Junior: The art and craft of writing. Cynthia Brantley. New York, NY: Random House, 1995. 214 pp. An introduction to clear, effective writing.

Putting it in Writing: Scholastic guides. Steven Otfinoski. New York, NY: Scholastic, 1993. 144pp. Exercises and models for preparing school reports.

Rachel Carson: The wonder of nature. Catherine Reef. Frederick, MD: Twenty-First Century Books, 1992. 68 pp. Follows the life of Rachel Carson, known for her writings on the environment.

Real Toads in Imaginary Gardens: Suggestions and starting points for young creative writers. Stephen Phillip Policoff. Chicago, IL: Chicago Review Press, 1991. 191 pp. Helpful hints for working with young writers.

Ride a Cockhorse: Animal rhymes for young children. Illustrated by Jenny Williams. New York, NY: Dial Books for Young Readers, 1987. 20 pp. Contains nursery rhymes about animals.

Riddles about Baby Animals. Jacqueline A. Ball and Ann D. Hardy. Morristown, NJ: Silver Burdett Press, 1989. 30 pp. Contains rhyming riddles about baby animals.

Scholastic Rhyming Dictionary, The. Susan Young. New York, NY: Scholastic, 1994. 213 pp. An easy-to-use source of 15,000 words.

Seasons. Warabe Aska. New York, NY: Doubleday, 1990. 44 pp. Contains poems about the four seasons.

75 Creative Ways to Publish Students' Writing. Cherlyn Sunflower. New York, NY: Scholastic Professional Books, 1993. 208 pp. Discusses various student publications.

Silver Seeds: A book of nature poems. Paul Paolilli. New York, NY: Viking, 2001. unpaged. A collection of nature poetry for children.

Sit Tight, and I'll Swing You a Tail: Using and writing stories with young people. Gregory A. Denman. Portsmouth, NH: Heinemann, 1991. 184 pp. Tips for writing with children.

Smart Learning: A study skills guide for teens. William L. Christen and Thomas Murphy. Bloomington, IN: Grayson Bernard Pub., 1992. 111 pp. Gives strategies for note-taking and organizing writing.

Snow toward Evening: A year in a river valley. Selected by Josette Frank. New York, NY: Dial Books for Young Readers, 1990. 32 pp. Contains poems about nature.

Space Songs. Myra Cohn Livingston. New York, NY: Holiday House, 1988. 32 pp. Contains poems and illustrations of outer space.

Still as a Star: A book of nighttime poems. Selected by Lee Bennett Hopkins. Boston, MA: Little, Brown, 1989. 31 pp. Contains 15 poems by well-known poets.

Special Species. Barbara Moran (Editor). Half Moon Bay, CA: 1994. 88 pp. Contains drawings, poems, reports, and essays about California's native plants and animals.

A Storyteller's Story. Rafe Martin. Katonah, NY: R. C. Owen, 1992. 32 pp. A children's author explains the interweaving of life and writing.

*Tails, Claws, Fangs, and Paws: An alphabeast caper. Terry Small. New York, NY: Bantam, 1990. 32 pp. Contains a rhyming text with animals for each letter of the alphabet.

Teaching Writing: A workshop approach. Adele Fiderer. New York, NY: Scholastic Professional Books, 1993. 112 pp. Contains suggestions for exercises.

Ten-minute Editing Skill Builders. Murray I. Suid. Palo Alto, CA: Monday Morning Books, 1996. 96 pp. Quick practices for strengthening editing skills.

Ten-Minute Real World Writing. Murray I. Suid. Palo Alto, CA: Monday Morning Books, 1996. 96 pp. Gives quick activities to strengthen writing skills.

Thinking Like a Writer: A handy guide guaranteed to inspire you! Lou Willett Stanek. New York, NY: Random House, 1994. 108 pp. A guide to creative writing.

Tiger Brought Pink Lemonade, The. Patricia Hubbell. New York, NY: Atheneum, 1988. 32 pp. Contains poems about both real and fantastic animals.

Time Is the Longest Distance: An anthology of poems. Selected by Ruth Gordon. New York, NY: Harper Collins, 1991. 74 pp. Contains many poems about time.

To Be A Writer: A guide for young people who want to write and publish. Barbara Seuling. New York, NY: Twenty-First Century Books, 1997. 110 pp. Provides advice for writers.

Trees: A poem. Harry Behn. New York, NY: Henry Holt, 1992. 30 pp. Celebrates the importance of trees.

Turtle in July. Marilyn Singer. New York, NY: Macmillan, 1989. 32 pp. Consists of poems that depict animals each month of the year.

25 Activities to Connect Writing and Math. Suzette D. Freedman. New York, NY: Scholastic Professional Books, 1996. 56 pp. Contains activities designed to help student communicate mathematically.

Tyrannosaurus Was a Beast: Dinosaur poems. Jack Prelutsky. New York, NY: Greenwillow Books, 1988. 31 pp. Contains humorous poems about dinosaurs.

Up in the Air. Myra Cohn Livingston. New York, NY: Holiday House, 1989. 32 pp. Contains poems that express the feelings of being up in an airplane.

Voices on the Wind: Poems for all seasons. Selected by David Booth. New York, NY: Morrow Junior Books, 1990. 40 pp. Contains poems about the seasons.

Water Pennies and Other Poems. N. M. Bodecker. New York, NY: Margaret K. McElderry Books, 1991. 51 pp. Contains poems about several different small creatures such as snails and moths.

What Should I Write My Report On?: 400 thematic research ideas for reports. J. A. Senn. New York, NY: Scholastic Professional Books, 1993. 88 pp. Ideas for report writing.

What's Your Story? A young person's guide to writing fiction. Marion Dane Bauer. New York, NY: Clarion Books, 1992. 134 pp. Explores such facets of writing as character, plot, point of view, and dialogue.

Whiskers and Paws. Fiona Waters (Editor). New York, NY: Interlink Publishing, 1990. 29 pp. Contains poems that feature animals.

Wild Country: Outdoor poems for young people. David Lee Harrison. Honesdale, PA: Wordsong/Boyds Mills Press, 1999. 48 pp. Nature poems young people will enjoy.

Wind in the Long Grass: A collection of haiku. William J. Higginson (Editor). New York, NY: Simon & Schuster Books for Young Readers, 1991. 48 pp. Contains haiku from all over the world.

Writers Express: A handbook for young writers, thinkers and learners. Dave Kemper, Ruth Nathan and Patrick Sebranek. Burlington, WI: Write Source Educational Publishing House, 1995. 452 pp. A useful handbook.

A Writer's Notebook: Unlocking the writer within you. Ralph J. Fletcher. New York, NY: Avon Books, 1996. 128 pp. Makes suggestions for how to keep a notebook.

Write Where You Are: How to use writing to make sense of your life: A guide for teens. Caryn Mirream-Goldberg. Minneapolis, MN: Free Spirit Publishing, 1999. 155 pp. Gives exercises to help become a more competent writer.

Writing. Peggy Burns. New York, NY: Thomson Learning, 1995. 32 pp. Gives tips on the writing process.

Writing, a Fact and Fun Book. Amanda Lewis. Reading, MA: Addison-Wesley, 1992. 96 pp. Discusses the history of writing and gives tips on writing stories, journals, and articles.

The Writing Bug. Lee Bennett Hopkins. Katonah, NY: R. C. Owen Publishers, 1993, 32 pp. Explains how daily activities and the writing process can be interwoven.

Writing Journals: Activities across the curriculum. Linda Western. Glenview, IL: GoodYear Books, 1996. 138 pp. A good source of interdisciplinary activities.

Writing Math: A project-based approach. Sharon Z. Draznin. Glenview, IL: GoodYear Books, 1995. 232 pp. Provides an interdisciplinary approach.

Writing with Style. Sue Young. New York, NY: Scholastic, 1997. 143 pp. Tips for writing exciting, well-organized reports.

Other Resources

A Child's Garden of Verses. Thomas Meehan. Van Nuys, CA: Family Home Entertainment, 1993. 1 videocassette. 26 minutes. Based on the classic writing by Robert Louis Stevenson.

Holiday Poems for December. Richard Laurent (Producer). Chicago, IL: Encyclopedia Britannica Educational Corp., 1988. 1 book, 10 pp. 1 videocassette, 6 minutes. Contains eight short presentations about three December holidays including Hanukkah and Kwanza.

Johnny Appleseed. Reeve Lindberg. Westport, CT: Weston Woods, 2000. 1 videocassette, 18 minutes. A video based on the famous poem about Johnn Appleseed.

13
Exploring science through art

Some people believe the worlds of "science" and "art" to be poles apart. This is not the case. The trained eye of the artist and the scientist may be very similar in their search for details and in their appreciation of symmetry, shape, color, texture, and pattern. Art can certainly be a means of deepening science appreciation and of communicating information.

An interested child or a class of students going on a hike to observe the autumn colors of changing leaves, to identify songbirds, to study different types of conifers, or to locate native wildflowers might do well to take along artists' sketch pads. For example, a careful sketch of a leaf, showing a bulging down on one side of the leaf base, will help the student know that she has identified a hackberry rather than an American Elm. Noting that the cones are prickly and sketching a bundle of only two pine needles that are 1 inch to 3 inches long will help identify whether a tree is a lodgepole or tarmac pine. Noticing the rusty orange patch on the back of a bird will separate the gray-headed junco from the slate-colored junco.

You may think that sketching is unnecessary, that you will remember what you see, but after a full day of hiking and observing, adults as well as children forget many details and become confused when trying to recall specifics. The sketch pad is very helpful to the young scientist, even if it's only a tiny spiral pad that slips easily into a pocket.

In addition to sketching in the field, there are opportunities of presenting science material in charts and graphs that can also involve artistic skills. Many a science fair project would be more impressive if, in addition to the thoughtful hypothesis, data, and demonstrations, the presentation of the print materials was pleasing to the eye, well-spaced, and easy to read.

Making a nature mobile

Sometimes, gathering material from fields and woods can be used in an interesting arts and crafts project. A nature mobile provides an artistic means of studying balance. On a hike to an area where it is acceptable to gather objects, have children collect small items that are of interest to them. Such objects might include a small pine cone, a branch with a piece of lichen on it, a colorful rock, a seed pod, a dried leaf, and any other small objects that may have pleased them and attracted their attention. Then provide time to construct the mobile.

Tie a short loop of sturdy, black carpet thread to the middle of a piece of wire that is about 8 inches long. This loop will hold up your finished mobile. Tie three other pieces of black carpet thread from the wire and let them hang down. Use the middle thread of these three pieces to tie to another piece of wire that is about 10 inches long. Tie two more pieces of carpet thread to this 10-inch wire.

Hook your loop on something so that the wires and strings hang down. Experiment with tying different objects to the four strings that hang down. You are trying to keep them in balance so that the two wires will hang in a horizontal position. For example, a twig with a piece of lichen on it may balance with a long, milkweed pod. A small pine cone may balance with a weathered piece of tree root.

The finished mobiles may hang from a light fixture, a plant hook, classroom ceiling lights, or any other place where there is enough room for them to hang.

Creating leaf bookmarks

If you can gather small, colorful leaves from a nature hike in the fall, you can use these materials to make interesting and decorative bookmarks.

Gather a half dozen small, colorful autumn leaves. Arrange them on a strip of waxed paper that is 3 inches wide by 8 inches long.

Put another piece of waxed paper over the leaf arrangement.

Use an ironing board and a moderately hot iron to melt the edges of the two pieces of waxed paper together. As you iron, go close to the leaf, but not over it with the iron.

Trim the bookmark and it is ready for use. You may want to use a punch to make a hole near the top where you can add a braided yarn string.

Assembling a shell garden

If, instead of living near the woods, you spend time exploring along the seashore, you can use shells that you gather for a variety of interesting art/science projects.

Take a walk along the beach to collect large clam shells. Also gather other pretty small shells, pieces of dried seaweed, and bits of driftwood.

Use the large shell for the base of your garden. Put a layer of clay into the shell. Press into the clay the objects that you gathered to make a miniature seascape garden. The driftwood will resemble a small tree. The seaweed will look like plant life. Sand dollars, shells, and other items you find will add to the scene.

You might want to cover the clay ground with a thin layer of sand so that it resembles the beach.

Inviting parents or friends to come to a science fair to see a classroom display of projects could involve designing an artistic, personalized invitation. You might include an original sketch of a tree, flower, or mountain on the front of the invitation. The invitations can be photocopies, or individually hand-crafted with a leaf or fern print on the front.

Making a fern print

Take a small fern leaf and press it overnight between two sheets of blotting paper.

Cut and fold paper to the size you wish for your finished invitation.

Place the pressed fern on the front of the invitation. Use an old toothbrush dipped into paint for your paint brush. Rub the toothbrush filled with paint over a fine mesh screen held about 6 inches above the fern. It will splatter the paint all around the area not covered by the fern. (You can splatter with more than one color if you wish.)

Carefully lift up the fern and you have the outline of the fern on your invitation. Because the paint will splatter beyond the invitation, be sure to cover the surface on which you are working to allow for easy clean up, and have the child wear a paint shirt to protect his clothes.

Even though you may immediately see ways in which "arts and crafts" can play a role in science studies, you may still shudder and maintain you can't do anything the least bit artistic. This is simply not true. While it's a fact that not everyone is a great painter, a fabulous quilter, or an accomplished sketcher, it is a rare individual indeed who does not have some skill that will be useful in arts and crafts.

Can you trace your hand? Fold a piece of paper? Take a photo? Sew on a button? Glue a pine cone? Cut out an airplane wing? If so, there are crafts you can do and that you can help children to do successfully!

Folding paper can yield interesting craft projects of many kinds. There are numerous books on making paper airplanes that can challenge the youngest to oldest reader.

Experimenting with paper airplanes

Take a wooden clothespin. Cut the wing for an airplane from lightweight cardboard. Decorate the wing with your favorite designs or paint it a bright color.

Slide the decorated airplane wing into the clothespin and wedge it into place with a toothpick or bits of cardboard. Have fun seeing how far it will glide. Experiment with different lengths and widths of the wing.

There are many books on folding lightweight paper airplanes. If you are studying aerodynamics, you might want to hold a paper airplane day. Give students time to try out a variety of designs. Number the planes so that you can keep simple but accurate records. Then go outside with a stop watch and tape measure. Clock to see how long and how far different planes will glide.

Creating shadow portraits

Shadows are often a topic of science study, and they are very intriguing to students. You may conduct a series of experiments using a sundial to measure time (see Chapter 7 "Exploring Astronomy"). Perhaps you will measure the shadow of an object placed in the same spot at different times of the day. This interest in studying shadows in science might lead you to want to do shadow portraits as an art project.

Shadow portraits are both easy and fun to make. Tape a piece of white construction paper to the wall. Have the student sit in a chair in front of the paper with one shoulder toward the paper.

Shine a bright light on the subject so that a sharp shadow of her silhouette falls on the paper. Turn off the other lights in the room. Trace the shadow onto the paper.

Then put a piece of black construction paper behind the white sheet on which you've drawn the outline. Cut through both sheets of paper. You will now have a black silhouette that can be signed, dated, and framed. It makes a great gift for a child to give a special friend or relative!

Children often are quicker than adults to use one idea as a springboard for another. Encourage these far-ranging artistic explorations. Providing the time, materials, and a place to work may be the adult's main contribution to the arts and crafts projects.

And let's face it—arts and crafts can be messy. It's a good idea to have some boxes where basic supplies are kept. A sturdy cardboard box could hold such items as scissors, ruler, needles and thread, stapler, gummed tape, paste, glue, tape measure, and any other pertinent material. Putting balls of yarn in another box with a lid, punching a number of holes in the lid, and threading the yarn out through the holes, puts a variety of colored yarns into availability without a tangle of knots. Yet another box may be home for ribbons, buttons, pine cones, nut cups, corks, walnut shells, and other small objects.

Depending upon the extent to which you want to be involved in arts and crafts, a box where large paper can be stored flat may also prove helpful. You might purchase a package of 12 x 18-inch colored construction paper and store the sheets in the paper box along with pieces of cardboard and packages of crepe paper. Tempera paints, brushes, and magic markers are also useful supplies to have on hand.

Some adults and children enjoy working with clay. Although many fine ceramics require baking in a kiln and special glazes, there are also simple clay crafts to make objects such as coil pots decorated with tempera paint and filled with dried wild flowers. Modeling clay can be used over and over to form and reform wild animals or zoo animals.

Taking a trip to the zoo

Give each child a lump of modeling clay. Invite the student to model a favorite zoo animal. Remind students that it works best to pull the legs, arms, trunks, and head out from the lump of clay rather than making little clay pieces and trying to stick them to the body.

Allow time for experimentation. Have magazine pictures of various zoo animals posted so that the child or class of students can look at them as they attempt their models.

Then make a zoo using shoe boxes, straws, and clay animals. Cut a "window" in the lid of a shoe box, about 1 inch from the edge on all sides.

Turn the shoebox on its side, and put the clay animal into the shoe box. Use striped plastic straws to make bars for the cage. Cut the straws so that they are 1 inch taller than the shoebox. Flatten the ends of the straws and tape them at the top and bottom at 2-inch intervals in front of the clay animals.

Put the lid back on the box and tape the lid in place. Make several, place them in a row, and you'll have a zoo.

You, or a child close to you, may be especially interested in photography, film strip making, or video recording. Some resources are listed at the end of this chapter that may be helpful in expanding on these artistic hobbies.

Today we also find a lot of "wearable art." You may want to use pens with washable inks or experiment with knots and dyes to create a fabulous T-shirt. This can be done in celebration of completing a hike or a camping trip and the art can depict a favorite nature scene.

If having lots of arts and crafts supplies on hand sounds disheartening to you, don't despair! Many of the resources listed require items that can commonly be found around the house, such as egg cartons, clothes pins, empty food containers, toothpicks, popcorn, and the like. Teachers can send home a list of wanted materials and have families donate supplies. Other projects require things that can be found on a hike in the woods, such as the mobile previously described that is made of twigs, pods, and leaves. Remember that arts and crafts can be as simple or as complicated as you want.

Using art to communicate science learnings is an effective and interdisciplinary approach to learning.

Resource Books

Adventures in Art: Art and craft experiences for 7–11 year olds. Susan Milord. Charlotte, VT: Williamson Publishing Company, 1990. 158 pp. Contains historical information and 100 activities involving printmaking, wearable art, portraiture, and sculpture.

African Animals in Origami. John Montroll. New York, NY: Dover Publications, 1991. 159 pp. Shows African animals created using origami.

Aircraft. Patricia Walsh. Chicago, IL: Heinemann Library, 2001. 32 pp. Provides instructions for drawing planes and helicopters.

*Alphabet Animals. Charles Sullivan. New York, NY: Ruzzoli International Pub., 1991. 56 pp. An A,B,C using paintings, sculpture, and photographs.

Amazing Animals. Penny King and Clare Roundhill. Crystal Lake, IL: Rigby Interactive Library, 1997. 29 pp. Gives directions for creating collages that feature animals.

Animals. Ting Morris. New York, NY: Franklin Watts, 1993. 32 pp. Gives instructions using craft techniques for creating animals from readily available materials.

Animals Observed: A look at animals in art. Dorcas MacClintock. New York, NY: Scribner, 1993. 56 pp. Shows animals depicted in drawings, paintings, and sculpture.

Animals: Through the eyes of artists. Wendy Richardson. Chicago, IL: Children's Press, 1989. 48 pp. Shows pictures of animals by notable artists.

Art From Rocks and Shells: With projects using pebbles, feathers, flotsam, and jetsam. Gillian Chapman and Pam Robson. New York, NY: Thomson Learning, 1995. 32 pp. Gives directions for making simple handicrafts.

Art From Sand and Earth: With projects using clay, plaster, and natural fibers. Gillian Chapman. Austin, TX: Raintree Steck-Vaughn, 1997. 32 pp. Gives instructions for making items such as a clay whistle and rock carvings.

Art From Wood: With projects using branches, leaves, and seeds. Gillian Chapman. New York, NY: Thomson Learning, 1995. 32 pp. Nature craft instruction.

The Art of Construction: Projects and principles for beginning engineers and architects. Mario George Salvadori. Chicago, IL: Chicago Review Press, 1990. 149 pp. Explains how to build models using home materials.

At the Zoo. Editors of *Better Homes and Gardens.* Des Moines, IA: Meredith Corp., 1989. 32 pp. Offers ideas for zoo handicrafts.

Autumn. Ruth Thomson. New York, NY: Franklin Watts, 1989. 32 pp. Presents arts and crafts that are based on the theme of autumn.

Balloon Sculpturing for Beginners. Bruce Fife. Bellaire, TX: Java Publishing Co., 1988. (Unpaged.) Contains easy-to-follow directions for making animals and other items from balloons.

Bats, Butterflies, and Bugs. St. Clair Adams Sullivan. Boston, MA: Little, Brown, 1990. 79 pp. Includes instructions for making toys that look like bats, butterflies, and bugs.

Capturing Nature: The writings and art of John James Audubon. Peter Roop and Connie Roop (Editors). New York, NY: Walker, 1993. 39 pp. Gives an account of the life and work of this nineteenth-century naturalist.

Cards. Clare Beaton. New York, NY: Warwick Press, 1990. 24 pp. Gives step-by-step instructions for making a variety of greeting cards.

Child's Play: 200 instant crafts and activities for preschoolers. Leslie Hamilton. New York, NY: Crown Publishers, 1989. Unpaged. Contains a collection of crafts, games, and activities.

Clayworks: Colorful crafts around the world. Virginia Fowler. New York, NY: Prentice-Hall Books for Young Readers, 1987. 150 pp. Gives instructions on making clay objects based on cultures both ancient and modern.

Colors. Philip Yenawine. New York, NY: Delacorte, 1991. 22 pp. Uses examples to examine the element of color and how it helps to convey feelings in art.

Color Zoo. Lois Ehlert. New York, NY: J. B. Lippincott, 1989. 28 pp. When placed on top of one another, the colors and shapes in the book illustrate animal faces.

Craft Painting Fun. Carolyn Davis. Tustin, CA: Walter Foster Publishing, 1991. 63 pp. Describes painting craft objects.

Crafts For Kids Who Are Wild about Deserts. Kathy Ross. Brookfield, CT: Millbrook Press, 1998. 48 pp. Gives instructions for 20 desert-related projects including making an egg-carton rattlesnake.

Crafts for Kids Who Are Wild about Dinosaurs. Kathy Ross. Brookfield, CT: Millbrook Press, 1997. 47 pp. Among directions for crafts in this book is instruction on how to make a triceratops ring-toss game.

Crafts for Kids Who Are Wild about Insects. Kathy Ross. Brookfield, CT: Millbrook Press, 1997. 48 pp. Contains instructions for 20 simple insect crafts.

Crafts for Kids Who Are Wild about Oceans. Kathy Ross. Brookfield, CT: Millbrook Press, 1998. 48 pp. Describes crafts, toys, and decorations made from common household materials.

Crafts for Kids Who Are Wild about Outer Space. Kathy Ross. Brookfield, CT: Millbrook Press, 1997. 47 pp. Contains directions for 20 projects such as making a planet mobile and space helmet.

Crafts for Kids Who Are Wild about Polar Life. Kathy Ross. Brookfield, CT: Millbrook Press, 1998. 48 pp. Contains directions for 20 projects including making a walrus mask and a harp seal puppet.

Crafts for Kids Who Are Wild about Rain Forests. Kathy Ross. Brookfield, Ct: Millbrook Press, 1997. 48 pp. Contains directions for 20 simple craft projects.

Crafts for Kids Who Are Wild about The Wild. Kathy Ross. Brookfield, CT: Millbrook Press, 1999. 176 pp. Contains directions for 75 projects including some that involve polar animals, insects, and reptiles.

*Creative Egg Carton Crafts. Nancy McClure and Janis Rhodes. Carthage, IL: Good Apple, 1991. 64 pp. Describes how to turn egg cartons into dinosaurs and caterpillars.

Creative Food Box Crafts. Nancy Giles. Carthage, IL: Good Apple, 1991. 64 pp. Contains ideas for making simple gifts and musical instruments for children from preschool to second grade.

Dinosaurs. Nina Kidd. Los Angeles, CA: Lowell House Juvenile, 1992. 63 pp. Teaches techniques for drawing dinosaurs.

Draw! Kim Solga. Cincinnati, OH: North Light Books, 1991. 48 pp. Discusses basic art principles and techniques.

Draw Desert Animals. D. C. DuBosque. Columbus, NC: Peel Productions, 1997. 63 pp. Gives step-by-step directions for drawing animals of the desert.

Draw, Design and Paint: Projects designed to foster individual expression in the visual arts. Jan Barry. Carthage, IL: Good Apple, 1990. 140 pp. Contains art projects in a fun-filled activity book format.

Draw! Dinosaurs. D. C. DuBosque. Molalla, OR: Peel Productions, 1993. 78 pp. Explains a variety of drawing techniques.

Draw 50 Birds. Lee J. Ames. New York, NY: Doubleday, 1996. Unpaged. Explains techniques for drawing birds.

Draw 50 Cats. Lee J. Ames. Garden City, NY: Doubleday, 1986. 60 pp. Shows how to draw domestic and wild cats.

Draw 50 Creepy Crawlies. Lee J. Ames with Ray Burns. New York, NY: Doubleday, 1991. 62 pp. Shows how to draw insects and spiders.

Draw 50 Endangered Animals. Lee J. Ames. New York, NY: Main Street Doubleday, 1993. 60 pp. Teaches drawing techniques.

Draw 50 Flowers, Trees, and Other Plants. Lee J. Ames. New York, NY: Doubleday, 1994, Unpaged. Shows techniques for drawing flowers.

Draw 50 Sharks, Whales, and Other Sea Creatures. Lee J. Ames with Warren Budd. New York, NY: Doubleday, 1989. 64 pp. Shows how to draw sea creatures step-by-step.

Draw Fifty Monsters, Creeps, Superheroes, Demons, Dragons, Nerds, Dirts, Ghouls, Giants, Vampires, Zombies, Other Curiosa. Lee J. Ames. New York, NY: Doubleday, 1986. 64 pp. Shows how to draw many strange creatures.

Draw! Grassland Animals. D. C. DuBosque. Columbus, NC: Peel Productions, 1996. 63 pp. Gives step-by-step instructions for drawing grassland animals.

Drawing. Anthony Hodge. New York, NY: Gloucester Press, 1991. 32 pp. Gives a variety of opportunities for projects involving line, light, shadow, and personal expression.

Drawing. Hilary Devonshire. New York, NY: Franklin Watts, 1990. 48 pp. Provides an introduction to drawing techniques.

Drawing Dinosaurs. Jerome Goyallon. New York, NY: Sterling Pub. Co., 1993. 80 pp. Gives instructions on how to reproduce drawings by hand and by computer.

Drawing Prehistoric Animals. Jerome Goyallan. New York, NY: Sterling Pub. Co., 1995. 80 pp. Explains drawing techniques.

Draw Insects. Doug DuBosque. Columbus, NC: Peel Productions, 1988. 63 pp. Step-by-step directions for drawing such creatures as bumblebees and yellow jackets.

Draw! Rainforest Animals. D.C. DuBosque. Molalla, OR: Peel Productions, 1994. 63 pp. A step-by-step guide to drawing animals.

Draw Real Animals! Lee Hammond. Cincinnati, OH: North Light Books, 1996. 80 pp. A step-by-step guide to drawing animals.

Easy-to-Make Water Toys that Really Work. Mary Blocksma. Englewood Cliffs, NJ: Prentice-Hall, 1985. 62 pp. Shows how to make toys that move in the water.

*EcoArt! Earth friendly art & craft experiences for 3- to 9-year-olds. Laurie Carlson. Charlotte, VT: Williamson Pub., 1993. 157 pp. Using recycled materials for art projects.

Experimenting with Art! 25 Easy-to-Teach Lessons in Design and Color: For grades 3–6. Shirley Kay Wolfersperger. Glenview, IL: GoodYear Books, 1992. 90 pp. Lessons in design.

Exploring Science through Art. Phyllis Katz. New York, NY: Franklin Watts, 1990. 63 pp. Suggests art projects using motifs from nature.

Fifty Nifty Dinosaurs to Draw. Bryan Baugh. Los Angeles, CA: Lowell House Juvenile, 1999. 96 pp. Gives directions for drawing dinosaurs.

Flowers. Peggy Roalf. New York, NY: Hyperion Books for Children, 1993. 48 pp. Explores 2000 years of art history.

Fold Your Own Dinosaurs. Campbell Morris. New York, NY: Perigee Books, 1993. 47 pp. Gives instructions for making 12 dinosaurs.

Free and Inexpensive Arts & Crafts to Make and Use. Nancee McClure. Carthage, IL: Good Apple, 1987. 112 pp. Contains at least 10 craft ideas for each month of the year.

Geology Crafts for Kids: 50 nifty projects to explore the marvels of planet earth. Alan H. Anderson. New York, NY: Sterling Pub. Co., 1996. 144 pp. Contains directions for a variety of crafts and projects.

Good Earth Art: Environmental art for kids. Mary Ann F. Kohl. Bellingham, WA: Bright Ring Pub., 1991. 223 pp. Contains directions for over 200 projects emphasizing recycling and natural materials.

*Handicrafts. Rosie Wermert. New York, NY: Random House, 1989. 32 pp. Contains 20 fun and easy projects you can make by tracing your hand.

Hand-Print Animal Art. Carolyn Carreiro. Charlotte, VT: Williamson Pub. Co., 1997. 144 pp. Gives directions for painting birds, wildlife, and sea creatures using fingers and hands as models.

*Hand-Shaped Gifts: Handmade gifts from little fingers. Diane Ronica. Carthage, IL: Good Apple, 1991. 138 pp. Consists of crafts for children from preschool through fourth grade using hand shapes as the basis for crafts.

Holiday Patterns. Jean Warren. Everett, WA: Warren Publishing, 1991. 237 pp. Contains a guide to a variety of handicrafts including paper work and decorations.

How to Draw and Paint the Outdoors. Moira Butterfield. Edison, NJ: Chartwell Books, 1994. 93 pp. Explains various painting techniques.

How to Draw Birds. Barbara Soloff-Levy. Mahwah, NJ: Watermill Press, 1987. 32 pp. Shows how to draw birds of prey, water birds, and exotics.

How to Draw Endangered Animals. Molly Walsh. Mahwah, NJ: Troll Communications, 1999. 32 pp. Directions for drawing endangered animals.

How to Draw Flowers. Janice Kinnealy. Mahwah, NJ: Watermill Press, 1987. 32 pp. Gives simple instructions for drawing flowers.

How to Draw Forest Animals. Barbara Soloff-Levy. Mahwah, NJ: Watermill Press, 1985. 32 pp. Gives step-by-step instructions for drawing animals.

How to Draw Sea Creatures. Barbara Soloff-Levy. Mahwah, NJ: Watermill Press, 1987. 32 pp. Shows how to draw fish and other creatures that live in or near the ocean.

How to Draw Zoo Animals. Jocelyn Schrieber. Mahwah, NJ: Watermill Press, 1988. 32 pp. Suggests different drawing techniques.

How to Draw Pets. Linda Murray. Mahwah, NJ: Watermill Press, 1995. 32 pp. Presents drawing techniques.

How to Make Your Own Video. Perry Schwartz. Minneapolis, MN: Lerner Publications Co., 1991. 72 pp. Tells how to use a camcorder and make home videos.

I Like Painting. Melanie and Chris Rice. New York, NY: Warwick Press, 1989. 44 pp. Provides an introduction to painting.

*Kids Create: Arts and crafts experiences for 3- to 9-year-olds. Laurie Carlson. Charlotte, VT: Williamson Publishing Company, 1990. 158 pp. Contains easy-to-follow instructions for 150 different craft activities.

Kidvid: Fun-damentals of video instruction. Kaye Black. Tucson, AZ: Zephyr Press, 1989. 96 pp. Shows children in nine lessons the basics of video production.

Lines. Philip Yenawine. New York, NY: Delacorte, 1991. 22 pp. Isolates the element of lines and examines how lines are central to art.

Lotions, Potions, and Slime: Mudpies and more! Nancy Blakey. Berkeley, CA: Tricycle Press, 1996. 110 pp. Gives directions for creative activities involving science, art, cooking, and concocting.

Make Prints. Kim Solga. Cincinnati, OH: North Light Books, 1991. 48 pp. Gives step-by-step instructions for printing.

Make Your Own Animated Movies and Videotapes: Film and video techniques from the yellow ball workshop. Yvonne Anderson. Boston, MA: Little, Brown, 1991. 176 pp. Contains instructions for making animated movies, operating a camera, and synchronizing sound.

Making Cool Crafts & Awesome Art: A kids' treasure trove of fabulous fun. Roberta Gould. Charlotte, VT: Williamson Pub., 1998. 160 pp. Suggests activities using music, cooking, storytelling, and nature.

Making Toys and Gifts. Stefan Lemke. Chicago, IL: Children's Press, 1991. 80 pp. Gives instructions for many projects for kids who are age 8 or older.

Masks. Clare Beston. New York, NY: Warwick Press, 1990. 24 pp. Gives instructions in how to make masks.

Monarch Magic! Butterfly activities and nature discoveries. Lynn M. Rosenblatt. Charlotte, VT: Williamson Pub. Co., 1998. 96 pp. Through text and photos describes monarch butterflies and includes suggestions for crafts and related activities.

More than Sixty Projects for Kids. Pat Roberts. Scotts Valley, CA: Mark Publishing, 1991. Unpaged. Contains a guide for parents/teachers to assist kids in making 60 projects.

My Camera: At the zoo. Janet Perry Marshall. Boston, MA: Little, Brown, 1989. 30 pp. Offers a crazy look at animals, first seen askew, and then clearly through a camera lens.

My First Camera Book. Anne Kostick. New York, NY: Workman Pub., 1989. 51 pp. Gives tips for taking pictures, making postcards, and so on, through a story of how Teddy Bear Bialosky shares.

The Natural World: Through the eyes of artists. Wendy Richardson. Chicago, IL: Children's Press, 1991. 48 pp. Filled with paintings by notable artists that reflect feelings about nature.

Nature in Art. Anthea Peppin. Brookfield, CT: Millbrook Press, 1992. 48 pp. Shows different techniques used by artists to depict nature.

Near the Sea: A Portfolio of paintings. Jim Arnosky. New York, NY: Lothrop, Lee & Shepard Books, 1990. 28 pp. Shows a variety of nature scenes of beaches, rocks, water, gulls, and fish.

1-2-3 Draw Dinosaurs and Other Prehistoric Animals. Freddie Levin. Columbus, NC: Peel Productions, 2001. 64 pp. Gives instructions for drawing dinosaurs.

Origami Dinosaurs. Yoshihide Momotani. New York, NY: Kodansha International, 1993. 64 pp. Shows how to make 14 dinosaurs out of folded paper.

Origami Sea Life. John Montroll. New York, NY: Dover Publications, 1991. 256 pp. Shows how to make fishes from folded paper..

Out of this World. Penny King and Clare Roundhill. Crystal Lake, IL: Rigby Interactive Library, 1997. 29 pp. Step-by-step suggestions for making space-related objects using common household items.

Painting. Anthony Hodge. New York, NY: Gloucester Press, 1991. 32 pp. Describes painting techniques and explores portraiture, still life, landscapes, and surrealism.

Paper. Erica Burt. Vero Beach, FL: Rourke Enterprises. 1990. 32 pp. Gives instructions for student projects using paper or cardboard that involve either folding, curling, cutting, or tearing.

Paper Sculpture. John Lancaster. New York, NY: Franklin Watts, 1989. 48 pp. Presents projects involving tearing, folding, and weaving paper.

Photography. David Cumming. Austin, TX: Steck-Vaughn Library, 1989. 48 pp. Gives an overview of British and American photography as art and discusses photography as a career.

Photography. Duncan Fraser. New York, NY: Bookwright Press, 1987. 32 pp. Tells how cameras were invented, their history, and how to choose a camera.

Photography: Take your best shot. Terri Morgan and Samuel Thaker. Minneapolis, MN: Lerner Publications Co., 1991. 72 pp. Gives practical techniques for photography and discusses dark-room skills.

Playing with Plasticine. Barbara Reid. New York, NY: Morrow Junior Books, 1988. 95 pp. Explains how to turn plasticine into flat pictures and three-dimensional objects.

Prehistoric Origami: Dinosaurs and other creatures. John Montroll. New York, NY: Dover, 1989. 143 pp. Explains how origami can be used to make prehistoric animals.

Prehistoric Rock Art. Marinella Terzi. Chicago, IL: Children's Press, 1992. 33 pp. Shows paintings and engravings made on rock by early people.

Prehistory from Australopithecus to Mammoth Hunters. Jean-Jacques Barloy. New York, NY: Barron's, 1986. 78 pp. Discusses the art of prehistoric people.

Projects for Autumn and Holiday Activities. Joan Jones. Ada, OK: Garrett Educational Corp., 1989. 31 pp. Contains autumn arts and crafts projects.

Redoute: The man who painted flowers. Carolyn Croell. New York, NY: Putnams, 1996, 40 pp. A look at flowers in art.

Science Arts: Discovering science through art experiences. Mary Ann F. Kohl. Bellingham, WA: Bright Ring, 1993. 142 pp. Filled with creative activities.

The Secret Garden: Dawn to dusk in the astonishing hidden world of the garden. David Bodanis. New York, NY: Simon & Schuster, 1992. 187 pp. Shows life in a garden including ants, caterpillars, and roots.

Shapes. Philip Yenawine. New York, NY: Delacorte, 1991. 22 pp. Isolates shape as an aspect of art, and explains the visual ideas that can be conveyed by use of shapes.

Sketching Outdoors in Autumn. Jim Arnosky. New York, NY: Lothrop, Lee & Shepard Books, 1988. 48 pp. Contains ideas for outdoor fall sketching.

Sketching Outdoors in Spring. Jim Arnosky. New York, NY: Lothrop, Lee & Shepard Books, 1987. 48 pp. Contains ideas for outdoor spring sketching.

Sketching Outdoors in Summer. Jim Arnosky. New York, NY: Lothrop, Lee & Shepard Books, 1988. 47 pp. Catches in sketches the various aspects of nature.

Sketching Outdoors in Winter. Jim Arnosky. New York, NY: Lothrop, Lee & Shepard Books, 1988. 48 pp. Catches in sketches the various aspects of nature.

Snow Shapes: A read-and-do book. Judith Moffatt. New York, NY: Scholastic, 2000. Unpaged. Gives instructions for crafts related to winter.

Television and Video. Ian Graham. New York, NY: Gloucester Press, 1991. 32 pp. Tells how TV and various pieces of video equipment work.

Terrific Paper Toys. Elmer Richard Churchill. New York, NY: Sterling Publishing Co., 1991. 128 pp. Tells how to make items from paper such as toys, hats, puppets, and flowers.

Things to Do. Editors of Time-Life Books. Alexandria, VA: Time-Life Books, 1989. 87 pp. Contains projects to make such as seashell mobiles, paper airplanes, peanut puppets, and other fun items in a question/answer format.

Time Out Together: A month-by-month guide to activities to enjoy with your children. Jan Brennan. Little Rock, AS: August House Publishers, 1990. 173 pp. Contains directions for creative activities.

Treasured Time with Your Toddler: A monthly guide to activities. Jan Brennan. Little Rock, AS: August House Publishers, 1991. 189 pp. Contains directions for a variety of creative activities.

You Can Make It! You Can do It! One hundred-one E-Z holiday craft activities for children. Ann Peaslee and Julien Kille. Union City, CA: Heian International, 1990. 128 pp. Explains how to make a variety of holiday decorations and crafts, and includes creative activities.

VCRs. Carolyn E. Cooper. New York, NY: Franklin Watts, 1987. 96 pp. Explains how to use video tape and VCRs with instructions for audio dubbing.

Water: Through the eyes of artists. Wendy Richardson and Jack Richardson. Chicago, IL: Children's Press, 1989. 48 pp. Shows different water scenes as they have been depicted by notable artists.

Whales, Sharks, and Other Sea Creatures. Nina Kidd. Los Angeles, CA: Lowell House
     Juvenile, 1992. 63 pp. Gives step-by-step instructions for drawing sea creatures.
Wild Animals. Nina Kidd. Los Angeles, CA: Lowell House Juvenile, 1992. 63 pp.
     Teaches drawing techniques.
Wildflowers, A garden primer. Anne Velghe. New York, NY: Farrar, Straus, Giroux,
     1994. Unpaged. An introduction to 30+ garden and meadow wildflowers.
Wood. Graham Carrick. Vero Beach, FL: Rourke Enterprises, 1990. 32 pp. Explains a
     variety of projects made by constructing with wood or by carving.

Other Resources

These magazines might prove useful to consult for craft ideas: *Crafts 'N Things,
American Craft, Ceramics Monthly, Art News,* and *School Arts.*

Art Lessons for Children: Easy watercolor techniques. Donna Hugh. Fallbook, CA:
     Coyote Creek Productions, 1991. 1 videocassette, 50 min. Shows lessons on how
     to draw flowers and the desert.
The Big A: Getting ideas. Lincoln, NE: Great Plains National Instructional Television
     Library, 1987. 1 videocassette, 15 minutes. Includes a visit to the zoo to draw an-
     imals and a visit to see a sculptor and a painter to learn how artists get ideas.
E-Z Bread Dough Sculpture. Torrance, CA: Morris Video, 1988. 1 video-cassette, 20
     minutes. For ages 4–8, shows bread dough craft.
Let's Create Art Activities. Parsippany, NJ: Let's Create, Inc., 1990. 1 videocassette, 45
     min. For ages 5–10, shows a variety of projects, including capturing nature in
     waxed paper.
Making Playthings. Los Angeles, CA: Concord Video, 1985. 1 videocassette, 60 min-
     utes. Shows how to make playthings for kids.
Nature Art. Edwardsburg, MI: Meuninck's Media Methods, 1996. 1 videocassette, 60
     minutes. Shows how to grow wildflowers and an herb garden and suggests
     flower-related art projects.
Painting without a Brush. Julie Abowitt. Torrance, CA: Morris Video, 1988. 1 video-
     cassette, 20 minutes. For ages 4–8, shows how to paint with string, sponges, and
     other objects.

14

Exploring science in the library

Exploring science through using the libraries in your area can be exciting for you and your curious child or class of students. Depending on the age of the children involved and your location, you may have several areas to explore: your public library, a school library, special libraries such as historical libraries, and college or university libraries. Thanks to the advances in computerizing information and its availability through networking systems, you may be able to access the holdings of libraries far distant from you. Resources may then be borrowed through interlibrary loan.

Learning library skills is much like developing any other skills. You need to ask questions, gain knowledge, and try out what you've learned. Because libraries have undergone so much change in recent years, many older adults are learning new library skills at the same time that children are learning them.

One part of learning to use a library is to familiarize yourself with the print holdings. These consist of fiction and nonfiction, reference materials, magazines, and vertical files. Most librarians would be pleased to show you and a child or a group of students around the library and help you feel comfortable there. If you don't have a library card, they will give you application forms and help you become a fully certified user!

Although you can check out materials for a special child on your adult library card or may be able to check out a collection of books on a teacher's card, getting children library cards of their own is a good idea. It is an important step in making the child an independent library user with responsibilities for the care and return of books.

Often the library's fiction holdings are simply housed alphabetically by author. Your special child may have "favorite" authors already. You can find that section of the shelf and check out a new book by that author or an old favorite to read again and enjoy.

Sometimes the child knows the name of a book but can't remember who wrote it. This is a good way to introduce the child to a computerized card catalog. Although it may be faster and simpler for the adult to enter the information, if the child is old enough, the adult can do a good deal to enhance the child's skills in independent learning by letting the child enter the data herself.

Each library system is different, but usually the computerized catalog will have a screen displayed that asks you to indicate whether you want to search for information by title, author, or topic. Once you make that choice, you type in needed information, and the computer screen will show a listing of holdings with call numbers so that you can locate a particular book. Sometimes a second screen shows more detailed information about a book, including the publisher, copyright date, number of pages contained in the book, and perhaps a brief description.

If your local library has not computerized its holdings, you will be able to assist the child by using the card catalogue, which has card sections alphabetically listed by title and by author.

Building this skill of locating a favorite title or author in the card catalogue or on the computer gives the child confidence in his or her ability to effectively use the library. It opens up a vast area of research information available to the knowledgeable seeker.

For the older child, the library is an excellent place for learning independent research skills. Perhaps there is a school assignment in which the child needs to write a "report." Perhaps in Scouts the child has been asked to investigate a topic. Maybe something on the television news or an article in the newspaper has suggested a subject that the child wants to independently study further. The child may have seen a bug, bird, or butterfly and wants to know what type it was. Any of these events may suggest that an exploration to the library is in order to investigate its nonfiction holdings.

Narrowing a topic and doing a materials search are learned skills, and the earlier a child begins developing these skills, the better. For example, if your child is a fourth grader and is asked to prepare a report on marine life, simply typing in "oceans" as the descriptor for a computer word search may yield a huge number or books. Typing "killer whale juvenile" may greatly shorten the list to a more appropriate number.

Many libraries use the Dewey Decimal Classification System. Although it is not necessary to learn the complete set of numbers, knowing the general classifications can be very useful.

Dewey decimal classification system

General Works	000–099
Philosophy	100–199
Religion	200–299
Social Studies	300–399
Language	400–499
Pure Science	500–599
Technology	600–699
The Arts	700–799
Literature	800–899
History	900–999
Biography	B
Fiction	FIC

Other libraries use the Library of Congress Classification. This is an alphabetical rather than a numerical system. For example: A = General Works; B = Philosophy, Religion; C= History and auxiliary sciences. If your library uses this system, you will want to help your child become familiar with it.

Depending on the topic, there are useful specialized dictionaries and encyclopedias. A few examples of specialized advanced reference books that can be very helpful when researching a specific topic are: *Dictionary of American History; What People Wore: A Visual History of Dress from Ancient Times to Twentieth-Century America; The New World Encyclopedia of Cooking; The Encyclopedia of Literary Characters; The Encyclopedia of Sports;* and *The Milton Cross New Encyclopedia of the Great*

Composers & Their Music. Your librarian can tell you if there is a special index of magazines on your topic such as the Art Index or National Geographic Index.

An interested child may want to locate and read interesting biographies of important scientific pioneers or learn more about possible careers in some science field. Perhaps a child wants to contrast the scientific views of early peoples as expressed through their legends and stories with modern day scientific discoveries. A library is a great place to explore all these topics.

If a child is interested in some aspect of local history, you may want to consult your library's newspaper section. Once a newspaper is no longer current, the pages may be copied on microfilm and stored in that form. Your curious child will need to learn how to access past issues and to find out if the paper provides an index by subject for each year. *The New York Times* is available from 1851 to the present on microfilm. It has an excellent index to help you find specific information.

Computers allow students to access current and past issues of newspaper and to copy and print articles from these papers. Various search engines are possible to help locate these Internet sites.

Other reference materials can be helpful, too. Rather than copy out a section from an encyclopedia and rewrite it in one's own words, a child may find more exciting and useful material in a current magazine such as *Oceans, Sea Frontiers,* or *Sea Secrets.* Each library has its own system for identifying magazines and periodicals, with back issues circulating more freely than current issues. Your child may need to use a *Reader's Guide to Periodical Literature* or a computer program such as *Un Cover* to locate appropriate magazines.

Your librarian may also have a vertical file of clippings and pamphlets on some topics of general interest that you can use. If your library does not have the information you need, the librarian can help you request it through an interlibrary loan.

Many libraries also house nonprint materials such as video and audio cassette tapes. These may be recordings of favorite books, popular movies, documentaries, and nature shows. One or more of these might provide information on a topic of interest.

Making a library treasure hunt map: Step One

Once you have reviewed all aspects of the library with your child, why not plan a "treasure hunt" in three steps to check on your curious child's progress in learning to make the most of a library?

Step one involves the treasure map. Prepare a floor plan map of your most frequently used local library. Ask your child to put the numeral of the items listed below in the correct location on the floor plan.

1 Card catalog (or computer access catalog)
2 Periodicals
3 Vertical or pamphlet files
4 Fiction
5 Biography
6 Special reference sections
7 Nonprint materials
8 Rest rooms and drinking fountain
9 Copy machines

When you feel your child is familiar enough with the local library and its contents, quiz him on more detailed components of the library

Giving a library treasure hunt quiz: Step two

Step two is a check for understanding of the Dewey Decimal Classification System that many libraries use. This short quiz will help assess your curious child's familiarity with it.

In what numbered section would you browse for books on the following topics:

Sculpture?	Ans. 700s
History of the United States?	Ans. 900s
A book on General Grant?	Ans. B
A chemistry book?	Ans. 500s
A collection of poetry?	Ans. 800s

Lastly, set up a fun treasure hunt game at the library, taking in all the information and details learned by the child with an ultimate treasure hidden amongst the stacks!

Finding a library treasure: Step three

Now you're ready for the final phase of the library treasure hunt. You can pick any books you wish for this final step, including your "treasure" tucked in the page of the final book.

Using the card catalogue or the computerized listing of books, ask your special child to locate a book by author or title.

You may substitute any books that you wish, but here is an example of how to do it:

1 Find any book written by Beverly Cleary.
2 Find a copy of *Ranger Rick Magazine.*
3 Find a book of poetry by Shel Silverstein.
4 Find a nonfiction book about whales.
5 Find a copy of *A Wrinkle in Time.*

The prize might be a ribbon attached to a small paper treasure chest with the child's name written on it and the words "I know how to find treasures in the library!" This can be tucked in the final book you include in the above treasure hunt.

Finding the information is only part of the independent research process. Often the child will want to share the information learned with others. Then it is necessary to decide on a format, organization, and presentation. Many of the references that follow will help a child make decisions about the sharing of information. Since a good library puts so much information at the child's disposal, your exploration here is tremendously important and deserves special care and attention.

Another chapter of this book that might be of interest while you are doing your library exploration is Chapter 12 "Exploring Science through Writing."

Resource Books

Activities Almanac: Daily ideas for library media lessons. H. Thomas Walker and Paula K. Montgomery (Editors). Santa Barbara, CA: ABC-CLIO,1990. 283 pp. Contains ideas compiled from a monthly column of School Library Media Activities.

Armando Asked, "Why?" Jay Hulbert and Sid Kantor. Milwaukee, MN: Raintree Childrens Books, 1990. 23 pp. Tells a story of how a family is too busy to take their child to the library, but after being introduced to the librarian, with help he is able to find the books he wants.

Art in Chemistry; Chemistry in Art. Barbara R. Greenberg and Dianne Patterson. Englewood, CO: Teacher Ideas Press, 1998. 280 pp. Contains 60 suggested activities to integrate chemistry and art.

Basic Library Skills (2nd ed.). Carolyn Wolf and Richard Wolf. Jefferson, NC: McFarland. 1986. 141 pp. Provides an orientation to the library.

Basic Media Skills through Games. Irene Wood Bell and Jeanne E. Weickert. Littleton, CO: Libraries Unlimited, 1985. 2 volumes. Contains games to teach library skills.

Benjamin Banneker: American mathematician and astronomer. Bobbie Hinman. Philadelphia, PA: Chelsea House Pub., 2000, 79 pp. A biography of this 18th century African American detailing some of his achievements.

The Big Book of Nature Projects. Len Rubenstein. New York, NY: Thames and Hudson, 1997. 128 pp. Contains suggestions for 53 experiments, field trips, and activities.

Books and Libraries. Jack Knowlton. New York, NY: HarperCollins, 1991. 36 pp. Gives a history of books and libraries.

Brainstorms and Blueprints: Teaching library research as a thinking process. Barbara K. Stripling and Judy M. Pitts. Littleton, CO: Libraries Unlimited, 1988. 181 pp. Provides useful reinforcement of library skills for secondary students.

Check It Out! The book about libraries. Gail Gibbons. San Diego, CA: Harcourt Brace Jovanovich, 1985. 32 pp. Offers an introduction to libraries.

Choose, Use, Enjoy, Share: Library media skills for the gifted child. Phyllis B. Leonard. Littleton, CO: Libraries Unlimited, 1985. 153 pp. Contains information skills.

Circuits, Shocks, and Lightning. Celeste Peters. Austin, TX: Raintree Steck-Vaughn, 2000. 48 pp. Projects and experiments related to electricity.

Complete Handbook of Science Fair Projects. Julianne Blair Bochinski. New York, NY: John Wiley, 1996. 221 pp. Suggests numerous projects for science investigation.

Computers All Around Us. Jim Drake. Des Plaines, IL: Heinemann Library, 1999. 32 pp. Explains the ways computers are used for different purposes.

Cooperative Research and Reports. Murray I. Suid. Palo Alto, CA: Monday Morning Books, 1993. 128 pp. Suggests a way for students in grades 2–6 to work together on reports.

Cruising through Research. John D. Volkman, Englewood, CO: Teacher Ideas Press, 1998. 207 pp. Contains reproducible lessons on teaching research techniques.

A Day in the Life of a Librarian. David Paige. Mahwah, NJ: Troll Associates, 1985. 32 pp. Follows a typical day of the chief librarian in an Illinois public library.

The Day the Sky Split Apart: Investigating a cosmic mystery. Roy A. Gallant. New York, NY: Atheneum Books for Young Readers, 1995. 156 pp. Tells about the Tunguska meteorite.

Decision Points: Boolean logic for computer users and beginning online searchers. Janaye M. Houghton and Robert S. Houghton. Englewood, CO: Libraries Unlimited, 1999. 155 pp. A useful tool in teaching on-line searching for students grade 5 and up.

Developing Library Skills. Ester Lakritz. Carthage, IL: Good Apple, 1989. 108 pp. Consists of an activity book on library skills for students in grades 4–8.

Dewey and the Decimals: Learning games & activities. Paige Taylor and Kent and Susan Brinkmeyer. Fort Atkinson, WI: Upstart Books, 2001. 80 pp. Presents skills to allow students to access information.

Dewey Dynamite. Sherry R. Crow. Book Lore (distributed by ECS Learning Systems, Inc.), 1987. San Antonio, TX: 32 pp. Presents research skills activities for each Dewey discipline for individuals or groups of children in grades 3–6.

Fantastic Flying Fun with Science: Science you can fly, spin, launch, and ride. Edwin J.C. Sobey. New York, NY: McGraw Hill, 2000. 90 pp. Suggests aerodynamics projects.

57 Games to Play in the Library or Classroom. Carol K. Lee and Fay Edwards. Fort Atkinson, WI: Upstart Books, 1997. 128 pp. Games to strengthen library skills.

Find It Fast: How to uncover expert information on any subject. Robert I. Berkman. New York, NY: Perennial Library, 1990. 330 pp. Tells how to find library information.

Find It! The inside story at your library. Claire McInerney. Minneapolis. MN: Lerner Publications Co., 1989. 55 pp. Describes the resources to be found in a library and tells how to use them.

The First-Timer's Guide to Book Reports. Danna Voth. Los Angeles, CA: Lowell House Juvenile, 2000. 64 pp. Explains how students can share what they discover through writing a report.

Folklore and Legends of the Universe. Isaac Asimov. Milwaukee, WI: Gareth Stevens Pub. 1995. 32 pp. Presents scientific beliefs of ancient peoples.

A Guide to Independent Research. Phyllis J. Perry (Editor). Mobile, AL: GCT Publications, 1990. 66 pp. Explains how to use the tools of library research.

Handling Data. David Kirkby. Crystal Lake, IL: Rigby Interactive Library, 1986. 48 pp. Introduces elementary statistical concepts.

Help Is on the Way for—Library Skills. Marilyn Berry. Chicago, IL: Children's Press, 1985. 46 pp. Provides an orientation to library skills.

Help! My Science Project is Due Tomorrow! Easy experiments you can do overnight. Janice Pratt VanCleave. New York, NY: John Wiley& Sons, 2002. 122 pp. Suggestions for quick projects.

Holidays: Lessons and activities for library media centers. H. Thomas Walker and Paula K. Montgomery (Editors). Santa Barbara, CA: ABC-CLIO, 1990. 285 pp. Contains selected activities that were published in *School Library* monthly magazine.

How to Become an Expert: Discover, research, and build a project in your chosen field. Maurice Gibbons. Tucson, AZ: Zephyr Press, 1991. 136 pp. Consists of a step-by-step guide on investigating research problems. With reproducible pages.

How to Write Super School Reports. Elizabeth James and Carol Barkin. New York, NY: Lothrop, Lee & Shepard Books, 1998. 90 pp. Explains how to choose a topic, find material, and organize the information into a report.

How to Write Terrific Book Reports. Elizabeth James. New York, NY: Lothrop, Lee & Shepard Books, 1998. 80 pp. Discusses how to write effective reports.

Hypermedia as a Student Tool: A guide for teachers. Marianne G. Handler and Ann S. Dana. Englewood, CO: Teacher Ideas Press, 1998. 360 pp. Explains how to use the World Wide Web as a research tool.

I Can Be a Librarian. Carol Green. Chicago, IL: Children's Press, 1988. 29 pp. Describes different types of libraries and the work of librarians.

Inventing, Inventions, and Inventors. Jerry D. Flack. Englewood, CO: Teacher Ideas Press, 1989. 148 pp. Suggests clever activities for students.

The Inventive Mind in Science. Christine Ebert and Edward S. Ebert, II. Englewood, CO: Teacher Ideas Press, 1998. 241 pp. Discusses creativity.

I've Got Your Number. Jane Tesh. Fort Atkinson, WI: Upstart Books, 1989. 4 pp. This short comic makes a good give-away to teach the Dewey Decimal Classification.

Kidsource: Science fair handbook. Donna Voth. Los Angeles, CA: Lowell House Juvenile, 1998. 112 pp. Discusses choosing and planning a project.

Know It All: Resource book for kids, The. Patricia R. Peterson. Tucson, AZ: Zephyr Press, 1989. 144 pp. Provides a valuable resource to improve independent learning skills, used much like a dictionary, with simple definitions, examples, and illustrations.

Learning About Books & Libraries: A gold mine of games. Carol K. Lee and Janet Langford. Fort Atkinson, WI: Upstart Books, 2000. 95 pp. Contains games designed to strengthen library skills.

Let's Go to the Library. Lisl Weil. New York, NY: Holiday House, 1992. 32 pp. Gives a brief history of libraries and describes what goes on in a library.

Librarians. Dee Ready. Mankato, MN: Bridgestone Books, 1998. 24 pp. Explains the daily work of a librarian.

Librarians A to Z. Jean Johnson. New York, NY: Walker and Company, 1988. 48 pp. Uses the letters of the alphabet to introduce the work of librarians.

The Librarian's Quick Guide to Internet Resources, 2nd Edition. Jenny Semenza. Fort Atkinson, WI: 2001. 94 pp. Gives quick access to resources by title, authority, and subject.

The Librarian Who Measured the Earth. Kathryn Lasky. Boston, MA: Little, Brown, 1994. 48 pp. Describes the life and work of Eratosthenes.

Library Lessons for Grades 7–9, Revised Edition. Arden Druce. Lanham, MD: Scarecrow Press, 1996.

Library Media Skills: Strategies for instructing primary students. Alice R. Seaver. Littleton, CO: Libraries Unlimited, 1991. 147 pp. Contains resources for teaching information gathering skills.

The Library of Congress. Gail Sakurai. New York, NY: Children's Press, 1998. 30 pp. Discusses the history of the Library of Congress.

Library: Your teammate. Philly Murtha. Mankato, MN: Creative Education, 1985. 32 pp. Offers a teenage orientation to the library.

The Life Stories of Stars. Roy A. Gallant. New York, NY: Benchmark Books, 2000. 80 pp. Describes what was believed in the past about the stars and the sun and contrasts it with what we know today.

Magnets and Sparks. Wendy Madgwick. Austin, TX: Raintree Steck-Vaughn, 1999. 32 pp. Suggests investigations with magnets and electricity.

Making Magnificent Machines: Fun with math, science, and engineering. Carol McBride. Tucson, AZ: Zephyr Press, 2000. 117 pp. Gives instructions for 17 mechanical projects.

*Mostly at the Library. Ruth Shaw Radlaver. New York, NY: Simon & Schuster Books for Young Readers, 1988. 32 pp. Tells a story of how a father and a 4-year-old check out 10 books from the library.

The Mysteries of Research. Sharron Cohen. Fort Atkinson, WI: Upstart Books, 1996. 135 pp. Teaches the use of basic reference books by solving mysteries.

New York Public Library Amazing Mythology: A book of answers for kids. Brendan January. New York, NY: John Wiley & Sons, 2000. 168 pp. Gives questions and answers about myths from many countries.

The New York Public Library Kids' Guide to Research. Deborah Heiligman. New York, NY: Scholastic Reference, 1998. 134 pp. Provides guidance on doing research.

The Night Rainbow. Barbara Juster Esbensen. New York, NY: Orchard Books, 2000. Unpaged. This collection of poems is based on ancient legends about the northern lights.

99 Jumpstarts to Research: Topic Guides for Finding Information on Current Issues. Peggy J. Whitley, Catherine Olson, and Susan Goodwin. Englewood, CO: Libraries Unlimited, 2001. 235 pp. Pin-points topics and suggests online databases and reference books for secondary students.

*Once Inside the Library. Barbara A. Huff. Boston, MA: Little, Brown, 1990. 32 pp. Tells a story in verse of the joys of books and reading.

100 First-Prize Make-it-Yourself Science Fair Projects. Glen Vecchione. New York, NY: Sterling Pub. Co., 1999. 208 pp. Suggests projects for science fairs.

On Line Searching in the Curriculum: A teaching guide for library/media specialists and teachers. Beverly Hunter and Erica K. Lodish. Santa Barbara, CA: ABC-CLIO, 1989. 219 pp. Tells how to do on-line library searches.

Pardon Me, But Your References Are Showing! 2nd Edition. Teddy Meister. Fort
  Atkinson, WI: Upstart Books, 1996. 48 pp. Suggests mini-projects to introduce
  students to using library resources.
Practical Steps to the Research Process for Elementary School. Deborah B. Stanley.
  Englewood, CO: Libraries Unlimited, 2001. 280 pp. Simplifies teaching the re-
  search process.
Practical Steps to the Research Process for Middle School. Deborah B. Stanley. Englewood, CO: Libraries Unlimited, 2001. 239 pp. Hands-on lessons designed to
  teach students the research process.
The Preschooler & the Library. Ann D. Carlson. Lanham, MD: Scarecrow Press, 1991.
Putting It In Writing. Steve Otfinski. New York, NY: Scholastic Reference, 1993. 144
  pp. Gives models as examples of reports.
*Ready-to-use Library Skills Games: Reproducible activities for building location and
  literature skills.* Ruth V. Snoddon. West Nyack, NY: Center for Applied Research
  in Education, 1987. 185 pp. Presents the reader with a variety of games to teach
  library skills.
Reference Puzzles and Word Games for Grades 7-12. Carol Smallwood. Jefferson,
  NC: McFarland, 1991. 190 pp. Contains a list of library activities.
The Research Book of the Fifty States. Nancy Polette. Book Lore (distributed by ECS
  Learning Systems, Inc.) 1991. San Antonio, TX: 32 pp. Offers research activities
  for students in grades 4–7 that can be applied to any state.
Researching Events. Maity Schrecengost. Fort Atkinson, WI: Upstart Books, 1998. 32
  pp. Explains tools best used to research important events.
Researching Issues. Maity Schrecengost. Fort Atkinson, WI: Upstart Books, 2001. 35
  pp. For grades 5–9, introduces the best tools for research and explains the
  process of writing effective papers.
Researching People. Maity Schrecengost. Fort Atkinson, WI: Upstart Books, 2001. 32
  pp. Explains how to carry out effective research on famous people.
Research It! Write It! A step-by-step guide to research and writing. 2nd edition. Di-
  ana Barnett. Fort Atkinson, WI: Upstart Books, 1997. 32 pp. A handbook on cur-
  rent research practices including using the Internet.
Research Made Easy: A guide for students and writers. Robert D. Matzen. New York, NY:
  Bantam Books, 1987. 248 pp. Provides an introduction to doing library research.
Research to Write. Maity Schrecengost. Fort Atkinson, WI: Upstart Books, 1994. 52 pp.
  For students in grades 3–6, teaches how to organize and present research reports.
Savy Student's Guide to Library Research. Judith M. Pask and Robert J. Kovac. West
  Lafayette, IN: Purdue University, 1990. 84 pp. Gives an orientation to the library
  for college students.
School Library Program in the Curriculum, The. Selected by Ken Haycock. Littleton,
  CO: Libraries Unlimited, 1990. 169 pp. Contains selected articles.
Science in Ancient China. George Beshore. New York, NY: Franklin Watts, 1998. 63 pp.
  Presents the achievements in many fields including astronomy of ancient China..
Science in Ancient Egypt. Geraldine Woods. New York, NY: Franklin Watts, 1998. 64
  pp. Discusses some of the scientific achievements of ancient Egypt.
Science in Colonial America. Brendan January. New York, NY: Franklin Watts, 1999.
  64 pp. Discusses the scientific contributions of early Americans in many fields,
  including astronomy.

Science of the Early Americas. Geraldine Woods. New York, NY: Franklin Watts, 1999. 64 pp. Describes the scientific accomplishments of Native Americans in many different fields such as astronomy.

Science Project Ideas about Air. Robert Gardner. Springfield, NJ: Enslow Publishers, 1997. 96 pp. Examines the properties of air.

Scientific Goofs: Adventures Along the Crooked Trail to Truth. Billy Aronson. 1994. 90 pp. Serendipity in science.

Search: A research guide for science fairs and independent study. Connie Wolfe. Tucson, AZ: Zephyr Press, 1988. 94 pp. Simplifies organization of research.

So You Have to Write a Term Paper! Nancy Everhart. New York, NY: Franklin Watts, 1987. 124 pp. Explains term paper writing through the steps of library research, note taking, making a rough draft, and editing.

Spring Science Projects. John Williams. Parsippany, NJ: Julian Messner, 1997. 30 pp. Suggests various projects and experiments suitable for springtime.

Super Science Projects About Weather and Natural Forces. Lorraine Jones. New York, NY: Rosen Pub. Group's Rosen Central, 2000. 48 pp. Suggests a variety of research projects.

Tales of the Shimmering Sky: Ten global folktales with activities. Susan Milord. Charlotte, VT: Williamson Pub., 1996. 128 pp. Gives folktales, background information, and suggests activities related to early beliefs about the heavenly bodies.

Teen Resources on the Web: A guide for librarians, parents, and teachers. Mimi Mandel. Fort Atkinson, WI: Upstart Books, 2000. 120 pp. Among others, provides tips for effective web searches.

The Thoughtful Researcher: Teaching the research process to middle school students. Virginia Rankin. Englewood, CO: Libraries Unlimited, 1999. 211 pp. Learning activities are presented to help students learn research skills.

Time. Andrew Haslam. Chicago, IL: World Book/Two-Can, 1996. 48 pp. Suggests projects that explore the mysteries of time and how it is measured.

Tracking the Facts: How to develop research skills. Claire McInerney. Minneapolis, MN: Lerner Publications Co., 1990. 64 pp. Explains how to do public library computer searches.

Turning Kids on to Research: The power of motivation. Ruth V. Small and Marilyn P. Arnone. Englewood, CO: Libraries Unlimited, 2000. 199 pp. Ways to motivate students and teach them information skills.

*A *Visit to the Library*. Sylvia Root Tester. Chicago, IL: Children's Press, 1985. 31 pp. Tells of how a group of children visits the library to see a puppet show, hear a story, and check out books.,

Wading the World Wide Web: Internet activities for beginners. Keith Kyker. Englewood, CO: Teacher Ideas Press, 1998. 210 pp. Gives step-by-step instructions for investigating using the computer.

What You Need to Know about Developing Study Skills, Taking Notes and Tests, Using Dictionaries, and Libraries. Marcia J. Coman and Kathy L. Heavers. Lincolnwood, IL: National Textbook Co., 1991. 91 pp. Discusses ways to develop study skills.

Winter Science Projects. John Williams. Parsippany, NJ: Julian Messner, 1997. 30 pp. Suggests various projects and experiments appropriate for winter study.

Word for Word I. Susan Hovis and Bonnie Domin. Tucson, AZ: Zephyr Press, 1988. 80 pp. Contains 10 units of activities that combine creative thinking and research skills.

Word for Word II. Susan Hovis and Bonnie Domin. Tucson, AZ: Zephyr Press, 1990. 80 pp. Contains 10 units of activities that combine creative thinking and research skills.

The World At Your Fingertips: Learning Research and Internet Skills. Heidi Kay & Karen Delvecchio. Fort Atkinson, WI: 2001. 80 pp. Teaches how to use a variety of research methods and techniques.

Write It! A Guide for Research. 2nd Edition. Betty Bankhead, Janet Nichols, and Dawn P. Vaughn. Englewood, CO: Libraries Unlimited, 1999. 56 pp. Step-by-step guide to the research process.

Writing with Style. Sue Young. New York, NY: Scholastic, 1997. 143 pp. Gives tips for writing exciting reports.

Other Resources

How My Library Grew by Dinah. Bronx, NY: H. W. Wilson, 1990. 1 videocassette. Neither Dinah nor her teddy bear have ever visited a library before until one is built down the street.

How to Use the Library. Mark Schaeffer. Bronx, NY: H. W. Wilson, 1989. 1 videocassette, 20 minutes. Explains basic research and how to use the periodical index.

Internet Searching Skills. Wynnewood, PA: Schlessinger Media, 1998. 1 videocassette, 23 minutes. Shows step-by-step strategies for using the Internet in doing research for students in grade 5 and up.

Glossary

acid Any one of a class of substances that is sour in taste, soluble in water, and will redden litmus.

aerate To combine or charge with gas.

aerodynamics The branch of dynamics that deals with the motion of air and other gases and the forces acting on bodies that move through the air.

altitude The vertical elevation of an object above a given level, such as sea level.

aluminum sulfate A colorless salt made by treating bauxite with sulfuric acid, commonly used for such things as purifying water or sizing paper.

aquarium A tank of water in which living aquatic plants and animals are kept.

astronomy The science that deals with celestial bodies such as the moon, planets, and stars.

azimuth An arc of the horizon measured clockwise between a fixed point on the horizon and the vertical circle passing through the center of an object.

baffle A circular, domed plate that hangs loosely above a bird feeder, preventing squirrels from getting to the seeds in the feeder.

barometer An instrument used to measure the weight or force of air distributed over the surface of the earth.

base A compound, such as lime or ammonia, that reacts with acids to form salts.

Big Dipper A constellation of stars, called *Ursa Major*, that resembles a drinking cup with a long handle.

bleaching Making white or lighter in color.

botany The science that deals with plant life.

calcite Calcium carbonate that is crystallized in hexagonal form.

call numbers The numbers assigned by an established system to books in a library collection so that they can be located on the shelves.

card catalogue A catalogue, with information entered on cards, which contain data about the title, author, and subject for all the holdings in a library collection.

carnivorous Meat-eating. The name given to designate those plants and animals that eat flesh.

cartography The art of making charts or maps.

Cassiopeia A constellation of stars found not far from *Polaris* that looks like a "W" in the sky.

chemical reaction The result or change made by combining two or more chemicals.

chemistry The science that deals with the composition of substances and the changes that they undergo.

chlorophyll The green coloring visible in leaves.

classify To organize by some established system.

climate The average condition of the weather in a place over a period of years, including information such as temperature and rainfall.

comet A luminous heavenly body, usually with a long tail, following an orbit around the sun.

compass A device for determining directions by means of a magnetic needle swinging on a free pivot and pointing to magnetic north.

conduction Transmitting heat or electricity by means of a conductor.

conductor A substance capable of transmitting electricity or heat.

constellation Any one of a number of groups of fixed stars.

crystals Bodies formed by chemical elements or compounds solidifying so that they have symmetrically arranged plane surfaces.

cyclometer An instrument for recording the revolutions of a bicycle wheel to measure the distance traveled.

Cygnus Group One of a number of fixed star constellations, which includes the bright star, Deneb, and which looks like a swan with outspread wings.

declination The angle that the magnetic compass needle makes with the geographical meridian.

dense Compact or having its parts tightly packed together.

density The quantity of anything per unit of volume.

Dewey Decimal Classification System A system used by libraries to group their holdings into large general and then more specific categories.

Dipper Group The constellations of fixed stars that contain both the Big and Little Dippers.

Draco Group The constellation of fixed stars that resemble the shape of a dragon in the sky.

drainage layer Often, a layer of gravel placed beneath the soil of a potted plant to allow water to drain away from the roots.

electricity One of the fundamental quantities in nature consisting of elementary particles called electrons and protons that gives rise to a field of force.

emulsion An oily mass in suspension in a watery liquid.

energy Power, efficiently and forcibly exerted, capable of performing work.

ethology The study of animal behaviors.

fossil Any trace of a plant or animal from past geological ages that has been preserved.

friction The resistance of motion between two bodies in contact.

geography The collective, natural features of an area.

geology The science that studies the history of the earth and its life, especially as recorded in rocks.

gravitation The phenomenon that two material bodies, if free to move, will be accelerated toward each other.

habitat The natural location where a plant or animal normally lives.

hand lens A magnifying glass that is held in the hand.

hardness test A test that determines the hardness of a substance by its ability to scratch the surface of another substance.

hydroponics The growing of plants with roots in a solution instead of in soil.

illusion A misleading image presented to the vision.

International Date Line The 180th meridian, which marks the point where one day ends and another begins.

ion An electrically charged atom or group of atoms.

kindling temperature The temperature at which a substance will ignite and burn.

latitude The angular distance on a meridian measured in degrees north and south from the equator.

light The essential condition of vision, the opposite of darkness, the emanation from a light-giving body.

Little Dipper A constellation of fixed stars, called *Ursa Minor,* located near the Big Dipper, and resembling a cup with a long handle.

longitude The portion of the equator, intersected between the meridian of a given place and the prime meridian, expressed in degrees.

lunar eclipse The shrouding of light, caused by the moon's entering the earth's shadow. A lunar eclipse occurs when the Earth is between the moon and the sun.

lune A three-line poem that contains three words in lines 1 and 3 and five words in line 2.

magnesium sulfate A compound of magnesium, sulfur, and oxygen, known as Epsom salts.

magnetic north The direction indicated by the north-seeking pole of the horizontal magnetic needle.

magnetism A property of the molecules of certain substances, such as iron, that can attract other nonmagnetic substances.

meridian The highest point attained by a heavenly body.

meteor A celestial body that enters the Earth's atmosphere with great speed, light, and heat generated by the resistance of the air.

meteorite A stony or metallic body that has fallen to Earth from outer space.

mineral Any chemical element or compound occurring naturally as a product of inorganic processes.

nerve cell A small mass of protoplasm making up the bands of tissue that connect parts of the nervous system with other organs and which conducts impulses.

new moon The phase of the moon when its dark side is facing the Earth. In this phase, the moon will appear invisible or as a thin, curved sliver.

northern lights Ionization of atmospheric atoms due to activity of the sun, producing a luminous phenomenon consisting of streamers of light in the sky. The northern lights are best seen in polar regions at night. Also called the *aurora borealis*.

odometer An instrument that measures distance traveled.

optics The science dealing with light; its genesis and propagation, the effects it suffers and produces, and other phenomena such as vision.

Orion Group A constellation of fixed stars resembling a hunter wearing a belt and followed by a dog.

oxidation The state of being oxidized.

oxidize To combine with oxygen.

oxygen An element occurring in the atmosphere as an odorless, tasteless, colorless gas.

paleontology The science that deals with the life of past geological periods.

Pegasus Group A constellation of fixed stars that resembles a winged horse.

physics The branch of knowledge that deals with the physical world and its phenomena.

planetarium A facility using projections on a ceiling to display the movements of celestial bodies.

Polar Group The constellation of stars around the Pole Star or North Star.

Polaris The name given to the North Star, found in the constellation known as the Little Dipper.

prime meridian An imaginary vertical line that runs from the north to the south poles, and from which degrees of longitude are measured. The commonly accepted prime meridian is Greenwich, England.

protractor An instrument used for measuring angles on paper.

radio waves The transmission and reception of signals by means of electrical waves without a connecting wire.

radium An intensely radioactive metallic element.

radius The distance from the center of a circle to the outside edge.

reaction A chemical transformation or change.

receptors A group of cells that receive stimuli.

reflection The return of light or sound waves from surfaces.

refraction The deflection of light from a straight path in passing from one medium to another.

salinity The degree of saltiness.

satellite An attendant body, revolving around a larger one.

Scorpio Group A constellation of fixed stars that resembles a scorpion in the sky.

sense organ An organ specialized to receive certain stimuli.

silver sulfide A combination of silver and sulfur commonly called "tarnish" or the dark stain that appears on silverware.

spatial Pertaining to space.

specimen A sample, or one of a number, designed to show something about the quality of the whole.

spore A reproductive body produced by plants.

stalactite A deposit of calcium carbonate hanging from the roof or sides of a cave.

stalagmite A deposit of calcium carbonate formed on the floor of a cave.

stimulus Any agent or environmental change capable of influencing the activity of living protoplasm. Plural stimuli.

suet feeder A bird feeder where pieces of suet, or fat, are placed for birds to eat.

sun dial An instrument to show the time of day by the shadow of its style, or *gnomon*.

terrarium An enclosure filled with earth for keeping or raising plants or animals indoors.

topography The configuration of a surface, including such features as its relief, and the position of streams and lakes.

transpiration The giving off of vapor from the surface of green plants.

true north The direction of the north pole from anywhere on earth.

vivarium An enclosure for keeping or raising plants or animals indoors.

volume Space that is occupied and measured by cubic units.

zenith The point of the heavens that is directly above the observer.

Index

About the author

Phyllis J. Perry is an award-winning author of over 40 nonfiction books for librarians, teachers, parents, and children. She has over 30 years experience as an elementary school teacher and administrator and has worked as an instructional design specialist, director of talented and gifted education, and has served in teacher training and supervision.

Dr. Perry earned her doctorate degree from the University of Colorado, specializing in curriculum and instruction, and did her undergraduate work at the University of California, Berkeley. She has won the Governor's Award for Excellence in Education and the Distinguished Leadership Award for her contributions to education. She is a three-time recipient of the Top Hand Award from the Colorado Authors' League for best published work in a year.

Dr. Perry lives in Boulder, Colorado with her husband, David.

About the
illustrator

Debra Ellinger is not only an illustrator, she also paints murals and absolutely everything presented to her. Internationally published and gallery featured, Debra finds inspiration from her two children, Kevyn (age 7) and Courtney (age 21) and the magic in her park-like gardens.